When Autism Comes to Roost:

A Family's Journey From Denial to Acceptance

by

Alicia Hendley, PhD

This book stems from my memory and perception of personal experiences. Thus, like any memoir, it is an imperfect account of actual events. Further, while family members and close friends are all accurately identified, certain names and details of other people described in the memoir (including certain dialogue, such as that between myself and a client) have been altered to protect their privacy.

Library and Archives Canada Cataloguing in Publication
 Hendley, Alicia, 1970-, author
       When Autism comes to roost : a family's journey from denial to acceptance
/ by Alicia Hendley, PhD.

ISBN 978-1-927637-23-4 (pbk.)

    1. Hendley, Alicia, 1970- --Mental health. 2. Parents of autistic children--
Canada--Biography. 3. Autistic children--Family relationships--Canada.
4. Manic-depressive persons--Canada--Biography. I. Title.

RC553.A88H463 2015   616.85'8820092   C2015-901628-2

First Published by Bridgeross in Dundas, ON, Canada

To Daniel, Meghan, Maxwell, and Samuel, who have each taught me how to be a better parent, and who, through their unconditional love, have helped me learn to forgive myself for all the times when I don't quite get it right.

Table of Contents

PROLOGUE

Let's start in the middle. It's the safest place to begin, after all. Think of the middle of a bed, away from its precarious edges. Or the middle of a pie, so much more inviting than any outer crust. Think of the middle of a life, wherever that might be, then dive right in.

Section One Denial

CHAPTER 1

I'm being pummelled by a hurricane that just so happens to have hit my kitchen. Not that I'm surprised. How could I be surprised? A similar storm passes through every morning at approximately seven thirty, give or take ten minutes. Unfortunately, like most hurricanes, it causes damage each and every time it strikes, no matter how expected. While my eleven- and fifteen-year-olds haggle over a Honey Nut Cheerios box and I try to physically force a wilful toddler into his booster seat, the wind begins to lick against the walls of the room, making its presence known in the form of a three-year-old boy who just so happens to be grabbing at my right leg and banging his forehead against it.

"Mom, I still need that form signed for me to go on the history trip," my teenager says. "You forgot on Friday and you forgot yesterday. Today's the last day!"

"Okay, okay. Just give me a minute here, Dan, please." With perhaps more force than is necessary, I push Sammy's fat little bum down on his chair and buckle him up. *Bingo.* I then turn and look at Daniel. "Do you have the form here? Hand me a pen and I'll sign it now."

My son stares at me. "I *gave* it to you on Friday, remember?"

"Okay, okay, I remember. I'll look for it after, honey, all right?"

I move towards the counter, Max still hanging onto my leg, and grab a loaf of bread. *Why can't I force myself to make lunches the night before, like all the wise mothers out there do?* As Max bangs harder, I can feel the storm start to rev up, but try to ignore it. I head towards the refrigerator and pull out a jar.

"Mom!" my daughter says. "Not the soy butter! Yesterday the lunch lady took away my sandwich because it looked like peanut butter. All I had to eat was that apple and one of Emma's cookies, which she licked first."

I glance at Meghan. "But I labelled that sandwich container soy butter. How could anyone mix it up?"

She shrugs. "Don't ask me. They're all peanut phobic over there."

I bend down towards Max and attempt to dislodge him from my leg. "Maxie, go sit down for breakfast, please."

"I need to pee!"

I turn to look at my eldest, who is now drinking milk out of his cereal bowl. "Daniel, didn't you try and take him to the potty when you came down this morning?"

My son keeps drinking, his Adam's apple moving as the milk slides down his throat. When did this kid speed through puberty and where was I while all of it happened?

"*Daniel!*"

"I asked him. He wouldn't go."

I finally peel Max off my leg and grab him by the hand. "Okay, Maxie," I say brightly. "Let's go to the bathroom."

Max twists his hand away from mine and begins to shout. "No! No pee! I don't want to pee! No! No!"

"Okay, Max," I say. "Let's just go change your pull-up then."

My child begins to slap my leg with his open palms, the movement rhythmic. "No! No! I need to pee! I need to use the potty!"

Again, I bend down. Again, I use my gentlest, sunniest voice, saved especially for Max. "Let's go to the bathroom, then."

"No! No!" Max turns his hands into fists and begins to pummel both my legs with them. I grab at his hands, but he pulls them away.

"No hitting, Max. Hands are for holding."

Suddenly my toddler wails from the table, having waited patiently for his breakfast for much longer than any eighteen-month-old should be expected to wait. In response to the noise, Max punches me harder.

"I scared," Sammy sniffs. "Hitting bad."

"It's okay, Sammy," Daniel says. "Max is just upset. Your dad will be down soon. Want some Cheerios?"

Sammy nods and his brother dumps a handful of cereal onto the table. Sammy picks up one Cheerio, then another. The fact that my youngest child is clearly placated by so little makes my chest squeeze with guilt. Where is his homemade oatmeal, his toast cut into buttered soldiers with the crusts all off? His substitute mother stands up and gets a sippy cup from the cupboard, fills it with milk, and then hands it to Sam. As I watch my daughter and baby interact, my chest squeezes again. *I'm sorry, Sammy. I'm sorry.*

Not content with mere head banging, Max begins to hit his entire chest against my legs. With each bang, he becomes more aggressive, reeling back further and further, before hurling at his target. "I need to pee!" *Bang.* "I need to pee!" *Bang.*

"Okay, Maxie," I say again. "Let's go use the potty." The winds are now wiping up everything around me, the noise deafening. I try and pull away from my child and push myself towards the open doorway. "Joel!" I shout at the stairs. "When the hell are you coming down?"

Max continues to bang, caught up in the middle of the storm. "No! No! No potty! The toilet! The toilet!"

Above the din I can hear my teenager trying to talk to me. "Mom, I really need that form signed today. Do you want me to forge it?"

Just as the gale overtakes the kitchen, my husband walks in. He heads over to Sam and tussles his hair, before turning toward me. "Why so much yelling?"

Max stops banging for a moment, his face covered in snot and tears. "I need to pee! I need to pee!"

"Why didn't you take the poor kid to the bathroom?" Joel asks me. "Can't you see he has to go?"

"Then why don't you try? We have case consult this morning and I'm running late and I've still got to make the kids' lunches!"

Sammy takes a handful of Cheerios off the table and stuffs them in his mouth. "Max naw-tee, Max bad."

My husband glances over at his youngest. "Max isn't naughty, buddy. He just needs to go to the bathroom. When you're bigger, you'll use the potty, too!"

Sam looks at his father with wide eyes, before stuffing more Cheerios into this mouth. Intent on having his father's full attention, Max begins to pummel Joel's legs with his fists.

My husband bends down, trying the same tactics that failed me moments ago. "Maxwell. No hitting your dad. Now, let's go to the bathroom. We can both pee!"

Max begins to scream, his hands no longer fists but rather sails that flap violently in the wind against his sides. "No! No! No! No pee! No pee!"

Somewhere, my teenager stands up, puts his empty bowl in the sink, and leaves the room, heading off to forge the signature of a neglectful parent. Somewhere, my toddler bursts into tears once more and my Mommy-in-waiting unbuckles him from his booster chair, using all of the empathy that her eleven-year-old self possesses to comfort him with a bear hug on her lap. Somewhere, my husband attempts to calm down his whirling dervish of a three-year-old son, whose pain is palpably stronger and more forceful than any storm that could ever hit would be. And where am I at this moment? Anywhere else, anywhere else but here.

CHAPTER 2

Looking back, there were signs. Infinitesimal, easy-to-miss signs I was able to wipe clean from my mind with reassurances that the parameters for what is considered normal toddler behaviour are wide indeed. Like the way that a two-year-old Max would stuff his mouth full of food until his cheeks puffed out and would then burst into heart-rending sobs if Joel or I dared to even gently remind him to "chew your food, honey, chew so you don't choke". It didn't matter how softly or sweetly we reminded him, it didn't matter what niceties we couched said reminder in. Eventually "chew" became such a loaded word that its mere utterance would trigger screams or sobs from Max even if he happened to overhear the word being said by others in an unrelated conversation.

Other signs existed, too. Like the way that a two-and-a-half-year-old Max would begin trembling if he saw other children upon his arrival at the local library or at the children's section of the bookstore, this despite the fact that as a daycare kid he presumably should have been used to same-age peers by now, and the fact that I always mentioned the possibility of seeing other children before we arrived at our destination. Such trembling would often be followed by shouting, shouting that I'd try desperately to hush, all the while feeling the disapproving glances of other parents against the back of my head.

"I don't *like* these kids!" he'd bellow, his hands shaking at his sides and his face getting redder and redder. "Make them go away! Make them go away, *now!*"

Like the way that our toddler son exhibited no interest in any stuffed animal, blanket, or other typical transitional object, instead becoming highly attached to the lid of a plastic container (affectionately christened "Liddie" by the rest of the family). Looking back, I recall how he would demand to sleep with that hard disc, and how he would scream in his car seat if he didn't have Liddie to bring with him to daycare. Cringing slightly, I also remember how my husband and I would smile indulgently at our clearly unconventional, thinking-outside-of-the-box child (*no stereotypical teddy bear for our boy, no sir!*).

Yes, looking back it's easy to see subtle signs and to wonder what would have happened if only we'd been called into action sooner, if only we'd sought professional help earlier. But what's the point of looking back? While it's true that you may not be turned into a pillar of salt, the guilt will still be enough to immobilize you nonetheless.

******

If I'm honest with myself, I have to admit that much more obvious signs also existed, signs that were writ large, had I been prepared to actually read them. The clearest one came in the form of a detailed developmental questionnaire that Max's preschool teachers completed about him at the age of sixteen months, something they were more than equipped to do, having spent each week caring for him since my maternity leave ended. Normally, the health professional in me would have been thrilled that the centre is doing such comprehensive monitoring of the toddlers in their care—what a great way to pick up on any early red flags! For the mother in me, however, it was a different matter entirely. Even the wisp of a suggestion that my beloved child could be anything but perfect was not up for discussion.

Max's daycare questionnaire could not come at a worse time, arriving as it did midway through the quite stressful pregnancy of his baby brother. Sam's conception was what one might refer to as a "happy accident", occurring for me at the age of thirty-eight, while still nursing a ten-month-old Maxwell on demand. Knowing the statistics regarding miscarriage and "advanced maternal age", Joel and I had barely begun to relax about the baby-to-be when results of blood screening tests came back positive for possible Down Syndrome. The weeks that followed involved meeting with a genetics counsellor, undergoing an amniocentesis, and reading all that I could about raising children with special needs. When the amnio results indicated that our baby was chromosomally normal, we began to relax once more. Such calm was again short-lived, however, as I developed problems with a heart arrhythmia and dizzy spells. After a few-day hospital stay, my heart received a clean bill of health but the dizziness continued, leading me to remain off work and to be told to keep my stress level to a minimum. As a result, I was using all of the relaxation and mindfulness exercises I knew to try and make sure the baby inside of me stayed put. Even the idea that there could be a problem with any of my existing three babies was too anxiety-provoking to contemplate.

The neatly folded questionnaire waiting for me in Max's cubby when I picked him up that October afternoon (next to his muddy outdoor shoes and a mismatched pair of socks) will forever be imprinted in my mind as the final marker of *Before*. Despite the fact that when it comes to Max there never was a Before and there never could be, that unopened questionnaire remains a signpost of sorts. *This is the moment when our train switched tracks, this*. As if it happened yesterday, I can see myself pick up the folded sheets of paper and stuff them into Max's diaper bag, before reaching over the room's baby gate to take my toddler from his teacher's arms and give him a healthy squeeze. If I concentrate, just a little more, I can watch myself head outside to my car, buckle my baby safely into his car seat, and then sit down to open up the questionnaire. Most of all, I can see myself read its words for the very first time, words that my eyes take in, only to be spit back out by an unyielding brain.

During my first read through, I learn that, in comparison to other sixteen-month-olds, Max exhibits delays in all areas of development, with significant lags noted in terms of communication and personal/social skills. *Something is wrong with my child*. The air in the car suddenly seems too thin, as if I am parked on the peaks of Mount Everest. I look over the pages a few more times, searching desperately for some sort of loophole. It's the former graduate student in me that finds it, in the form of what others might consider a mere technicality. The questionnaire with the power to change my son's life is called the "Ages & Stages Questionnaires: A Parent-Completed, Child-Monitoring System".

A parent-completed, child-monitoring system. *Parent* completed. *Parent Completed*! Meaning mother or father, or perhaps even legal guardian, but not (definitely not!) a childcare teacher, no matter how qualified she or he might purport themselves to be. Loophole in hand, I neatly refold the questionnaire, stuff it into Max's diaper bag, and begin the brief trek back home, having successfully used my psychology credentials as a convenient shield to protect myself from anything with the potential to harm.

After arriving at my house ten minutes later, I burst through the front door, Maxwell in my arms, and shout for Joel.

"What's wrong?" he asks, coming down the stairs to meet me. "Is Max ill?"

I hand him our toddler, then begin pacing back and forth. "Wait until you see what we got from the daycare today!" I say. "Wait until you read this schlock about your son!"

"Schlock? Did you actually just say schlock?"

"The questionnaire was designed for parents to complete, not teachers. Parents! Do you know what that means?"

"Alicia, what are you talking about? What questionnaire?" Joel kisses Max on the cheek, who in turn grabs at his father's nose.

I run out to the car to get the diaper bag, then begin waving the questionnaire in my husband's face. "This! His teachers gave me this screener about Max's development. It was left in his cubby, without any explanation whatsoever. No note or anything!"

"Okay."

"Well, it's not okay, actually, because most parents aren't qualified to know when results such as these are valid or not. Other parents might read these results and think there's something horribly wrong with their child!"

"Something's horribly wrong with Max?"

I shake my head. "No! You're not listening! I need to tell you about the questionnaire, not his results! It was developed specifically for parents to fill out, but the daycare used it for teachers! That means the results are likely totally bogus! How could they assume normative data from parents would be valid for results made by teachers?"

I keep on ranting and raving for a few minutes more, until Joel gently places Max on the floor, and then takes the papers from me.

"My guess is that it still could have some useful information..."

"None of the information is useful! That's what I'm trying to explain! It's basis statistics, Joel! You can't use the wrong normative sample to interpret data, it invalidates everything!" I let out a snort. Feelings of righteous indignation wash over me, obliterating any lingering twinges of fear.

"Hmmm. This says Max can't stack even one block on top of another. That's true, I think. And this says he doesn't stand up by himself. It also says he has no interest in trying to walk or ever speak. That he won't say even four words. Alicia, all these things are true." He looks up at me.

"That's not my point!" I can tell my voice has gotten screechy, but I don't care.

Meghan pokes her head around a doorway, the telephone receiver against her ear. "Mommy, can I sleep over at Emma's tomorrow night?" she asks. "They're going to go to a Greek restaurant and I've never tasted Greek food! Her dad can't even believe it!"

"Not now, Meg," I say.

"But she's got to know now! She's on the phone! She'll invite someone else!"

"Not now, Meghan!" I wave her away.

"Why can't you just say yes or no?"

"Fine." I face my child. "If you can't wait five minutes, then the answer is no."

Meghan gives me her best wounded look, before heading back into the other room, phone still glued to her ear.

I turn back to Joel. "As I was trying to say, my *point* is that you can't compare Max's results to the sample used to create the damn questionnaire in the first place, because that sample had parents answer the items. Parents and not teachers!" My heart beat starts to feel like a dying fish flopping on a deck, and I place both hands against my chest to will it back to normal.

Joel takes a step towards me and puts his arm around my shoulders. "It's okay, I get it. It's bogus. I'll just read it later, when the kids are in bed. As long as you aren't concerned about Max, then I guess I'm not, either." He pauses, then reaches out to touch my belly. "Let's order take-out tonight. You pick!"

The next Saturday during a visit with my parents, I persuade my mother to redo the questionnaire with me, using a red marker to scratch out the daycare teacher's careful responses and messily replace them with my own.

"She said here that Max doesn't say four words! He can say four words!"

We both turn to look at my son as he sits contently in his playpen, chewing on the cover of a waterproof book.

"Well, I'm not sure if I've heard him say that many," my mother says.

"What about Mama and Dada? He says those!"

"But, honey, it says here that you aren't to include those."

"Well, I think that's ridiculous. I mean, sometimes he just says 'Ma', and that's different than 'Mama', right? At least one of those words should count!"

My mother nods her head. "I suppose you could make an argument for that."

"Exactly!" I glance at Max again, who is now chewing on a rattle in the way that any *normal* baby would chew on a rattle. "Anyway, I think he does say at least four other words at home, don't you? He's probably just really shy around his teachers, just like Daniel used to be when he was little."

"I remember someone asking me if Daniel had a hearing impairment, because he was too shy to say hello to them," my mother says. "Now it's hard to keep him quiet!"

"Ha!"

My mother looks thoughtful. "I *do* know that Max understands quite a bit of what I'm saying. The other day when I took him in the stroller and spoke about birds, he looked up at the sky. Does that count?"

"I think it should!" I say, crossing out the "Not Yet" response the teacher had endorsed, and replacing it with a bright red "Yes". I smile at my mom. "See? He now has ten more points just by changing that one answer. Imagine how well he'll do once we're done!"

After about twenty more minutes and almost as many revisions, I tabulate the results and find out that, surprise, surprise, when a *parent* actually completes the Ages & Stages Questionnaires: A Parent-Completed, Child-Monitoring System, Max receives scores that are far more typical for a toddler his age. Yes, some fine and gross motor difficulties are still noted (I can't red-marker away his lack of standing, for example), but these problems are mild, a mere trifle in the grand scheme of things. More importantly, Max scores within the normal range when it comes to communication, problem solving, and personal-social skills, areas where most of the developmental red flags tend to be planted. After my mother leaves, I triumphantly show Joel the revised questionnaire, then file it away in a locked cabinet, stuffing it next to a picture of a Thanksgiving turkey his teachers had made out of his hand print and an inky impression of the little soles of his feet.

And so, life goes on, as life tends to do. Max continues going to daycare, my eldest two children continue going to school, and I continue spending my days trying to relax and keep my final baby from hatching too soon. October flows into November, which flows into (for us) the double holiday season, which then flows into a brand new year and the scheduled caesarian section birth of eight pound, twelve ounce Sammy. After I hear his APGAR score (a perfect 10), I finally let out my breath. I know that I am lucky, that we are lucky, that for some unknown reason, we have been allowed to have one final perfect baby. With my tubes firmly tied, we know not to tempt fate again.

******

With winter firmly upon us and our nights and days flipped around by a squalling baby, Joel and I decide to continue having twenty-month-old Max attend daycare, at least until his baby brother figures out how to sleep through the night. During this hazy winter, some of Max's behaviour begins to seem more worrisome (his "temper tantrums" last longer and longer), but such concerns are balanced by the clear progress he's made in terms of walking, climbing, and grasping.

Soon winter edges into spring and April arrives. With it comes another Ages & Stages Questionnaire, once again left in Max's cubby. This time it is Joel who comes across the neatly folded pages and it is Joel who reads through the results first. When he arrives home that day with Max, he walks into the den where I sit nursing Sam, and hands me the questionnaire.

"I think we need to talk," he says.

I unfold the papers and read through the findings. Just like six months before, significant delays are again noted in all areas of Max's development, with his teachers making a point of commenting about his limited verbal skills and his ongoing preference for crawling. I read through the questionnaire one more time, then put it down on the sofa. I turn away from Joel and begin gently stroking Sammy's nearly bald head.

"You need to talk, so talk," I say.

Joel perches on the edge of the sofa. "I think something's wrong."

I shrug, continuing to touch my baby's velvety skin.

"Don't you?" Joel asks. "It's two in a row now."

"Ages and Stages is still meant to be for parents only," I say. "How can we know if the thing's reliable or valid?" Tears start falling down my face, and I hide behind my hair.

Joel sighs. "Do you think this is serious or not?" he asks. "I'm taking my cues from you, here. Is this something we should investigate?"

I lean over and press my lips against Sam's head, as he continues to suckle. "I think it means we should keep an eye on things, really watch how he's doing." I turn my head to look at my husband. "Maxie's not even two, Joel. He's not even two!"

Joel nods, then scoops Max off the floor and carries him into the living room to play with Daniel, before heading upstairs to get out of his work clothes. I continue to hold Sam, who is still nursing in his sleep.

******

In the weeks that follow, I keep a more vigilant eye on Max, making a mental note when he does something that seems not quite right. And the more I watch, the more I become aware that *not-quite-right* happens much of the time. The marathon temper tantrums, the outbursts at the library when other children show up unexpectedly, the tendency to "zone out" and seem unreachable, only to smile and laugh again several minutes later. I begin questioning Daniel and Meghan every few days about what they've noticed, hoping each time that they'll only give me positive feedback about their baby brother.

"I think he's okay," Dan shrugs as I corner him near the pantry. He pulls out a box of Oreos and shakes it. "This is empty. Who'd put it back on the shelf?"

"Daniel!" I take the box from him and toss it on the counter. "Please focus! When you say you think Max is 'okay', what do you mean exactly?"

My almost fourteen-year-old stares at me, confused. "I dunno. I mean okay, like fine, like no problem. You know. Okay."

"But do you notice anything unusual?"

"If I did, I would have said unusual!" Daniel starts riffling through the pantry once more. "I think you worry too much. Seriously. You're like always worrying, even when there's nothing going on. Maybe you need to work more at stopping that."

My conversation a few hours later with Meghan proves more fruitful but also more troubling.

"I definitely think something's weird," she says as we sit on her bed together. "I mean, do you realize that each time I walk into the den he screams at me? Sometimes he even hits me with his head! What's that about?"

"Maybe he's surprised to see you come in."

"But don't you think that's weird? I'm his sister. He sees me *all the time*." She picks up a Barbie and begins making it dance. "The last time Emma was here he yelled in her face, too. It freaked her out."

Most concerning to me isn't Max "freaking out" his big sister and her BFF, however, but his continued lack of speech, a lack that becomes more obvious as he approaches his second birthday. While it's true that his vocabulary has grown since his first questionnaire, and it's also true that his comprehension of language is quite good, when compared to other little boys or girls we run into at the park or the local Early Years Centre, his ability to actually verbalize what is going on inside of him remains quite limited.

Every so often, Joel and I make a point to have a parental huddle and hear what the other thinks. Yes, more problems seem to exist than before, we agree. Yes, we need to continue keeping an eye on things. Yes, if they become more serious, we'll make sure to bring them up with the family physician, at some undefined point in the future. We'll definitely bring up any serious concerns, someday, if needed. Max is not quite two-years-old, after all. He needs to be given the chance to grow at his own pace, before pinning him down with any possible diagnoses. Everyone who knows him (and especially his four loving grandparents) point out what an affectionate, curious child he is, how intelligent he seems. So what if he also beats to the sound of his own drummer? Look how quirky his parents are, ha, ha! We need to give the little guy a break!

Soon after we receive the second questionnaire, Max leaves daycare, to instead be at home with me and Sammy. In the months that follow, our days become fluid and simple, the hours forming their shape and structure around such predictable activities as eating, sleeping, bathing, and having the older children leave for school and then return home again. While I become more aware that Max seems to be a highly sensitive child, to me such sensitivity still fits within the framework of normal, my daughter and her friend's "freaked out-ness" notwithstanding. What child wouldn't be upset when the birth of a younger sibling usurps his status as baby of the family? While the way Max expresses his feelings may be unusual (e.g., screaming for up to an hour when given a green spoon instead of an orange one), isn't the fact he's been more upset since Sam came on the scene proof of what an incredibly normal kid he is?

Then comes the end of my second maternity leave, and with it, a return to daycare for Max (this time with his baby brother Sammy in tow). On the surface, everything seems to run in an organized, smooth fashion. On the three days a week that I work, I leave the house at seven thirty each morning, leaving Joel in charge of getting breakfast into all four children, sending Daniel and Meghan on their way (with lunches and homework packed), and then driving the little boys to daycare. Assuming the weather and traffic cooperate, I end up sitting in my office by eight thirty, ready to face my first client. My workday ends at four thirty (sharp!), with me picking the boys up from daycare by five thirty. I'm then in charge of the early evening shift, making sure that all children get watered and fed, and that homework is done. Putting Max and Sam to bed is a shared affair between Joel and I, followed by me collapsing on the den sofa, trying to convince myself to get up and prepare the lunches ahead of time for tomorrow, but inevitably failing miserably.

Such days are long ones for me, but not unreasonably so. One could argue that they are no longer than anyone else's work day, and likely much shorter than many. Yes, I have the demands of four children to somehow fit into my day, but such is the life of any working parent. If anything, I have it easy, as we are financially able to have me still stay at home with the little boys two days each week. However, while it's soothing to think that our lives actually run in such an organized, smooth fashion, the daily emails that my husband and I send back and forth to each other start to tell another story altogether.

On the days I go to work and Joel is in charge of the morning routine, he usually gives me a thumbs-up as I wave goodbye, the gesture so earnestly optimistic I have to look away. For, despite his early morning confidence, I know that within hours I will inevitably receive an email describing the chaos that was breakfast and daycare drop-off. In each message, the content may be different, but the theme remains the same.

"This morning Max wanted a blue tea towel on the couch to sit on. He must have remembered the one I'd used a few days ago to soak up a spill," Monday's email reads. *"He then changed his mind and got upset, then wanted blueberry yoghurt, then changed his mind and wanted plain yoghurt, then got upset and wanted no yoghurt...then starting telling me I was a 'bad boy', and starting hitting me..."*

Then on Tuesday: *"Why the heck does he get so upset almost every single day? It's like his little brain just 'snaps'".*

Then on Wednesday: *"The truth is, I find it harder to deal with his 'silly' meltdowns than his 'upset' meltdowns...I got very impatient with him, which I don't normally do, when he wouldn't let me dress him or put on sunscreen...suggestions on how to deal with this?"*

I typically read such missives between seeing my clients, a stunningly stupid thing to do, as it makes it that much harder to clear my mind and exude calm for the next person who arrives at my office door, seeking my help. I begin to find it impossible to shut out home while at work, or work while at home. It seems as if both settings require all of my focus and energy, and that someone will be let down no matter where I am.

The emails Joel receives from me each Thursday and Friday when at home with the boys match his in terms of desperation, mirroring as they do the messages he's recently sent me:

"Feeling defeated. Went for nice walk downtown with little guys. Max good doing errands and then went to bakery for a treat. Had asked him before what cookie he wanted, but unsure, so knew to choose it myself. When woman handed him his peanut butter cookie (a kind he's loved before), he of course totally freaked out and refused it. He kept screaming about it and trying to hit me as I pushed the stroller back outside, me still holding the cookie. He still refused it, screaming down the sidewalk. He kept sobbing all the way home—people looking at me. Sam happily ate his. Max refused to come in house, still yelling. Had to pick him up and force him in house. Hitting me. Then suddenly yelled he wanted me to rub his back. I picked him up and did and he instantly slumped against me and was fine. Now sipping a juice box. Sigh."

As the email exchanges between Joel and I increase, our actual conversations decrease. While it's true that our busy days have left little time for us as a couple, they have left some, but we each chose to fill up that remaining time away from the other, me plopped in front of the den TV, watching reality shows with Meghan, and Joel holed up in his office with his computer. We have both begun to admit in our emails that something is wrong with our child, something serious and real, something we as parents possibly cannot fix on our own. We have even gone so far as to agree that if Max's meltdowns don't lessen by the time he turns three, we will go seek help from our doctor. Despite such virtual communication, however, when actually face to face with each other, Joel and I seem to be at a loss for words, each trapped in a private turret of grief.

CHAPTER 3

As Sam grows into toddlerhood, he becomes the unwitting control group in our house, his ever-improving verbal, physical, and social skills highlighting the fact that Max's abilities have never been within the normal range, after all. When Sam's Ages & Stages Questionnaire is left in his cubby at the age of sixteen months, he receives a near perfect score, with no need for me to pull out my red marker. At home I watch as my youngest child not only speaks, but asks four-word questions and then waits for the answers. I listen to him laugh at a simple joke Meghan tells him, see him have a tickle fight with Daniel and somehow understand how to play. I then turn my gaze to my third born, who is carefully arranging pieces of toy food in a neat, precise line on the floor, and has no time for such shenanigans, and realize that something is truly wrong with my beloved planned baby, with Max.

With the arrival of Max's thirty-six-month developmental questionnaire (still designed for parents to complete and not teachers!), everything shifts. Without denial obscuring our vision, Joel and I are able to see that the teacher who answered each item clearly cares about our child and took the responsibility of filling the questionnaire out seriously, not only checking off the appropriate boxes, but spending the time to add comments, including "Runs with arms at chest level, on his tip toes", "Rarely talks, unless he is one-on-one", "Fine motor skills [a problem]", as well as "Still does mostly parallel play".

The findings of ongoing delays in terms of fine motor, gross motor, and social/emotional skills, combined with our acknowledgement that, when it comes to our sweet son, we are clearly in over our heads, finally kickstarts Joel and I into action. We speak to our family physician, the dreaded daycare questionnaires in tow, and receive a referral to a pediatrician. When I learn the referral wait will take months rather than weeks, I decide to use my knowledge of the mental health system to our benefit and short-circuit the whole damn process by making an appointment to meet with a child psychologist, knowing that at least she'll speak my language.

Within days of our first appointment with Dr. Christie, our family is in the thick of the assessment process. Somewhat ironically, a large part of the assessment involves Joel and I completing parent questionnaires, because we are *parents*. For a few weeks, everything revolves around Max's assessment. Forced to actually communicate face to face once again, summer evenings are spent sitting at the kitchen table, completing detailed questionnaires about our beloved child. Joel and I become a mini-UN, a world organization of two, each item before us needing to be discussed, debated, and laboured over. Does Max "almost always" or "always" dislike a change in his routine? Does Max "sometimes" or "occasionally" do imaginative play? So much rides on our responses, Max depends on us to be accurate. Here is our chance to finally *do* something, to finally help. What will it mean if we get it wrong?

In addition to the parent questionnaires, there are several appointments with Dr. Christie, first for her to interview Joel and I about our impressions, next for her to actually go through detailed testing and observation with Maxwell himself. Thankfully, Max seems to be happy with the process, possibly perceiving the various activities he is asked to do within the framework of play, and responding positively to Dr. Christie's gentle, warm nature. From the first meeting onward, it is clear that the psychologist views Max as his own person, not as a specimen to dissect or classify.

Once the assessment itself is over, comes the waiting. Weeks and weeks loom in front of us until the September feedback appointment with the psychologist. Weeks and weeks of not knowing whether Max is merely a quirky kid, or is a quirky kid with a diagnosis. Joel seems to handle this uncertainty with aplomb, relating to our son in the same easy, effortless way he has always done. In contrast, I find myself increasingly ill at ease, suddenly worried that I do not truly know my child. On more than one occasion Joel pulls me aside, letting me know that I am acting a bit "too" with Max. Too enthusiastic, too complimentary ("Great job sitting up straight, Max!", "Wow, you sure played with that toy car well, honey!"), too artificial. I attempt to rein my nervous energy back in a bit, but find it almost impossible to do. *I need to know!*

In the midst of the wait, I'm temporarily distracted by our August trip to a cottage. We go with my father-in-law to a little town on Lake Huron, a place imbued with happy memories for me, as I spent repeated vacations there when my eldest two children were small.

Soon after arriving in Southampton, the knot in my stomach loosens and something is released. *I know this place, I know it.* I find myself relax more as I watch Max's initial reaction to exploring the cottage, to building sandcastles at the beach, to walking in the waves. He is thrilled, just like any child would be.

And yet. On the second day he gets triggered when asked to choose an ice cream flavour, *any flavour at all, honey.* As we wait in line I notice his fingers start to flutter against his sides, like an engine getting revved up. *Shit.* The tone of my voice becomes overly gentle and calm, as if trying to coax a wild animal back into its cage, rather than talk to my three-year-old child. Regardless of my words, regardless of what his father crouches down to whisper in his ear, Max explodes. And though I try to ignore it, I can't help but notice the reactions of other vacationers as Max screams hysterically at being offered a chocolate cone, then becomes even more hysterical when his grandfather suggests swapping ice creams with him. I can't help but notice how easily his toddler brother picks his own flavour, then licks at it with no complaint. Through the other vacationers' eyes, I am reminded that such a meltdown is not typical, not expected, not normal. *What the hell is wrong with my child?*

******

There's two more weeks to go until the feedback session with Dr. Christie. I sit in front of the computer screen in my office, my hands hovering above the keyboard, each finger bent and frozen in its own specific position. I lift my hands to rub my face, then reposition them again. A year ago I would have been able to whip off five session notes within an hour and still have had time to repeatedly update my Facebook status. Now I find myself incapable of even remembering, let alone typing, today's date. My hands stay frozen over my ergonomically correct keyboard until a buzzer sounds on the wall in front of me, causing me to jump about fifty feet. *Exaggerated startle response. That can't be good.* I flick a switch above my computer, get out of my chair and head to the door. I walk down a long hallway, as I've done hundreds of times before, to the waiting room. A few other counsellors pass by me in the other direction, smiling or nodding. On a normal day they'd receive a smile or nod in turn, whether I felt like they truly deserved it or not. *But today is not a normal day. Nothing is normal, anymore.* When I reach the waiting room, I scan the faces for my client. Slowly from the left to the right I look, with each move of my eyes feeling increasing panic. Despite knowing that this client is a returning one coming for her fifth session, at this moment, at this crucial, get-a-hold-of-yourself-you-idiot moment, I have no idea what the hell she looks like.

Eventually a young woman stands up, smiling, and her face becomes familiar to me.

"Sandy! Good to see you."

"It's Sara," she says. "I always come on Tuesdays."

I try to smile, but the best my mouth can do is grimace. "Of course! Where is my brain today? Sara. Good to see you again! Let's go back to my office!"

I lead the way back down the hall, Sara following. Too soon, we reach my office, and I open the door. Sara walks in and I close the door behind us. As always, I wait for my client to get comfortable before sitting down across from her. While relieved beyond belief that I finally *recognize* this person, the room in my head that stores all of each client's particular facts and figures, his or her stories and secrets, has been inexplicably shut and bolted. I've always taken for granted my ability to access each client's personal narrative from my mind. I've always believed that by the sheer act of *remembering,* rather than by obnoxiously flipping through a person's file in front of them as their grief spills onto the carpet, I'm able to make a meaningful connection with them. Now suddenly, for reasons unknown, my knowledge of this particular client sitting on my loveseat, of *Sara,* has been locked away. *Shit, shit, shit.*

I smile at the client for a moment too long, before starting. "So, why don't we begin with you filling me in on what's been going on since our last session?"

"Can we do that later?" Sara asks. "I really want us to work on my cognitive restructuring sheets, like you said we would. I did all the homework." She reaches into her knapsack, pulls out a handful of papers, and then passes them to me.

"Of course!" I say, using my chirpy Max-voice. "I'm just so pleased that you did your homework! Not everyone does, you know. Life of a university student, eh?"

Sara shrugs and bites on a cuticle.

"So, did you find the process of coming up with examples of negative thoughts to be difficult?"

"Nope. That's kind of all my head's filled with, anyway. It's the challenging them part that I need your help with."

"Great!" I say. "Let's do that today, then."

"Yeah, that's kind of what you said last time, remember? I was supposed to come up with four examples of negative thoughts and then today we'd use those steps you have to analyze them. That's what I was kind of counting on."

"Of course we will. Let's look at your first example..." I glance down at the page I'm holding, but the writing seems all fuzzy. As I try to focus more, the words begin moving on the page, mocking my attempts at concentration. I look up at Sara. "Do you know what would be most helpful? Instead of having me read what you wrote here, why don't you talk about each negative thought in your own words and then together we'll evaluate them for their accuracy."

Sara frowns at me. "But they're already in my own words on the paper." She points at the pages. "That took me a long time to do. I skipped studying for my Anthro quiz to complete this." She pauses. "One of the examples I wrote down talks about how stupid I was to do that."

I smile at my client, but hold the pages out to her. Eventually she takes them, her frown digging deeper into her skin.

"I know it might seem strange," I say, "but this method really does work the best. Trust me on this."

"Okay," Sara says. She reads the page in front of her. "Well, my first example is that I was supposed to meet this new friend for drinks at the campus pub but she never came. The bitch stood me up, excuse my language. So my negative thought was that she sucks and that she must think that I suck and that I'll never have any friends and that my life is basically a waste..."

"Was it the new campus pub with the dance floor or the old one?" I ask.

Sara stares at me. "Um, does that really matter?"

"Probably not. Sorry! Just curious, I guess."

"Oh. Well, it was the old one."

"They make great fries, don't they? They're really thick and they come in those big baskets..." I can feel my stomach growl. Maybe I should go there for lunch?

"So, anyway, that was my negative thought."

"What was?"

Sara frowns again, this time her eyes involved. "I just *told* you. My new friend stood me up at the *old* pub and then I had the thought that I was basically worthless, which is kind of how I'm feeling right now!"

"You're feeling worthless right now? We definitely need to analyze that. It sounds like you might be engaging in dichotomous or catastrophic thinking. Possibly fortune telling as well. Do you remember what those types of cognitive distortions are? Why don't we start there."

Sara stands up, stuffing her papers back in her knapsack. Suddenly the door unlocks and all of my secrets about her come tumbling out. *Struggled with an eating disorder in middle school but has worked hard at overcoming it. Is a high achiever but is much too critical of herself. Has bouts of feeling mildly to moderately depressed. No suicidal ideation. Was raised by a single mother and is fiercely proud of it. Believes that everyone will ultimately let her down.*

"I think we should do this another time," she says, her face flushed. "Something is obviously weird with you, because you've never been like this before!"

"Sara, I'm sorry! I've got a lot on my mind. Please don't go. I'll focus better now, I promise."

Sara shakes her head. "No, I think I'll rebook for another time. But here's some advice: Whatever you do, don't see any new clients today, because they'll think you're the worst therapist ever, when you're actually pretty good, when you're not being weird. No offence or anything."

"No offence," I nod. "Again, I'm sorry."

Sara heads to the door and opens it. "Yeah, I know." She walks out, gently closing the door behind her. I stare at the spot she used to be sitting in for a few minutes, trying to rewind what just happened.

******

The therapy session clearly aborted, I leave my office and head straight for the small conference room. The lights are off and I don't bother to turn them on. The chairs, which are all arranged in a perfect circle, are deep-seated and welcoming. I randomly pick one, and settle in. I close my eyes and try to think of nothing. No clients, no session notes, no Max. Suddenly the door opens and the overhead lights turn on. Again I jump about fifty feet.

"Alicia! You startled me! I didn't see you there in the dark!"

"Sorry, Anne," I tell my fellow counsellor, a pleasant, affable woman.

Anne walks into the room and sits down a few seats away from me, clearly wanting to give me space in case I need it. While I *know* I should appreciate this gesture, as it likely comes from a very good place, all it serves to do is irritate me. Must we play therapist all of the time when any of us are together? Are we never allowed to turn down the volume on the empathy, even a teeny, weeny bit, perhaps for a measly five seconds, and let ourselves just frigging *be*? It's as if none of the other counsellors have ever counted the minutes until a therapy session is finally over or have hoped against hope that a particularly difficult client will be a "no-show". To put it even more bluntly, it's as if no one (myself included) is willing to give off the scent of being human.

Anne holds a notebook and pen in her lap. "No need to apologize!" she says, cheerfully. "Are you waiting for the case conference?"

"Um, yes. I thought I'd just come sit in here. My last client left early."

"Early?" She cocks her head to the side. I look away. "Well, it's always nice to have an unexpected breather in the middle of a busy day, now isn't it?"

I force myself to turn towards her once more, my internal Pollyanna kicking in, despite itself. "It is nice," I respond.

Anne nods, then draws in a deep breath, a slight spot of pink surfacing on each of her cheeks. "I hate to bug you, but did you happen to bring any cases to present today? I don't think we've heard one from you in a while."

"No. Sorry."

More nodding. "That's all right. It means your sessions must be going well for you." Pause. "I have a feeling that no one else will have any cases to go through either, to be honest. None of the others got back to my email about it at least. I suppose there will be a lot of time for our check-in, then." Her cheerful resolve returns.

I give a half-smile, then look towards the door, hoping for more people to materialize as quickly as possible. Thankfully, other counsellors start arriving, some singly and some in groups of two or three. After a few minutes pass, the chairs are filled with about thirteen women, anyone with a penis mysteriously absent, despite four males working on staff.

Anne clears her throat. "All right, everybody, why don't we get started? As I was just telling Alicia, as far as I know we don't have any cases to present today, so why don't we spend the extra time focusing on check-in?"

All around the room women nod. I sit on my hands, to avoid smelling my fingers. Ever since childhood I've had the tendency to smell them whenever I'm bored or uncomfortable. It's like the poor man's version of biting one's nails, just more revolting.

"Great," Anne says. "Who wants to get started?"

A woman in her forties raises her hand. "I do."

"Go ahead, Hillary," Anne says.

"Well," Hillary begins. Her voice sounds tight, small. All eyes turn toward her, our counsellor antennae vibrating. Despite myself, I begin to feel concerned as well. "Work here has been pretty stressful," Hillary says, "but when is it not? I'm finding my caseload growing and growing. I have double the clients I did when I started here, fifteen years ago. And now Gary has been laid off again, which ramps up the stress." She stops, her voice so tight I'm afraid its strings will pop. I can feel my own throat become smaller, taut. "I know we've gone through the same thing before and gotten through it, but you never know what'll happen this time."

The woman next to her reaches over and pats her shoulder. "Have you found anything that helps you cope? I know the last time Gary was laid off it was quite a tough go for both of you."

Hillary looks around the group. "I've started taking a yoga class to try and balance things more. That's helping a bit. That and a nightly glass of wine."

A wave of gentle laughter laps against her and she smiles slightly.

Another woman speaks. "Chocolate does the same for me." She pauses. "Is it okay if I go now?"

"Definitely, Susan," says Anne. "As long as Hillary is finished."

Hillary nods, then sighs, her entire body looser.

"Well, work is going fine for me. I find jogging is really helping me manage stress. I mean, my mother is having such a rough time with my father's Alzheimer's and I want to be there for her, but I find hearing about it every night on the phone can be too much, you know? Especially after a day with clients who are also struggling. It's hard, because I want to be there for both of my parents, but also take care of myself."

I feel myself start to zone out, twenty minutes being the upper time limit for my concern about the woes of coworkers. While the more selfless part of me recognizes the importance of having these monthly meetings, of the need for counsellors to have a chance to regularly vent with people who *get it*, the fact remains that my font of empathy is getting close to empty and there isn't a damn thing I can do about it. I fight the urge to leap out of my chair and out of this room and instead find myself doing something incomprehensible for me, given that I am an introverted, pessimistic, painfully private woman who perpetually protects her *true* self from hurt by using a plastic smile as a barricade: I find myself raising my hand.

"Alicia?" Anne asks. Her voice sounds surprised, even skeptical, and I can't say that I blame her. When have I ever volunteered to share any of my self with the other female counsellors? I'm more like the ones with the penises who consistently hide themselves away in their offices when these meetings occur, too "busy" for the messiness of check-in. While always here in body with my fellow vaginas, I too am typically absent.

I look around the room. All the other women are looking at me encouragingly. *Oh shit.* I clear my throat. "Um, I don't really know why I'm even talking about this here, because it'll probably turn out to be nothing at all, but, um, we're in the process of getting our son Max tested for Autism." Suddenly I burst out sobbing and cover my face with my hands. *So much for the barricades.*

"How incredibly difficult for all of you," Anne says softly.

I wipe at my face with my fingers, which become wet with tears and snot. "Um, I don't know *why* I'm crying right now. I never cry in front of people! And besides, the chances are that he doesn't even *have* Autism, right?" I'm aware that my voice sounds angry, defiant. *Where is this coming from?*

I watch as each head around the circle nods. What other choice have I given them?

"It's just that he's been doing things for a while now that don't seem normal to me or to Joel," I continue. "And I used to test kids for Autism when I was a grad student, so I'm more aware of the symptoms. But my awareness could also make me see symptoms that don't exist, right?"

"That's always possible," Hillary says slowly.

"Exactly! I mean, he *does* have problems, like freaking out if he has to choose between two flavours of ice cream, or screaming if I don't go the correct route home from daycare, or having a meltdown if you say 'shop' instead of 'store'. Stuff like that. He likes to line up his cars a lot, too. You should see how perfect the lines are! And he often zones out, like he's deaf, when we know that he's not. He also flaps his hands against his sides when excited and bonks me when he's upset."

Anne interrupts. "Bonks?"

"You know, um, bangs his chest or head against me, in a rhythm. Bonking. Anyway, his daycare teachers have been concerned about some things for a while, so we decided we'd better get an assessment done. We've had a few sessions with a child psychologist for the testing and we're also going to meet with a pediatrician. Covering all of the bases, I guess." For some inexplicable reason, I laugh. *How is this funny?*

The one woman in the group whom I consider to be a friend gets up and sits down next to me. She touches my hand. "You know, when I last visited your house, Max seemed like a pretty normal little kid. Really shy, but so sweet too, and very smart."

I take a deep breath, then slowly let it out. I face my friend, snot and all, and smile slightly. *I'll bet she often hopes for no-shows, too.* "Thanks, Erica."

A woman from across the room speaks up. "Even if your son *does* have Autism, does that have to be a bad thing? I've heard that a lot of these children have special gifts, that some are geniuses at math or piano or art."

I can feel myself start to shake from the inside out, my arms beginning to tremble. Will I be able to stop myself from throttling this woman? "No!" The word comes out as a roar. "No! Maxwell doesn't have any special gifts! He's just this quirky little kid who gets really upset and can't be calmed down and who might have something seriously wrong with him and I can't do a damn thing about it! He's not a genius with pseudo savant abilities! There's no positive way to spin this!"

"I wasn't trying too..."

Erica touches my hand more firmly and I regain control. "No, sorry, I know you weren't. I'm sorry, I just..."

I begin crying once more and lower my head. I can feel Erica pat me on the back, but her touch remains on the surface of my clothing, my body refusing to absorb any real comfort.

******

A week before our September feedback session with Dr. Christie we meet with the consulting pediatrician, ostensibly to rule out any medical concerns. The pediatrician is an intelligent, inquisitive woman with kind eyes. Quickly bored by the appointment, Max turns his focus onto my hair, running his fingers through it in his gentle, familiar way and rubbing his face against my head. *A Max-hug.* After making notes at her computer while Joel and I yammer on about our concerns for

32

forty-five minutes, the doctor takes her hands off the keyboard and turns to us.

"It's clear to me that Max is in the Autism spectrum," she says. "Based on what you've told me, he seems to be in the moderate range."

"The moderate range?" I blurt. "But how is that possible? He's incredibly verbal, he's curious, and he's affectionate!" I pause for a moment, feeling Max's hands on my head. "See? Look at how affectionate he is now, holding onto my hair!"

"Does he look at you when he touches your hair?" she asks.

I think for a moment, realizing the answer quickly, but not wanting to say it. "No."

"This might be hard to hear, but I think what he is doing is more for self-stimulation than being affectionate."

"Oh," I say. *Not a Max-hug, after all.* Suddenly the room becomes flat, the air thin. Everything is two-dimensional. Without meaning to, I move away abruptly from my child's gentle fingers. *Stop it, already!*

For the rest of the appointment, I'm not there, not really. While I know words are being said about waiting lists and private therapies, about play sessions and gross motor skills, I'm not listening. My thoughts are caught in a web of hair, imprisoned by the thick strands of loss.

******

After the appointment with the pediatrician, Joel and I jump face-first into denial. Where else is there for us to go? We both loudly agree that the doctor had no right to give us any sort of diagnosis, without spending any time one-on-one with Max. How preposterous! Besides, we only went to the appointment to rule out possible medical concerns. The psychologist is the professional whose opinion will matter, whose formulation will carry weight. After all, her report will be based upon hours spent with Max doing testing, observing, and interpreting detailed questionnaires! No, we will not allow the pediatrician's words to absorb through our skin, into our hearts. After all, hope can always be found in what remains unsaid. We will wait another week until the *true* professional involved says her piece.

Except that I soon discover I can't. I can't play the denial game any longer, and I also can't wait. My heart has already begun grieving and won't listen to reason. With the pediatrician's quick words and kind eyes, the ground has shifted under my feet. Or rather, I've suddenly discovered that there is no ground, that there never has been. I'm like a Saturday morning cartoon character who was only able to walk blithely on air until she looked down and saw the truth. At the pediatrician's office I made the mistake of looking, and since then I haven't been able to stop falling.

*****

We sit beside one another in a bright, cheerful room, filled with colour and toys. Dr. Christie sits across from us, her gaze direct and her voice clear. She patiently goes through every result leading up to the actual diagnosis in detail, taking the time to answer each of my husband's questions, seemingly aware that he is not yet fluent in Psychologist patois. I start to crack my knuckles and then bite down on my lip, forcing myself not to shout at my husband to *please stop asking so many damn questions!* I bite down harder and taste blood. Doesn't Joel realize that the psychologist holds the whole world in her hands?

The cut, when it happens, goes deep. It turns out that the pediatrician was right. It turns out that my gut was right. It turns out that every single patronizing stranger that ever looked pityingly at me while Max had yet another meltdown at the playground was right. My son, my sweet, beloved baby, has Autism. Specifically, he has Autism in the Mild to Moderate range in terms of severity, with the qualifier that he is often high functioning and is also quite bright, end stop. As if anything will ever start again.

I don't know when or how I left the psychologist's office, with its bright, cheerful colours and its atmosphere of optimism. All I know is that I end up standing on a busy street corner with my bewildered husband, who merely suggested that we take a walk to clear the air, and did not expect his wife to begin sobbing into the front of his jacket as cars rushed by. All I know are these tears and the feeling of utter, bottomless despair and helplessness that accompanies them.

Section Two Anger

CHAPTER 4

In the days following Max's diagnosis, I begin to wonder if I might be losing my mind. Is it possible that I've gone insane and everyone is just too polite to mention it? How else to explain why our child has just been given a life-changing diagnosis, and yet nothing is happening. *Shouldn't something be happening*? I feel like Joel and I have just been tossed a hand grenade with the pin pulled out, but have no idea what to do with it. And so, grenade in tow, we continue to go through each hour as if nothing has changed. Lunches keep getting made, homework is reviewed, and dirty little bums are wiped. The older children still get taken to and fro to piano lessons, swimming lessons, and ballet, and the younger children continue to be read bedtime stories and bathed. Joel still churns out his requisite number of columns at his office and I still counsel clients at mine. As if life were still normal, I keep mediating the silly little arguments which erupt almost daily between Meghan and her equally dramatic best friend, and I keep at least feigning interest when Daniel comes to talk to me in excruciating detail about his new video game. I still follow a wily Sammy around as he toddles throughout the house, intent on terrorizing the cat, and I still try to stay connected to my sweet Maxwell, pulling him into frequent hugs and holding on tight.

By the end of that first post-diagnosis week, occasional ripples start to appear on my surface to suggest to those around me that all may not be well, but these go as quickly as they came, occurring most often in the form of unexpected fits of sobbing. A few days after Max's diagnosis, for example, I end up monopolizing most of a case conference check-in to cry once again in front of my coworkers, who in turn show themselves to be the compassionate, caring, lovely women they truly are. A day later I can be found standing in the driveway of one of Meghan's friends, weeping into his mother's arms as she gently rubs my back, and my alarmed daughter waits for the mini-van to swallow her whole. Jump forward a few days more, and I am sobbing in front of my kind but bewildered ex-husband, who had just arrived to pick up Daniel for a visit and had only asked me how Maxwell's feedback session had gone.

Despite my tears, everything else on the surface of our lives initially remains the same. Yes, we now have a diagnosis in hand, but little else. If we must wait, so be it. Officially knowing Max has Autism is merely the first step in a long journey, after all, a journey which the six of us will take together, hand in hand, like those plucky Von Trapps. My roles as a mother, wife, daughter, sister, and psychologist remain unchanged. I may be sad, I may even experience grief, but I will soldier through this, I will blossom and grow. We all will! And yet, throughout that first week, a sense of foreboding begins to seep in, filling me from the bottom up with what Thoreau once referred to as 'quiet desperation'. *Things are going to get worse. Much, much worse.*

The only thing I can compare the first post-diagnosis week is to how the earth must feel just before a tsunami hits. On some level it must sense that a fundamental shift has happened, somewhere, deep within. On some level it must know that in a very few moments, a wave of unfathomable change will be triggered by that inner shift, and that nothing will ever be as it once was. Pretending life is the same will not make it so. However, for a blessed few moments when one looks at the surface, all that can be seen is a glorious blue sea and those occasional ripples.

At the end of the week, I decide to try and make sense of what Max's diagnosis means to me by making a list. Given that only seven days have gone by since we were told our son has Autism, it may seem a tad premature to create such a list, but the reality is that the seven-days-ago-diagnosis merely put a pretty label on experiences that have existed for years. Further, list-making is what I do when feeling anxious, upset, helpless, on the verge of a total breakdown, or in this case, all of the above. In other words, in situations in which there is not a damn thing I can do in the moment, I make lists. And so, after putting my babies to bed and hugging Max perhaps a bit too tight, I head downstairs to my computer, create a new word file, and begin to type.

MAX DIAGNOSED WITH Autism MEANS THAT:

1)   Max is still the same little boy he was as before the diagnosis.

2)	The meaning of Max being the same little boy is more complicated that it appears. Yes, Max is still my bright, funny, curious child who loves to help me bake banana bread, who finger paints me beautiful pictures, who has entire stories memorized, and who says things like "That was an absolutely delicious dinner, Mommy" (this said with a plate of uneaten food before him).

BUT

It also means Max is still the same child who hits me with his fists or head when upset, who often seems locked in his complex rituals, and who has meltdowns for seemingly nonsensical things, such as the jam on his bread being spread wrong, me driving the incorrect way home from preschool, or his sister's hair up in a ponytail. It also means there are moments (shameful moments, but real ones, nonetheless) when I wonder if I gave birth to a wild, rabid animal, rather than a boy.

3)	Max still being Max means all of it, the brightness and the dark, the lightness and the heaviness. All of it is Max and all of it makes him who he is.

4)	Moments of optimism can come bubbling up when least expected, filling me with the certainty that I know I can do this.

5)	Moments of despair can come bubbling up when least expected, filling me with the certainty that I am completely over my head.

6)	I have the inner capacity to inflict bodily harm. Please don't misunderstand. I have never hit anyone, nor do I ever plan to. I just mean that if before the diagnosis I was a mother lioness when it came to my children, now I am a mother lioness on steroids, hyper vigilant of any situation that could hurt my baby and ready to make use of a mean left hook, if need be. Enough said.

7)	The kindness of so many strangers and acquaintances who have shown their concern and support seems limitless and has made all the difference in the world (included in this grouping are many of my fellow counsellors, this despite my crossed arms cynicism towards the lot of them).

8)	The ignorance of a few strangers who have openly shown their pity or disapproval (e.g., when Max is having a meltdown at the playground), also knows no bounds (please refer back to #6 for clarification on my feelings about this).

9)	I have never been more grateful for having gone through school to become a psychologist, as I at least already know the language of Autism, being fluent in terms like echolalia, perseveration, and self-stimulation.

10)   I have never been more aware of just how limited me being a psychologist truly is in this situation, as much like a student who has textbook knowledge of French but has never actually lived in France, I remain absolutely clueless to the culture, customs and laws of this strange new land I find myself in.

11)   This is just the beginning and that there are many miles to go before I sleep.

CHAPTER 5

While clearly devastated by Max's diagnosis, in the weeks that follow our meeting with Dr. Christie, Joel seems able to integrate this information into his life and to keep moving forward. Yes, moments of pure grief suddenly creep up behind him and knock him down when he least expects it, but unlike me, he somehow picks himself back up, wipes himself off, and carries on. It could be differences in our personalities that play a role in how we cope, or it could be our backgrounds themselves. Joel comes from a large, vocal, Jewish family, the eldest of five children, four of whom were boys. Since as far back as he can remember, the norm for him has been to talk about anything that enters his mind, particularly if what is on his mind is bothersome (in other words, Joel is a card-carrying member of the kvetching club). As a result, if you spend more than an hour or two with my husband you are more likely than not to hear him vent. If for some reason some obstacle or social nicety prevents him from venting (and it would have to be a pretty damn important social nicety for this to happen), Joel will become increasingly agitated and may even pace a room or mutter under his breath about inconsequential things. Once he's gotten what he wants to express out, however, he becomes cheerful and good-humoured again, no longer carrying whatever baggage had been feeling too heavy inside of him.

When talking about my husband it's also important to mention that he's a journalist, a fact that has come in handy when it comes to processing feelings about Max. Months before we even considered having our son assessed, Joel began writing a family column for the newspaper he works for. Every two weeks I'd see our family's hijinks splashed across the local paper, Joel's descriptions of our somewhat chaotic life always humorous and with more than an element of truth. Over time, more and more people mentioned his column to me, how they felt as if they actually knew our family as a result. And then came the diagnosis of Autism, hitting us all as gently as an anvil to the head. At first, Joel considered stopping the column. How could he write about Max anymore without mentioning Autism? And how could he write a humorous column about such a serious, devastating topic? But somehow, he did. Somehow, he does. Somehow, he manages to incorporate Max's diagnosis in a way that is equal parts respectful, poignant, and funny, and in so doing, I think that as a father he has begun to heal.

I've also turned to writing, but what comes out of me are dark, despairing poems that merely add to the weight of my grief and leave me even more mute and inexpressive. Why inexpressive? Blame my own socio-cultural upbringing (it's an easy target, after all). Conjure up your biggest stereotypes about WASPs and you won't be close off the mark. I come from an academic family, my mother a librarian and my father first a philosophy professor and later a Dean at the local university. While feelings were considered important both at home and in the Anglican Sunday School I attended, it was mostly the feelings of *other* people that were emphasized. I learned from an early age to try and be respectful of others, to be kind, not to be hurtful, and to turn the other cheek, all very good lessons which I've also tried to instill in my children. Venting one's own feelings, however, wasn't something that was often modelled. It's not that my parents tried to make us keep stiff upper lips, per se. It was more that what seemed to be the most important things to express inevitably came from the limitless world of ideas. If you happened to spend a meal at our dinner table, then more often than not you might find yourself engaged in an interesting debate. As a result, I've always loved to question and discuss, to have verbal volleys for pleasure. As a child, I was encouraged to think for myself and to question things, as long as I did so in a polite, well-mannered way (my mother was from Connecticut, after all!). But venting about this, that, and the other emotion? Not so much. Imagine the culture shock when Joel and I began dating and found to our mutual chagrin that I hated talking about my *feelings* and he despised having endless debates about *ideas*.

Despite knowing this about each other, on occasion we still attempt to draw the other one to our side. I have been known to follow my husband from room to room, needling him with my questions, trying to get into the core of his thoughts. "But why do you believe in not eating pork or fasting on certain days, when you aren't even all that religious? Why is that important to you?"

"Because I'm Jewish," he'll respond, clearly exasperated at having to give the same answer for the fiftieth time.

"But you are Jewish regardless of whether you do those things. You could do nothing and still be Jewish. I want to understand, I want to know!"

At this point, Joel will typically go upstairs to his office and firmly shut the door behind him, annoyed that I have yet again tried to bully him into explaining his most private and personal beliefs.

For his part, Joel has been known to search me out whenever I seem overly quiet or withdrawn and demand to know how I'm feeling. "What's wrong?" he'll ask, sitting down close to me and invading my personal space.

"Nothing's wrong," I'll say. "I just want to watch this TV show."

"But I can tell that something's wrong. What are you feeling?"

"Nothing is wrong," I'll repeat.

"Alicia, something is clearly wrong. You have barely spoken to me all night. What's going on? Are you mad at me about something?"

"What's wrong is that you keep asking me what's wrong!" I'll finally snap. "Can you just please leave me alone? Can you please just do that?"

And so it goes, the emotionally expressive person colliding with the introverted thinking one and both getting left with bruises. In recent years, however, Joel and I have reached an unspoken agreement that basically entails me not interrogating him quite so much about why he believes whatever he believes and he not pestering me quite so often about whatever the hell I'm feeling.

This arrangement has worked swimmingly for both of us until Max's diagnosis. While Joel seems to benefit from turning to the typical Woody Allen school of venting in order to cope, I've found little solace in the limitless world of ideas, and, as September turns predictably into October, have become even more withdrawn and shut down. It doesn't take a rocket scientist to figure out which coping strategy can cause the most harm. Thus, without the time-honoured skill of kvetching to help pull me out, I've somehow gotten stuck in the proverbial muck and it is here that I remain.

* * * * * *

Having one's child receive a diagnosis of Autism elicits different emotions for different parents. Grief, shock, denial, anger, guilt, you name it, some mother or father out there has felt it. And while I of course can't speak for all parents, I do think that for many of us, a diagnosis brings with it some relief. Relief that finally (*finally!*) there is an official, recognizable term to describe what has, until this point, seemed so overwhelming, so isolating, so stressful, and so damn idiosyncratic. Finally, we know what we're dealing with. Finally, we can begin taking the appropriate, universally acknowledged steps necessary towards helping our child. Finally, we can learn how to cope with what seems like inexplicable rages, nonsensical rituals, minimal social skills, or even a total lack of communication. Finally, we are ready to stop wringing our hands and to start *doing*.

Except here's the rub. Here's what really smarts. It turns out that there are no appropriate, universally acknowledged steps in which to start placing one's feet. They don't exist. In their place is a mishmash of credible treatment possibilities with less credible, researched protocols with the untested or alternative. There's behavioural, biomedical, relational, even equestrian. It's snake oil mixed with science, natural mixed with sterile, double-blind studies mixed with desperation, all stirred into one pot. What's more, from left, right, and centre comes the message that time is of the essence, that even before a child has received his or her diagnosis the clock had begun ticking.

Within weeks of Max's diagnosis, the well-meaning and the less well-meaning start flooding Joel and my inboxes with suggestions, recommendations, links to the perfect remedy. What are we waiting for? Why aren't we changing our son's diet/giving him massive amounts of vitamins/undergoing chelation therapy/refusing any additional vaccinations/swimming with the dolphins/signing him up for ABA or RDI or the Son-Rise program/running off to Mongolia to commune with nature already? Why are we hesitating and trying to gather more information when time was passing us by? What is stopping us from diving right in? What kind of parents are we, anyway?

I become paralysed by the sheer amount of conflicting information coming my way and find my inherently skeptical nature and training in the scientific method at odds (again!) with Joel's more open mind and willingness to at least *consider* methods that other parents (often readers of his column who have taken time out of their days to email him) have found helpful, alternative or not. It's too much, too soon, and while my better half and I waste time debating the merits of this treatment or that, our little boy continues to spiral into meltdown mode.

When we try to access possible, publicly funded treatments we find that endless bureaucratic red tape and waiting lists block our path. This is our Canadian tax dollars at work? Seriously? I become increasingly cynical about the entire Autism Intervention field and laugh bitterly when we receive a letter in the mail stating that even if Maxwell meets screening criteria for thirty hour a week Intensive

Behavioural Intervention program (a program that could be accessed quicker if we go the private route but would then cost us $40,000-50,000 a year), the wait could be up to three years. While our relief knows no bounds when the psychologist who diagnosed Max reassures us that our child is too high-functioning for such a program and that he will be better off accessing the four-hour-a-week Applied Behaviour Analysis (ABA) program, an intervention that involves a wait that is in months rather than years, I can't help but wonder what a several year wait *would* be like for parents of lower functioning children?

Trying to access other presumably available services proves almost as difficult, with representatives from two different agencies telling me to contact the other for help. We are told by some to be patient, that there are many, many children in need and that this is an under-serviced area. We are told by others that the clock is continuing to tick and that the window for early intervention will close if we don't put things into gear and *get started* with treatment already. I notice my anxiety and desperation continue to increase as weeks and weeks pass post-diagnosis and nothing seems to be happening. Why is nothing happening? Can't anyone see that our little boy and his hapless parents need help?

Until. Until Joel and I realize that while we can't do everything, we can at least start to do something and we lay down our own first step by contacting Elaine, a highly recommended occupational therapist in private practice. It is in her therapy room, during our first appointment together, that I discover that Maxwell's frequent outbursts and seemingly nonsensical behaviour have a rhyme and a reason behind them. It's explained to me that, like many autistic children, Maxie becomes emotionally "dysregulated" when faced with things that I take for granted—loud noises, bright colours, a crowded room, direct eye contact, sudden movement—and needs help learning how to calm himself down. I'm taught simple holds that seem to actually relax my jack-in-the-box child, as well as different strategies to help encourage him to have two-sided interactions, to actually *be present* with me rather than zoned out. During that first session, I watch as my normally shy, passive little boy connects with Elaine, shares a giggle with her, and actually begins to *play*. And although in that therapy room there is no miracle cure hiding in a corner somewhere for me if I just search hard enough, what I do find is something that's perhaps more valuable, something that I thought might be gone forever. I find hope.

CHAPTER 6

There's a new emotion I've been experiencing lately and I can't quite find the word for it. It's an odd mix of sad and grateful, pulling me back and forth, up and down, here and there. Sometimes it's a little more of one than the other, sometimes it's an equal balance of both. Sadly grateful or gratefully sad? Neither sounds exactly right. This new emotion has been visiting me a lot lately, as the bureaucratic wheels of various special services machines have suddenly started moving at the same time, catching me unawares.

Take a few weeks ago. Like many parents, I attended the annual autumn open house/barbecue at my daughter's school. While ostensibly there to mingle with Meghan's teachers, I also went in order to find out whatever I could about next year's kindergarten class. By the time all of the hotdogs had been eaten, I'd learned that for Max a "transition" meeting with the school will have to be scheduled next spring, including not only Joel and I, but also the various professionals involved in his care. For the opportunity of being able to plan Max's transition so smoothly, I am grateful. For the *necessity* of such planning, I'm incredibly sad.

It was recently suggested to us that we set up a Registered Disability Savings Plan for Max, a new program that gives us financial peace of mind for his future, should he need it. For this program, I am grateful. Having to even ponder that Max might ever require this money (versus being gainfully employed), makes my heart ache. We have also been encouraged to apply for a grant from the March of Dimes to help subsidize the cost of diapers, as Maxie is over three (going on four), and still in pull-ups. Again, the fact that such a program exists makes me grateful. Actually applying for it for some reason has made me so sad that I can't do it (Joel has agreed to apply instead).

Not too long ago I talked on the phone with a professional from the community referral program involved in developmental services. This phone call (as well as the various brochures which arrived in the mail soon after) provided helpful information about numerous programs out there and has led to new referrals for Max. For this I am grateful (and yes, once again, also sad).

And then there's this morning. A coordinator for family support programs arrived at our house to help us fill out government forms for "special services at home" funding. While the wait list is lengthy (three years), such funding would permit us to purchase services of a support worker, who would provide an hour or two of weekly respite in our home, or it could fund certain programs that focus on "personal growth and development" goals. Again, I feel such gratitude that these programs (and such funding) exists, and that the coordinator actually came to our home (a house-call!) to fill out the forms with us. During this morning's conversation, I was also told about additional services we might choose to access in the future, such as an actual respite home in the community, where children aged six to twenty-one can stay anywhere from a night to a month. The community residence is meant for children who are experiencing behavioural and emotional challenges, due to their developmental disabilities, and is likely a godsend for their exhausted parents.

Before the family support coordinator had finished explaining about the residence, I was already shaking my head, trying to make her words fall back out before I truly *heard* them.

"But we won't ever need something like that," I said. "Not for Max." Joel also shook his head.

The woman smiled respectfully and nodded (clearly she had heard this before). She then carefully explained that it is hard to know how Max's behaviour will be as he gets older (and his fists get bigger). She added that because of the fun, recreational activities there are to do, many children actually love going to the community home (probably as much as my cat *loves* being boarded at the kennel whenever we go away).

As the woman continued smiling at me, I wanted to protest again, but how could I, when I had just described all of Max's aggressive behaviour when upset (hitting with elbows and fists, slapping himself and others in the face, head-butting, pushing, hair pulling), and she had just watched as Max behaved how he often behaves when I'm talking with another adult (especially a stranger). During this visit, my child pulled out all of the stops, including violent bonking, grabbing my hair and pulling it out by the fistfuls, as well as avoiding all eye contact with the woman, other than to scream "NO!" in her face. Not an extreme meltdown, not an episode of out-of-his-mind silliness, but still.

After the papers were signed and the coordinator had left, the image of a future Maxwell in a group home kept sliding into my brain. How could I ever put my child in such a place, even for a night? He's my baby, my little boy. As I looked at a three-year-old Maxie playing contently with his toy trains, it seemed unimaginable. But what about if he's eight or twelve and the aggressive behaviour continues? What about then?

While every part of my being tells me that we will never need it, how can I really know? How can I be sure that one day I too might be overwhelmingly grateful for a place like this residential home, whether it's "fun" for Max or not? And it's this realization, this shitty, horrible realization that as mother causes me the most sadness.

******

Despite my mood, I'm trying to live in the moment, to keep up with my child, but it's difficult. Max leaps from this emotion to that with alacrity, his whole being focused purely on the experience directly in front of him. Whatever may have happened just before is already forgotten, pushed to the side by a new feeling. Max in action is like someone jumping from stone to stone in a river, all attention on the rock that he's balancing on now.

Overjoyed to see me one moment when I pick him up from preschool, outraged and slapping me full in the face one second later for reasons often unknown (perhaps his teacher opened the classroom gate for him to walk through, rather than pick him up and hand him over, as expected?). Skip to a few moments later, and he's now shrieking in the car, completely inconsolable ("I DON'T LIKE YA! I DON'T LIKE YA! GO RUN AWAY!"). Within minutes we are back home and Max turns a bright red face up at me and cheerfully asks if he can help with the dinner, the tears still not dry on his cheeks. When I say yes, my own eyes full, he dances to the kitchen, all sweetness and light.

Unlucky for him, unlucky for us, I'm not built this way. While I *try* to pull it together quickly in order to appreciate the joyful, connected moments, a part of me is still back at that preschool, grief-stricken that yet another unreachable moment has happened, and all too aware that their frequency seems to be increasing.

In contrast to my stone-jumping son, my memory is like an endless prairie, each experience rolling seamlessly into the next, all moments connected into one continuous whole and easily recalled. Ask me to remember what it was like to be eight-, eleven-, fifteen-, or thirty-one-years-old, and bingo, bango, I'm there. Whether the emotions and experiences are completely accurate is irrelevant; what matters to me is how they *feel*, and how they feel is immediate and true, full of colour and shadow.

Hence, while I'm thankful that Max seems able to recover from his internal explosions with aplomb and return to his sunny self, I find myself starting to drown in the accumulating fears and sorrows that I experience whenever he leaps onto a more jagged stone. Will the violent outbursts get worse? Will he ever become aggressive towards people outside his family? To other children? Will his unreachable moments stop being like small stones in a river to be jumped across and instead grow into endless ridges of impenetrable rock?

So yes, I'm trying to live in the moment, to keep up with my often affectionate and joyful child, but sometimes, dammit, I just can't seem to make the leap.

* * * * * *

I'm standing next to the minivan, holding Sam in one arm and Max by the hand. All around me in the daycare parking lot are perfect parents and their perfect children, all doing the same. To a passerby, there is nothing unique about my little family unit, nothing to make a person pull a rubberneck or gawk. And yet, other than breakfast time, the daily preschool pickup has become my most dreaded time of the day.

It typically starts out well, like most dreaded things do (the hell that is birth begins with a sweet pink line or two on a stick, after all). Sam is his typical chirpy self and Max is eager to share with me all that's happened in his day. So far, so good. The truly ridiculous thing is that, just like the moronic Charlie Brown and his football, I always fall for the initial pleasantries, the ease in which I get to strap my little ones into their car seats and start our familiar journey back to the house. Everything seems fine, everything seems good. *Maybe this time it will actually go well.*

Today's just like any other. Once Max and Sam are safely buckled in their seats, I turn on the radio to a favourite station and then turn my head back quickly to ask my sons about their days. Each time it always begins the same, as these things do.

"Did you guys have a good day at school?" I ask.

Sam speaks first. "I missed Mommy."

Max interrupts, happy as can be. "I had a great day! There were new cars and a new parking garage and I got to play with it at free time and it is like the parking garage at Papa and Yaya's house and Papa likes to play it with me and sometimes Papa takes his old cars and plays it with me!"

"That's wonderful, Maxie!" I say, turning on the ignition. "Are you both ready to drive home?"

"Yeah!" they shout, and we're on our way.

I drive down one road, then another, eventually reaching a busy intersection. I'm attempting to turn left during the traffic light's last moment of orange, doing anything and everything possible to shorten this drive.

"Mommy!" Max calls out, his voice still cheerful. "What's that, there?"

I make the turn on red and keep on trucking. "What are you looking at, Maxie?"

Anxiety starts to creep into Max's voice and I press on the accelerator. "There! There! With the slides!"

I quickly look out the window and see a large park. "Oh, that's the big park," I say.

"Yeah. The *big* park."

I speed through an orange light just as its changing colour and then turn the volume of the radio louder, my fingers tightening around the steering wheel. *When the hell will some genius get around to inventing teleportation already?*

"Mommy!" Max says. "What's that, there?"

I quickly turn my head to look out the window and almost rear-end the car in front of me. "Um, the ice cream shop?"

"Yeah, the ice cream shop."

My heart start to race against my breastbone and I press my foot down harder. Sam begins to hum in the backseat and I try to focus on that.

"Guess what I'm making for dinner tonight, guys? Pasta and garlic bread!"

"Yummy pasta! Yummy pasta! Yummy pasta!" Sam crows.

"What's that, there?" Max again.

Again, the quick head turn. "That's the fire station, Max."

"*No!*" Max shouts, all the oxygen in the car being sucked up with his anger. "What's that, there?"

"Max, all I saw was the fire station. What did you see?"

In response, Max grabs one of his shoes (*damn you, Velcro*), and throws it at my head. Thud. He then grabs the other and whips it at the windshield. A direct hit. I turn my head to look at him and see him begin thrashing in his car seat, hitting himself in the head with his little fists.

"No! No! What's that, there?"

Knowing that if I stop I will only prolong all of our agony, I again step on the gas. I can hear Sam start to whimper and my chest squeezes. "Honey," I say, in my Max-voice, "I don't know what you mean. Please tell Mommy what you mean!"

"No! No!" Max shrieks. "I'm not honey! Tell me! Tell me! What's that, there?"

"Max, I don't know. I'm sorry, but I don't know! Help me, here, dammit! Please!"

Sam stops crying for a moment, to reprimand me. "Mommy say bad word. Mommy naw-tee."

Max continues screaming, completely out of his head. "No! No!"

Finally, like a mirage, our house appears, and I quickly pull up to the curb, my front wheel going over it with a thump. I jump out of the car and take Sam out of his car seat, running him to the porch. I then head back for Max, who has become a thrashing, fist-thumping, shrieking mess of boy. I carry him to the porch, trying to avoid his hits when possible, and begin ringing the door repeatedly, desperately. After what seems like a lifetime, Meghan answers.

"Hi, Mom. What's for supper?" A normal question, but when was the last time that my family was actually *normal*?

While I'm aware that tears are flowing down my face, that I am sobbing in front of my eleven-year-old *child*, all that I care about at this moment is that there is a human being in front of me who is big enough to take Max from me, if only for a few minutes.

"Take them!" I cry, pushing Max towards my daughter. "Please take them for me!"

Meghan instinctively holds out her arms and I thrust Max towards her. "Mommy?" she says.

I lift Sam into the house, then run to the downstairs' bathroom, shutting the door behind me. I slide down to the ground and begin sobbing into my knees. *What's the point of all of this? What's the goddamn point?*

A minute or two later, there's a knock at the door. "Go away!" I shout.

The knocking becomes louder, more demanding. *The knock of a man.* "Alicia," Joel says. "Let me in."

"I just need some time. Please go!"

"The kids are going berserk. I've got Max with Daniel right now, and Sammy with Meghan. I can't believe you left both kids with an eleven-year-old. Please tell me what's going on!"

I reach up and open the door, then slide back down onto the floor. I don't look up as my husband enters, just curl into myself more.

"So, what happened?" Joel asks, bending down.

"It's these drives home from daycare! I can't take it anymore! Each time it's the same. Max starts out in a good mood and then he loses it. He asks me questions and if I don't say the *exact* correct thing, he has a meltdown. He was throwing his shoes at me while I was driving. I could have gotten into an accident!"

"He said something to me about you saying fire station and not fire house."

I look up abruptly at my husband and then burst out laughing. I laugh harder and harder, a shrieking, guffawing, snot-flowing mess of a woman (*like mother, like son*).

"Honey?" Joel asks. He puts his hand on my shoulder and my laughter turns to sobbing.

"Oh my god! I'm going crazy, aren't I? Did you ever see *The Snake Pit*? I'm actually going crazy!"

"You're not going crazy, but you should see Dr. Seidler about how you're doing. I'm getting worried about you."

From behind the door we can both hear sudden shouting and then the sound of something hitting the floor. Joel quickly stands up, his hand on the doorknob.

"Remember what Max's OT Elaine said during our first visit. This is to be expected, you know? He's high-functioning enough to hold it together all day at preschool, but at some point he has to let it out, all that stress. Unfortunately, he seems to let it out most with you."

Joel kisses the top of my head, before heading out into the hallway. I slowly stand up and look at my face in the mirror. Makeup is running down my cheeks and my eyes are blood shot. My hair is standing at crazy angles, the remains of Max's attempts at pulling it out from the scalp. I turn on the water and splash handfuls of it on my hot face.

"A damn fine mother you turned out to be," I say, before giving myself the finger.

******

At Max's next occupational therapy session, I pull Elaine to the side and describe what's been happening during our rides home from daycare and how I've come to dread the drive. The OT informs me that what Max is experiencing is something common for children with Autism. Called mind-blindness (although I prefer to call it by its other name—Dante's Seventh Circle of Hell), my little boy truly cannot "get" that whatever he is thinking or expecting to happen isn't exactly the same as what another person is thinking or planning to do. Thus, if you answer his question in a way Max didn't expect, he actually believes that you are being cruel, upsetting, and basically messing with him intentionally. *Why don't you just give me the right answer? Why do you have to be so mean*?

This extreme difficulty at perspective-taking causes more than a few problems for my little boy and those who love him, to put it mildly. As the OT and I watch Max climb into a plastic kiddie pool filled with rubber balls, his expression pure joy, I can't enjoy the moment. Instead, I turn my focus inward, my brain circling around and around the question that scares me the most: What if this "blindness" never ends, and thirty-pound Max eventually morphs into a one-hundred-and-seventy-pound man, still hitting and kicking at anyone who answers him incorrectly? What then?

CHAPTER 7

My friend Alisa calls and I actually answer the phone. I say actually, because my need to talk to anyone outside of my immediate family has inexplicably vanished. Despite being an introvert, in the past I've always craved regular social contact with my closest friends. In the last month, however, such craving has been replaced by an almost desperate need to be left alone. A bubble has been growing around me, expanding daily. Its skin is impenetrable, allowing only my children (and sometimes my husband) entry. Planned get-togethers with friends have fallen by the wayside, with me cancelling anything that had already been scheduled, often at the last possible minute. The fact that the excuses I give are flimsy matters little. To be honest, I no longer care what anyone else thinks or feels unless they reside under my roof. I no longer want to hear anyone else's voice or have to listen to their mundane problems. I really don't give a damn if one friend has gained seven pounds or if another had a lousy coffee date with some goof from an on-line site whose profile picture turned out to be ten years old. These are not real problems, people!

But today for some reason, I pick up the phone and actually talk to the friend on the other end of the line. During the call, I use all of my energy to steer the conversation toward superficial, surface topics, filling the air with my thoughts on the weather, reality TV shows, and municipal politics. Alisa follows my lead, at least until I'm about to hang up the phone. Just as I'm about to say a chirpy goodbye, she blurts out a meaningful question, forcing me to dunk my head below the surface, despite my best efforts.

"What's the hardest thing right now?" she asks.

"What?"

"Alicia, this is me, okay? Not some telephone solicitor. *Me.*" Alisa sighs, the sound causing my eyes to suddenly fill. *Dammit.* She sighs once more. "You're my best friend, and you're hurting. I just want to, I just hoped to..."

"What?"

"What's the hardest thing right now...about Max?"

"Um..." I glance at the gigantic clock on our wall. I've given her fifteen minutes of my precious time already. Why isn't that enough?

"I know you don't want to talk about it, but that's what worries me," she says. "I know you, and I know when things are bad, you withdraw."

"So you're the psychologist now?" I laugh. Even I can tell how fake my voice sounds.

"Alicia, I want to know. What's the hardest thing for you?"

"Ah," I say. My eyes fill and I can no longer see the clock's time. "Not now, okay?" I say, carefully hanging up the phone. I wait for Alisa to call back, sitting at the kitchen table with my hands neatly folded. If she calls back, I'll let voice mail get it. Who does she think she is anyway, her with her damn questions? If she thinks I'm going to answer again, she's crazy!

She doesn't call back.

I sit there a while longer. Thoughts start bubbling up, each one darker and heavier than the one before. Eventually I reach towards the counter for a piece of paper and a pen, and begin list-making.

What's the hardest thing?

The more I think about it, the more I realize that it isn't any one thing, but rather a collection of things, shards of glass that are incredibly hard to hold singly, let alone as a group. I'm trying, doing my best to avoid having anyone else get cut, but my best isn't working.

What's the hardest thing?

I put the pen to paper, and begin.

Mornings. During the last few days Max has woken up upset. This used to happen in the spring, but then suddenly stopped. While we've been told that going from being asleep to being awake is a transition and transitions can be difficult, Joel and I can't figure out how one morning our son will wake up happy and cheerful, and the very next day the mere act of waking triggers a landslide. Take this morning. Before Max had even opened his eyes, he was muttering in a grumpy kind of way. Within seconds, his muttering changed to open-eyed anger. Despite Joel and I doing all of the OT strategies that have worked in the past, such keeping the curtains shut, doing "leg hugs", and foot rubs, Max exploded with an out-of-control meltdown within about two more minutes, our little boy quickly stuck in what we call mind-lock.

Mind-lock. Even though this is a term I've invented, it's one that I wish I could wipe from our entire family's vocabulary forever. Now that I think about it, *this* may be the hardest thing. So how do I feel about mind-lock? Let's just say that if mind-lock were a person, I'd take him or her behind the school and beat the crap out of them. Mind-lock is when Max seems paralysed between two choices and screams for the first option, only to start shrieking when it is offered to him, hysterical for the other choice. Mind-lock is what happened at the ice cream store at the cottage, but can happen anywhere. It can be about two pairs of socks, two chewable vitamins, two TV shows, or two types of hugs. Mind-lock may occur for up to an hour, regardless of whether we try to distract our child, soothe him quietly, or ignore the behaviour entirely (and good luck with that last option). Mind-lock can be triggered when Max is already upset (as it did today), but just as often it will begin despite our son having been happy and calm just moments before. Like someone tiptoeing across an old minefield, you can never be confident about what may happen with your next step. When in the midst of a mind-lock situation, I truly believe that I may go insane.

This morning's mind-lock was typical. Once Max had calmed down enough from his meltdown for me to open up the blinds and turn on the light, I helped him out of his bed and began pulling off his pyjamas. I then took off his nighttime diaper, to replace it with a morning pull-up. It was in that moment, in that ordinary, routine moment, that a key in Max's brain suddenly turned and a door shut, locking my child inside and me out.

"No! No! I need a diaper!" he shouted, as I began to put his foot in one side of the pull-up.

"Okay, Maxie," I said. "You can wear a diaper today, if you'd like. Let me just get one." I reached up to the changing table and grabbed a fresh one, then showed it to him.

"No! No diaper! I don't want a diaper! No! No!"

I took a deep breath, then another, willing my heart to slow down. "All right, Maxie," I said. "Let's put on a pull-up, then."

"No! No pull-up! A diaper! A diaper!"

"Okay, Max," I said again. "Let's put on this diaper. It's all ready for you!"

"NO!" Max began jumping up and down, his body naked and his face bright-red. He ran to his bed and began throwing toys off it. He grabbed his favourite stuffed animal and pitched it at my head. Ignoring this, I followed him with a diaper in one hand and a pull-up in the other. I could tell my little boy was in agony and that he had reached the point of no return. Despite this, I still tried to reach him. I *still tried*.

"Let's put on a nice pull-up, then," I said. "Look, it has Diego on it! Let's hurry, okay? Sammy is already downstairs, eating breakfast. Wouldn't you like to go eat breakfast, too?"

Instead of answering, Max began to jump up and down faster and faster, beating his ears with his fists. Watching him pummel himself with such force made my stomach turn over. *Oh no, sweetie. Please not that. Anything but that*. The screaming turned into a shriek that I knew must have made his throat hurt. I attempted to force Max into a deep pressure hold, but he kept pulling away, no longer able to let me soothe him. After a few minutes Joel entered the room. He met my eyes and I silently told him all that needed to be said, before handing him the pull-up and the diaper. I then left the room, not allowing myself to cry my useless tears until I was safely out of ear shot. So yes, mind-lock should be at the top of my list of hard things.

The other children. Now that I think about it more, how Max's Autism impacts his siblings should be number one in terms of what's the hardest thing. If I focus on this hard thing too much, however, I know I'll get pulled into a despair that's not so different from what Max experiences. This one is just so hard. To possibly make it a bit easier, I need to break it down into its three component parts.

Daniel. Ah, Daniel, my eldest, my first-born, my mother-maker. My fifteen-going-on-forty-year-old son, the kid who asks for so little lately and puts up with so much. In the last several months I can't help but notice that Daniel has been trying to make as few waves as possible, especially when a meltdown is erupting in our house. When I've talked to Joel or my parents about this, they try to put a positive spin on my son's behaviour. Having an autistic little brother will help him become a more compassionate, caring man! While this is true (how could it not be true?), it doesn't make things better. If anything, it makes things worse. When I remember myself at fifteen, the world I recall was inhabited by me and my friends. We were mercurial, mouthy, self-centred teens, doing exactly what teens typically do. No, not just typically. What teens should be permitted (within reason) to do. We were going through that second developmental stage (the first being toddlerhood) when everything revolved around us. Given how fleeting that stage is, no one begrudged us our drama, our need to be on centre stage.

Not so for my teenager. Instead, my fifteen-year-old is becoming a compassionate, caring man at a time when he has no business doing so. Sometimes I want to shake him, to yell at him to swear more, to break curfew, to drink orange juice straight from the carton, dammit! Do something (anything!) to demand my attention. But because of the reality of our lives, I find myself not even having the time to give him that quick shake. While in a perfect world we would have the necessary time and space to talk privately about his drama project, or the screenplay he's been writing for his "vlog", or even get into an occasional moody teen/clueless parent sparing match, the truth is that most days the best I can do is to nod in his direction while he passes by. So yes, how Daniel's been affected is a hard, hard thing.

Meghan. My eleven-year-old daughter, the only girl in a sea of boys. Meghan is at that age where she's on the brink of everything, and needs a mother more than ever. A kid who wants her two baby brothers to worship her, not abuse her. While I can tell that Meg loves Max, it's obvious that she's incredibly frustrated and hurt by his behaviour, as his aggression is often directed at her. If she attempts to say good morning to him, he may hug her or he may growl in her face. If she tries to talk to me (and this is during calm times), Max may head-butt her or shout repeatedly that *he* is the "talker", laughing hysterically between yelps. While we don't let him get away with this, and we remind him that of course Meghan gets a chance to speak, his screaming is usually enough to shut her down. How could it not? Meg is still a *child* and as a child she takes these outbursts towards her personally. While I make sure to make time for her every evening, mornings like today are hard and she too is given a quick nod over the screaming and the banging.

Sammy. Oh my god. This hard thing may be the hardest one of all. Sammy is almost two and has grown up only knowing these meltdowns. While most of the time he acts immune to the screaming, this morning was a reminder that he is not. After cheerfully eating his breakfast, he suddenly asked Max if he was "sad" and then proceeded to sing him a lullaby. Hearing your baby trying to comfort his shrieking brother with *tura lura lura*, rather than just focus on being a baby, is a hard, hard, hard thing indeed.

As I look at this list of hard things, I realize that when it comes to the order of items, I might have messed things up. Because, you see, there actually is something that is harder than all of the things I've already listed. A thing that is so hard, it makes me want to wail and keen, rending my garments with one rough pull.

Maxwell. Yes, yes. How all of this impacts Maxwell is the hardest thing by far. For you see, more than half the time Max is a sunny, curious, affectionate child. He's a boy who tries *so hard* to make connections, to form friendships. He's a child who brims with confidence many mornings as he tries to use the potty, a newly learned skill for him. A child who, when he wakes up happy, will start telling a story midway through as you open his door to get him, and will continue chattering throughout his breakfast. A sweet, sweet little boy, who says "Please, Mommy", and "Thank you so much, Daddy", and doesn't deserve to experience the pain of a meltdown and the terror that comes from running around naked, screaming and unreachable, not knowing how to calm down (and all too aware that his parents, his Mommy and Daddy, the two people who *should know*, for god's sake, don't have a clue, either). A child who, once today's morning meltdown had run its one-hour course, slumped against me on the couch, took my hair in his hand to twirl, and began talking calmly about a show on TV, all of his terror forgotten.

So in answer to my friend's question, the hardest thing right now is how this impacts Max. That is the hardest thing of all and the one that, as a parent, is pulling me further and further towards a dark, frightening place that no one should have the audacity to ever go.

Section Three Bargaining
CHAPTER 8

In retrospect, deciding to follow through on a plan to take Max for a weekend to Trenton, Ontario (a city over three hours away from our home) and to stay by ourselves in a hotel when I was on the verge of a nervous breakdown may not have been the wisest decision to make. In my defence, the trip was piggy-backing an already set in place plan to drive my daughter to Trenton to spend time with her father, stepmother, and new baby brother. In my mind, Meghan had put up with so much recently, that I couldn't cancel the trip. The idea of reconfiguring my plans in some way so that, say, I leave Max at home with my highly competent husband and thus give myself a well-needed weekend to myself, never entered my mind. Driving Meg to Trenton, dropping her off at her dad's house, and then checking into the local Holiday Inn for a weekend with my boy was the plan and it was iron-clad. Besides, ever since hearing Max's diagnosis, my desire to spend some quality one-on-one time with him had intensified until it had reached a fever pitch. I'd developed an unacknowledged fear that I was somehow losing my child to a scary entity called Autism, a fear that came out as me *needing* to be with Max and believing that Max needed to be with me, without the busy bustle of home life to distract us.

Initially, the plan goes off without a hitch. We arrive in Trenton in record time, leave Meg safely ensconced in her father's house, and then go to our hotel before dark. Max is a model child that first night, clearly excited about having so much of his Mommy's undivided attention. He spends time exploring our room, which is actually a loft suite. I picked this two-story room both because I inexplicably got a cheap rate for this weekend and because I knew it would allow Max to have enough space in which to play. And play he does. After running up and down the small flight of stairs to our loft bedroom multiple times, he settles on the bottom floor with his Hot Wheels, blocks, train tracks, and random Thomas the Tank engines that I had the foresight to bring with us. As I sit on the sofa and watch him race cars and chatter happily to himself, I expect to feel content. This is what I have driven three hours for. Except the problem is, I don't feel content. Instead, as I sit on the sofa and watch my child I am struck by the realization that being completely responsible for my small son for an entire weekend while I am on the brink of a mental breakdown may not be the wisest move as a mother. I focus on slowing down my breathing and practising the relaxation exercises I have foisted on multiple clients in the past. *Calm down, calm down. This too will pass.*

After a picnic supper on the living room floor, I turn on a kiddie show for Max and decide to call home. Maybe Joel can make me feel better. The phone rings a few times before Daniel answers.

"Yeah, hello?" he mumbles. *We've got to work on telephone etiquette.*

"Hi honey, it's Mom," I say, instantly settling into Upbeat-Mother mode. "How are you?"

"Okay," he says.

"Did you have a good day at school?"

"Yeah...say, do you know where Joel is? I haven't had supper yet."

"Joel's not there?" I grip the receiver in my hand. "Are you sure?"

"Nope, not here." Daniel yawns in the phone. "I was taking a nap and when I came down all the lights were out in the house. No one's here but me."

"Did he leave a note? Is his coat in the hall?"

I hear Daniel walking around the house with the phone. "Nope and nope."

"Maybe he took Sam out for a walk," I suggest.

"Nope, the stroller's still here."

"Can you look outside and see if his car is parked in the street?"

"Do I have too?" Daniel asks. "I'm kind of in my socks."

"*Please!*" My voice comes out high-pitched.

"Okay, okay, just a sec." I hear the front door open and the sound of cars driving past. "Nope, no car."

"You're sure?"

"Mom!" I hear him walk back inside and shut the front door.

"But where could he be? It's after seven o'clock and Sam needs supper. He should have been home with him over an hour ago!"

"*I need supper, Mom,*" my teenager reminds me. "I'm hungry!"

"Okay, here's the plan," I say. "I'm going to try calling our home phone to see if there are any messages on it. It's possible Joel tried to call you when you were sleeping and you just didn't pick up. Whatever you do, don't answer the phone in the next five minutes, okay? I'm also going to try his cell. I'll call you back in ten minutes, all right? Make sure you answer in ten minutes but not five!"

"But what about supper?"

"Just make yourself a sandwich or something, I have to go!" My voice comes out in a sob and I hang up the phone. I look over at Max, thankfully transfixed by a Dora the Explorer episode. I try calling Joel's cell, but there is no answer. I dial my home number again and eventually the machine picks up. *You have no new messages.* I hang up and try Joel's phone once more. At this point I'm in full-out panic attack mode. Tears have begun streaming down my face, as images of my husband and my baby in some sort of car crash or at the hospital fill my mind. *Why did I have to pick this weekend of all weekends to go away? Why? Why? Why?*

"Hello?" Joel's voice fills my ear and for a moment I don't know who it is. "Hello?" There is a lot of noise and muffled talking in the background.

"Where are you?" I nearly shout into the phone. "I talked to Daniel and he hadn't heard from you and now it's after seven o'clock and he hasn't had any dinner and he was worried and I thought you were dead and where is Sammy?"

"Calm down, calm down," Joel says. "I'm at Walmart and can't really talk right now. We're at the checkout."

"But where's Sammy? Where is he?" I find it hard to breathe and cry loudly into the phone.

"Sammy is with me, of course! I wanted to get bean bag chairs and big pillows for Max's quiet spot, like the OT suggested. We stopped in here after daycare and I guess it's taken longer than I thought. Sorry I didn't call Daniel—I guess I forgot."

"But I thought you were dead!" Now I'm not just crying, I'm sobbing. *What's with me and the hysterics, lately?* The racket I'm making is enough to pull Max out of his TV trance. He gets off the carpet and climbs onto the sofa. He starts banging my back with his upper chest, a sign that he's getting agitated.

"Look, sweetie, I'm sorry if I upset you. I can't really talk right now. Can we talk later?" Joel asks.

"Fine!" I whisper, then hang up. I reach an arm around Max and pull him onto my lap. He now starts to bang me with his back against my chest. "It's okay, it's okay," I whisper into his hair, my tears falling onto his head. "It'll be okay." If only I could will it to be so.

******

For the next two days, I'm a nervous wreck, despite the fact that Max continues to be on his best behaviour, eliciting indulgent gazes from other vacationers as he purveys the hotel's breakfast buffet with obvious delight ("Look, Mommy! Pancakes! And more than one!"). True, throughout the weekend there is the occasional odd or ritualistic behaviour, but never a meltdown. Max clearly loves our time together and his blatant joy is the only thing that keeps me going. We spend most of the two days in the hotel, either playing with the trains and cars in our room, eating in the restaurant, or splashing in the pool. During the few times we venture outside, I experience unadulterated panic.

One of the times starts innocently enough—we drive to a huge bookstore in a nearby town and spend over an hour reading books and playing with various toys in the children's section of the bookstore. Max seems to particularly love playing with their train table and I end up agreeing to buy him a train book that makes noises when you press certain buttons. His booty in hand, we make our way to a very small line at the front of the store. Before I take my place, I give Max a quick hug. Having to wait in line makes no sense for my child and thus can be a huge trigger for meltdowns. I remind myself to breathe, relieved to see that the line is moving quickly. Max stands next to me, holding the book against his chest and humming an unrecognizable tune. Suddenly, for no reason I can fathom, he takes a few steps away from me and begins to walk backwards.

"Maxie," I say. "We need to stay in line if we want to buy the book!"

Max keeps stepping backwards and begins to talk in a loud voice to no one in particular, a strange look in his eyes. "*You're* not my Mommy!" he blurts out, his voice rising. "Where's my Mommy? Where are the other kids? *You're* not my Mommy!"

The woman in front of me in line turns around and stares at me face, her mouth forming a frown. I try and smile back, shrugging.

"Maxie!" I call out. "Come back to Mommy, now! Enough with being silly!" I attempt to catch his gaze but his eyes now look unfocused, unreachable.

"*You're* not my Mommy!" he says again, grinning slightly. Seeing that look on his face, a look which, fair or not, I've come to think of as

61

being quintessentially autistic, I start to feel lightheaded and find it hard to breathe. I step out of line and begin walking towards my child, trying to smile reassuringly.

"Of course I'm your Mommy," I say, increasingly aware that strangers are beginning to take notice, to take notice and perhaps get ready to make a move.

"*You're* not my Mommy!" he says, almost shouting.

I will myself to ignore the people around me and to just focus on Max, but find it impossible to do. My thoughts dart around my brain like sparks from a match. *What if someone calls the police? What if they accuse me of kidnapping and try and take my son away from me? What will I do? What will I do?*

"Maxwell," I say softly. "Let's buy your book and then go back to the hotel and have a snack. I'll bet you're hungry for a snack."

"*You're* not my Mommy!" he yells. He starts to bounce on his toes, his hands flapping at his sides. This is never a good sign.

"Come on, sweetie," I say desperately. "Let's get back in line and buy your book, okay?"

Without meaning to, my use of the endearment "sweetie" instantly jolts my child back into himself. His slightly crazed grin turns into a deep frown and his eyes become angry and focused. "I am not sweetie!" he shouts at me. "I am Maxwell Thomas Hendley-Rubinoff, Mommy! Don't call me sweetie, Mommy! Don't call me that!"

"Of course, Maxie, I'm sorry," I say, holding out my hand to him. He takes it and we get back in line. *Side show's over, folks.*

CHAPTER 9

There are few things more humbling as a psychologist than developing a psychological or emotional problem oneself. Didn't all of those years spent slogging through graduate school and eating bowl after bowl of Mr. Noodles while my former high school friends blithely started their careers account for anything? If nothing else, didn't all of that wasted time mean that I would now and forever be protected from the onslaught of ailments such as depression or anxiety, the common colds of mental health? Aren't my neatly framed Master's and Ph.D. degrees meant to do more than prettify my wall? Aren't they shields against mood dips or panic attacks, armour that's supposed to be there for me when I need it?

The answer, of course, is no. Surprising no one except perhaps myself, it turns out that I am human. What is more, I am a human with a fairly messed up history of depression and anxiety in late adolescence. An *almost-forgotten, so-far-in-the-past-it-now-seems-irrelevant-la-la-la* history, true, but a history nonetheless. This history puts me near the front of the line for future problems, a fact that no degrees, no knowledge of cognitive restructuring, progressive muscle relaxation, exposure response prevention, grounding techniques, or mindfulness can mitigate. I am, in fact, the opposite of immune and will always be at risk of experiencing future depressive episodes or symptoms of anxiety, no matter the years that have passed or the number of degrees I've stacked in front of me like a wall of dominoes for protection.

Despite my teenage flirtation with depression (okay, so maybe it was more of a down-and-dirty, drawn-out affair), despite the fact that in the last year I've *known* that I've been juggling too many balls in the air (mother of four, wife, psychologist, Super Woman), and have now been given another (Max's diagnosis), despite the promise I made to myself at the age of eighteen to always be on the lookout for future problems, I ignore the signs and forget the basic golden rule in the world of mental health: Nothing is a given. Despite knowing that for me, the cost of continued happiness and mental stability is to periodically look over my shoulder and not take anything for granted, I stop paying the toll.

Having gone through a few decades in which, other than pretty normal ups and downs, my mood has seemed stable and resilient, I begin to count on my ability to ride the waves of daily life with expertise. What's more, I become cocky, my arrogance a stick I use to poke at a sleeping bear. Look at me! I can get a Ph.D. in Clinical Psychology because I'm so mentally stable! *Poke*. Look at me now! I'm working full-time as a clinical psychologist, helping people in need because I'm just so mentally stable! *Poke*. And here I am again, floored by my little son's behaviour and recent diagnosis, true, but able to cope with the uncertainties of life with aplomb! If given lemons, you make lemonade, right? *Big frigging poke*. And then, surprise, surprise, the giant, burly bear finally wakes up from its lengthy hibernation to give me a poke back. And another, and still another.

In the last several months, my typical work day has consisted of this: Trying to cope with Max's meltdowns each morning as I attempt to leave for my job, all the while pretending that my child's high-pitched screaming doesn't bruise every single part of me, rushing off to a campus in another city in order to focus (fifty minutes at a time) on my clients all day, and then swooping back home again to try and make supper, help with my eldest two children's homework, and cuddle my littlest, all the while trying to cope with Max's evening meltdowns. And then finally, when the house becomes blessedly quiet, nodding to my equally beleaguered husband from across the room before dragging myself off to bed, where I am destined to spend the next hour or so staring at the ceiling, cursing my recent unwelcome house guest, Insomnia.

This has been my modus operandi, this has been my entire family's modus operandi and would have likely continued indefinitely, if only I had not opened an ordinary, professional email while at work the Monday after my weekend away with Max, an email that I find myself unable to read. I stare at the screen, blink several times, then stare again. While I can see that there are neat little words typed in paragraph form, I have no idea what they say. I turn the screen off, then on, and look once more. *What the hell does it say?* Whether the message is written in English, Latin, or Esperanto, it makes no difference to me. I can't understand what I am expected to read, let alone what I'm supposed to do with the information once I read it. *Not such a Super Woman, after all. Not a super-anything, really.* It is this knowledge, this moment of clarity, that forces my obstinate self to finally hold up the white flag. Hold it up and wave it frantically.

Within minutes of turning off my computer, I contact my physician's office and make an appointment to be seen that day, suddenly overwhelmed with the knowledge that not only is my concentration poor, but my sleep has been next to nil for weeks, my appetite nonexistent, my mood off the charts, my willingness to even speak with friends gone, and my interest in the simple pleasures in life nonexistent. What's more, I've had mini-crying jags in my downstairs bathroom and the staff washroom more times than I can count. The fact that I've been on auto-pilot as a therapist for at least a few weeks and thus not all that helpful to the clients who put their trust in my skills doesn't strike me until later, but when it does finally hit me, I add it to the ever-growing pile of things to feel guilty about.

Fast-forward a few hours and I'm off work for two weeks, a prescription for an anti-anxiety med/sleeping pill in hand, as well as instructions to go for a nice, brisk walk for an hour each day (*What am I now? Eighty-three?*). During the first week things don't go as swimmingly as I'd hope, with the highlight being me bursting into tears in a high school gymnasium filled with other adults, during a routine parent-teacher interview. The woman I sob in front of is someone I've never met before and is likely not the type whose demeanour typically elicits tears from parents. Rather, she is my fifteen-year-old son's by-the-book, no-nonsense computer teacher.

"I'm not one to mince words, Mrs. Hendley," she begins.

"Ms. Hendley," I interrupt.

"Pardon me?"

"Um, it's Ms. Hendley," I explain. "Mrs. Hendley is my mother! You could say Dr. Hendley, if you choose, although that would be a bit odd, given that I'm not your psychologist. I guess Alicia is also okay, although it might seem a bit over-familiar, if you know what I mean..."

Mrs. Wallace gives me *the look*, and I feel about fourteen-years-old again. "As I was saying, *Ms*. Hendley, I'm not one to mince words. Your son is making quite a nuisance of himself in my class, disrupting other students, trying anything to get a laugh. It's quite a change from last year, when I had him for Computer 101. He was quite shy and hardworking then."

"Oh."

"Do you have any explanation for his recent behaviour?"

Did I just say that I feel fourteen? Consider that to be a wild over-estimate of my current confidence level. I clear my throat, a grown-up thing to do. "Um, while I don't want to try and um, *excuse* Daniel's behaviour in any way," I say, "I think his acting out might be because lately he's expected to be so responsible at home."

"Oh?" the teacher cocks her head at me, her face unsmiling. Not *another* helicopter parent trying to get their child off the hook.

"You see, um, my husband and I have been turning to him more and more to help out at home because his little brother has been diagnosed with Autism." With that declaration comes the now predictable tears, accompanied by loud, unpleasant sobbing noises. "I'm not trying to excuse his behaviour!" I eventually get out, wiping my face with my sleeve. "I'm just, um, just trying to *explain* it."

"And have you mentioned this to the guidance counsellor? This is the type of information that would be helpful for the school to be aware of."

I shake my head, then wipe my face with my sleeve. I can hear the shuffling of feet from the parents standing in line behind me. "I guess I should do that. A great idea, in fact."

"Yes, well, if you don't mind my saying, it might also be helpful if you found someone to speak with as well."

This time I begin shaking my head so vigorously I'm lucky it doesn't fly off. "Oh, no, no! Thanks so much for the advice, but given that I *am* a psychologist, it's really not necessary..."

Mrs. Wallace nods slightly, then glances at the endless line of parents behind me.

"I guess that's my cue to go, eh?" I laugh, now at a maturity level of about seven. I stand up, knocking my chair over in the process, and hitting the father behind me in the legs. "Oops!"

I hurry out of the gym, going down this hall and then that. I haven't felt this anxious and lost since I was in high school myself. Eventually I find an exit door and push it open. I step outside and bend forward, my whole focus on learning how to catch my breath once more.

******

Other than possibly freaking out a teacher by becoming so unhinged, this little episode shows me just how bad my mood and anxiety level have actually gotten. As someone who takes being a lifetime member of the WASP club very seriously and who is teased mercilessly by her Jewish husband for never crying in movies ("How did this not make you sad? Who doesn't cry at *Love Story*, for god's sake? What is your heart made of? Wood?"), crying in front of a somewhat intimidating stranger is *not* the norm for me.

The severity of my depressed mood is further highlighted the very next day when I start sobbing while watching an upsetting news clip on the internet about a toddler who is hit by a car repeatedly, with no one coming to her aid. As a mother and as a human being this video would have upset me regardless. How can the world be so callous? What if that had been Sam innocently wandering onto a street? Seeing this video may have elicited tears on a normal day, but I would have been able to then move away from the upset, to somehow compartmentalize the traumatic footage I'd seen, shake my head at the heartless world we all live in, and then keep going. Today I find myself crumpled in a corner howling, tears and snot flowing out of me, unable to breath.

"Why? Why? Why?" I shout to no one, hitting my fist against the wooden floor. Finally, after twenty minutes of wailing, the rational part of my brain blessedly takes over and I decide to call my husband on his cell phone, in the hopes that he can somehow calm me down.

"She was hit! She was hit and no one cared!" I blurt out as soon as he answers, sobbing all the while.

"Who was hit?" Joel asks into the receiver. "Is everyone okay? Is Meghan hurt?"

"No! No! The baby!"

"Sam? Is Sam hurt?"

"The baby on the computer!" I cry, my wails getting louder. "A car hit her and she lay in the street and people walked by and she was hit again and more people walked by and she lay there dying and no one cared!" I start sobbing even harder and begin to feel dizzy. "Help me, please! I can't stop! Help me! Help me!"

"Okay, sweetie, it's going to be okay," my husband says in a reassuring voice. "You're just having a tough time right now and you saw something very upsetting. It's going to be okay." He keeps murmuring encouragement into my ear as I attempt to slow down my breathing. Eventually, the sobbing turns to gasping, which turns to occasional tears. "How are you feeling now?" Joel finally asks as I let out a few deep breaths into the phone.

"A bit better," I say. "Very sad for the baby."

"I know. Do you think you're going to be all right now if I hang up? I'm kind of in the parking lot at work."

"Yes," I whisper. "I'm sorry."

"Don't be sorry, sweetie. I'm glad you called."

"Okay."

"Promise me you won't watch any more news right now."

"All right." I nod to myself.

"I love you," he says.

I nod again, then take another deep breath. "Okay."

After I hang up the phone I get up off the floor and move onto the den sofa, where I end up sleeping for over an hour, completely depleted. When I wake up I feel calm once more, but in an eerie, unnatural way, like I've been shot through and through with Novocaine. *This can't be normal.* It is then that I make an appointment to see my physician as soon as possible.

* * * * * *

If keeping my commitment to take Meghan to Trenton with Max in tow proved to be an unwise decision, then deciding to follow through with plans to go to Toronto the very next weekend with my husband, despite now being on a stress leave, was a choice that can only be categorized as monumentally stupid. To be fair, Joel and I had been looking forward to seeing Cirque Du Soleil's Immortal Tour for almost a year now, as the tickets were something I'd given him the December before as a Hanukkah/Christmas present. For me, the tickets had a "Gift of the Magi" feel to them, given how I knew my husband loved Michael Jackson's music, while I personally couldn't stand it. How would I ever showcase the selflessness attached to my gift if we didn't even end up going to the performance? And so, despite some hesitation on Joel's part (*"Are you sure you're ready for another night away, sweetie?"*), on October 21st we set off for Toronto the Good, my parents waving at our living room window, each holding a tearful little boy in their arms.

The ride to Toronto was a positive one, the vibe between us both almost giddy. How could it not be, given that we rarely ventured out of the house without at least one child, and certainly not for a night out on the town! This evening away held other meaning for us, too—if it was a success, it might lead to other occasional nights away, breaks that Joel and I already knew we'd need periodically, in order to best parent four children, including a child with special needs. Once we checked into the hotel Joel had chosen, I found myself feeling even more at ease. The place he'd picked for us was perfect, a tiny boutique hotel with a room barely large enough to hold a bed, but decorated in simple elegance. I spent time taking a luxurious bath, while Joel read the paper.

Feeling relaxed for the first time in weeks, I walked into the room to dress. I carefully slipped my dress over my head, put on a necklace, and then turned to face my husband.

"What do you think? It's not new or anything, but because I never dress up, it should be okay."

Joel stared at me.

"Is anything wrong?" I turned this way and that in front of the mirror. "Do you think the necklace might be a little...too much?"

"Sweetie, I think the whole thing might be 'a little too much'."

"What do you mean? You don't think this is pretty?"

"The dress looks beautiful, *you* look beautiful, but sweetie, this is the Air Canada Centre."

"Isn't that like Centre in the Square?" I asked, thinking of Kitchener's performing arts centre, an enchanted place I used to go to with my mother to see The Nutcracker every Christmas, sitting in the mezzanine and watching ballerinas as they worked their magic. I remember the thought that went into both her outfit and my own, from the stockings to the Sunday coat I wore over my neatly ironed dress. Wasn't this going to be a similar place?

Joel put down his paper. "Alicia, the ACC is an arena. It's home to the Leafs and the Raptors! They've had Britney Spears, Taylor Swift, Pearl Jam, you name it. They sell Tim Hortons, Pizza Pizza, and lots and lots of beer."

"Pizza Pizza?" I look down at my dress. "But I thought Cirque du Soleil was more...refined."

"The show will be great! Just not like Centre in the Square. Do you have anything else to wear?"

"Yeah." I head into the beautiful bathroom, and put back on the clothes I wore in the car.

When I come out, Joel looks me over once more, nodding at my jeans. "Perfect."

Within hours, we're in what reminds me of the former Milwaukee County Stadium, a place I went to every year to see baseball games when visiting my grandparents in Wisconsin. As a kid, I remember loving being with my dad and grandfather and being a part of the crowd. I recall loving the noise that surrounded me, noise which broke into cheers whenever the mascot had to "dunk" himself in a gigantic mug of beer as a Brewer hit a home run. I also remember getting swept up in the smell of hot dogs and beer and sweat.

That was then.

Now, sitting in what turn out to be the nosebleed seats (all I could afford), assaulted on all sides by the unbelievably intense sights and sounds of the Michael Jackson tribute, the crank on my anxiety gets turned tighter and tighter until I think I may explode. Whether the show was actually good or not (and I'm reassured by Joel that it was not just good, it was magnificent), I cannot tell you, as I spent most of it with my eyes shut and my fingernails digging into the skin of my upper arms. To say that going to such a stimulating, crowd-packed event when on the cusp of a free-fall into depression may have been the most asinine thing I have ever done in my life would be an understatement, but no one has ever accused me of being wise. Determined, yes. Obstinate, absolutely. But wise? Afraid not.

******

Following my next visit with my doctor I am placed on an indefinite leave of absence, a prescription for an antidepressant in my fist, as well as the contact information for a therapist. Me, see a therapist. True, I saw a patchwork of therapists as a teenager, but that was different. That was because I was a mere *child*, not a Ph.D.-level clinical psychologist who has herself treated hundreds (hundreds!) of depressed clients of many ages, ethnicities, and creeds. It is a testament to my present mental state that I don't see the brilliant irony in being referred to a therapist now. What I do find ironic, however, is the fact that finding help for a forty-year-old depressed woman who seemingly has at least a few coping skills to draw upon is infinitely easier and quicker than finding services for a vulnerable three-year-old boy with Autism.

My therapist's office is located in a residential community for older adults, a somewhat strange situation that makes sense when I learn that the company which owns the retirement community also has a grant for outpatient counselling. This complex welcomes both wealthy retirees looking for interactive condo living and those with medical issues, in need of long-term care. I'm told to go to the reception desk of the River Glen Centre and to wait for my therapist there. I find the building easily, situated as it is in the back of the grounds. I park my car and enter the front door of the River Glen Centre, fully expecting to see clear signage to direct me to the counselling offices. No such luck. There are signs for the Great Hall and even for the more whimsically named Muskoka Lounge and the Carousel Lounge, but nothing I can find for counselling.

It may be my current state of mind, but I've found few

experiences more disorienting than taking my first steps into the River Glen Centre. I walk into what is clearly some sort of assisted living facility for the elderly. The floor alternates between thinly carpeted and not, the lights above over-bright. Decorating the walls are orange and black streamers and the occasional balloon. There's a subtle smell of over-cooked meat and boiled vegetables, not an unpleasant smell, certainly, but one that I associate more with the school cafeteria lunches I used to wolf down as quickly as possible in order to get my pudding the year my family lived in England, than to a therapy office. Directly to my left is what is called the Great Hall, a banquet-type room filled with what are obviously residents, many of whom are sitting in wheelchairs. Someone is playing a piano in what can only be called an over-enthusiastic manner, pounding the keys in a way that would have led me to get my knuckles rapped as a child. Someone else (or perhaps the same individual) is singing in a loud, lusty voice and admonishing the audience between songs to sing along. The songs are also unusually cheerful and seem to be straight from a Glenn Miller songbook. *Chattanooga Choo Choo* and *Don't Sit Under The Apple Tree* predominate. Occasionally a few brave souls join in, their warbling voices drowned out by that of the vocal cheerleader. I stand transfixed in the hallway, feeling a deep sense of sadness and loss. For them? For me? Suddenly I want to be anywhere but here.

I glance around further ahead for a sign, but still find none. A hundred feet in front of me is what a sign calls the Carousel Lounge, an indoor courtyard of sorts, with what may or may not be real plants, as well as a few merry-go-round horses inexplicably decorating the ground, with signs also on them, reminding guests to please not climb aboard. The wide halls are clearly designed for wheelchairs in mind. In a corner sits a large reception desk, but it seems more for the River Glen Centre itself. I walk hesitantly over and try to smile at the woman in front of me.

"Hi—um, I'm not sure if I'm in the right place or not. I'm here to see one of the counsellors. Her name is Gail?" I say. I hate how my words have come tumbling out in question form and wish I could have a redo.

The woman looks at an appointment book in front of her and shakes her head. "I'm afraid you must have the wrong day. Gail doesn't work on Mondays."

"I know, that's what I was told on the phone, but I was also told that she made an exception for me." I notice my heart rate start to increase at the word "exception" and unzip my coat. How hot do they have the thermostat in here, anyway?

"No appointments listed," the woman says again, still not looking up. Another woman comes into the reception area from a back door and the two have a brief chat.

"I have an appointment for sure," I say, interrupting them. "I was told to come fifteen minutes early to fill out some paperwork. The appointment is for four o'clock on the thirty-first, which is today." My voice has become shrill, beseeching. I stand in front of the counter, uncertain of my next move. "Um, is there somewhere I should go? A waiting room or anything?"

Finally the woman looks up, her face blank and officious-looking. "You may sit over there," she says, gesturing with her hand. *I am dismissed.*

I glance across the hall to where she pointed. There are two chairs pushed close to each other. Both are made of dark wood, their seats deeply padded, and appearing perhaps more appropriate for an elegant hotel lobby than an office, per se. I sit down in one, no paperwork in hand. My coat is still on but unzipped. I can feel sweat forming around my hairline. Down the hall I hear the door to the sing-song room open up, the exuberant voices briefly floating out towards me, before being muffled by the door once more. An elderly woman starts coming down the hall, each step clearly an orchestrated effort between herself and the walker which she grips in both hands. She stops in front of me, turns her walker carefully around, and slowly settles down in the chair that's a twin of mine. Once sitting, she lets out a slow sigh that sounds like I feel—completely depleted of all energy, emotional or otherwise. She notices me looking at her and gives a small smile, which I return. I then close my eyes for a moment, willing the lightheaded feeling to pass already. *Breathe in, breathe out, breathe in, breathe out.*

Suddenly I hear the sound of purposeful footsteps coming down the carpeted hallway and open my eyes once more. *Gail?* A woman clearly of retirement age but youthful for the current surroundings stops in front of my new acquaintance and I. Whether she is an employee at the Centre, a volunteer, or another resident, I don't know.

"Doris! There you are!" she says loudly, her hands on her hips. "Why did you leave the sing-song? Did you know that it's not over yet?"

Doris gives another little smile and then shrugs. *Of course she knows it's not over, you idiot! Don't you realize that's probably why she left in the first place?*

"Do you want to come back? You could probably pick the next song!"

Doris looks at her lap but shakes her head, ever so slightly. This small act of defiance makes me proud of my new-found friend and I feel like giving her a high five or maybe even a fist bump.

"Did you know that they are giving out lollipops?" the loud woman asks. "They're the rainbow kind!" She suddenly reminds me of Brown Owl in my long-forgotten Brownie troop, a larger than life character who demanded cheerful obedience at all costs.

Doris makes a nervous chucking noise, still looking at her lap.

"Well, lucky for you I snuck one out of the basket ahead of time. Here it is!" The woman reaches into her pocket and pulls out a cellophane-wrapped candy. She holds it out to Doris, nearly waving it in her face.

"No, thank you," Doris says softly. "Not for me."

"Oh, please take it! I was told that everyone at the sing-song gets a lollipop! It's for Halloween!" The woman pushes the lollipop towards Doris's hand. I hold out hope that Doris will give her a left hook, but no such luck. I watch instead as she gingerly opens her hand and takes the proffered treat. How could she do otherwise?

"Well?" the other woman asks.

"Thank you," Doris says quietly.

"You're welcome!" the other woman trills. "Part of why I love volunteering so much!" She gives Doris a wide smile, then strides back down the hall. *Mission accomplished.*

I glance at my sitting companion once more as she stares at the brightly coloured candy, clearly astonished that it is now in her hand. Anger begins to build within me, pushing away the lightheaded feeling. Is this all one is to expect after living to the ripe old age of eighty-five or ninety? That you'll be offered a rainbow coloured lollipop and that you'll not only be badgered into accepting such a paltry gift, but that you'll have to feign gratitude as well? Is this what life comes down to in the end, this?

* * * * * *

I sit in silence, willing four o'clock to come and go already so that I can get back in my car and drive home, away from this place. I think about what I'll tell Joel and my parents, about how I'll explain that while I was at the office at the specified time, sadly the therapist was not. What else could I do, but eventually leave? Could anyone blame me if my efforts went unnoticed?

The door to the sing-song room opens once more and the audience begins spilling out and heading my way. Two elderly people slowly walk by my chair, one wheeling an oxygen tank behind him while his companion is dressed in a witch costume. A few more elderly witches pass by, as well as a ghost, a gypsy, and two pirates. I also see three people in wheelchairs, each neatly dressed in a blouse and a pair of slacks, and one with a pretty broach pinned to her chest. I soon figure out that the way to tell who is healthy in this place and who is not is by costume. When it comes to the River Glen Centre, it is the normally dressed people who are clearly the sick ones.

Four o'clock. Just as I'm planning how to look as disappointed as possible for Joel, a woman carrying a clipboard but wearing no costume comes walking towards me, her smile leading her. *Damn.*

"Are you Alicia?" she asks, her voice kind. I pause for a moment before nodding. "Why don't you follow me?" she says.

I stand up and head towards her, turning back one time to look at Doris. She remains sitting with her hand in front of her, the lollipop still unwrapped.

"I hope you found us all right," Gail says, opening a door and heading into another hallway, this one much more office-like and not smelling like a boiled dinner. "I know it can be a bit confusing, especially on a holiday day like Halloween."

"It was fine," I say.

Gail opens the door to her office and gestures me inside. The room has a physician's examining table in it, which strikes me as strange, but no stranger really than a hallway filled with geriatric goblins and portable oxygen tanks. I sit down in the chair provided and wait for Gail to begin the requisite speech about confidentiality, privacy of personal health information, and the circle of care, a speech that will inevitably be accompanied with overly detailed forms to sign. I'm prepared to listen politely for a moment or two before reminding her that this speech is not at all necessary, given, that *ahem*, I am a psychologist, after all.

To my surprise, no such speech is forthcoming and no forms are pulled out to be signed. My confidence in this therapist instantly plummets, while my assurance in my own abilities starts to grow once more. No matter how bad a psychologist I consider myself to be at this point, even *I'm* a better therapist than this.

Except it turns out that I'm not. Within fifteen minutes of being with Gail I realize that she is an infinitely better therapist than I will ever be. For despite not asking me specific, often irrelevant questions about myself the way I would have done (must get all that background information for the chart!), and despite not using a pad of paper in which to write down everything that I'm saying (must make sure that even the tiniest, extraneous detail is accurate!), Gail somehow manages to create an immediate space of safety and caring, something that I doubt I have ever been able to do. Yes, I've had clients tell me how helpful I've been or how connected they have felt with me. But never this quickly, never this effortlessly.

Having come into the session worrying that I would have nothing to say, I find myself filling up each available moment with my rambling thoughts, each idea starting out in one direction and then ultimately going nowhere. Never mind. It seems that Gail is able to follow my disjointed musings and not only to follow, but to stay with me as I go here, there, and everywhere. By the end of the session, I feel heard, but also even more exhausted than I did when I came in. For with the awareness that Gail is a natural, gifted therapist, comes the heavy knowledge that I am not. When it comes to therapy-making, Gail could be in the major leagues, while I linger listlessly in the minors. And given that this knowledge feeds a problem with no immediate solution, my mood drops even lower than before.

******

I'm rinsing the supper dishes and stacking them into the dishwasher while Joel stands in the doorway, watching. I can hear the sound of Dora the Explorer behind him, an indication that we won't be disrupted for at least seven minutes.

"So?" Joel asks.

"So what?"

"So, how was your appointment? Did it go well?"

I shrug, continuing to rinse. "The place the counselling office is in is kind of ridiculous. I mean, it's this long-term care facility for elderly people. Could be a great place, but it doesn't exactly make a depressed person feel too relieved to be there. Or maybe it would make some people relieved, to be in a place where everyone has one foot in the grave already. I guess it would give some people evidence that all the crap does eventually end, that you don't have to stick it out forever..."

Joel interrupts. "While this is quite a cheery conversation topic, what I wanted to know is how your appointment with the social worker went."

I stick the last plate into the dishwasher then turn it on. I go and sit down at the table. "Well, you know…" I say.

"No, I don't know. Can you please feel me in a bit here?"

I shrug again. "It went fine. The social worker is really good. Her name is Gail and she listened to me ramble on and on for at least an hour. She went over-time by twenty minutes, which is something I would never do. Not that it's a bad thing or anything."

"So you like her?"

"Yes, I like her. She's an excellent therapist, actually."

Joel sits down across from me. "Did she give you any good advice?"

I use my "I'm-a-wise-psychologist" voice. "That's not really what psychotherapy is all about, Joel."

My husband sighs, his "look-what-I-have-to-put-up-with" voice. "Let me say it differently, then. Did she give you any new strategies to work with?"

I shrug again. "Well, she did tell me one thing that helped. She said that each person has a kind of cup that is filled with ways to cope. When something stressful happens, what's in the cup gets lower and lower. That's okay, as long as the stressful thing is followed by a good thing, or even just reduced stress. Then whatever's in the cup can start to fill back up again. When problems happen is when you have stressful thing after stressful thing. Eventually your cup gets empty. That's when you become basically screwed emotionally." I smack my palms on the table and Joel jumps in his chair.

"That's a good analogy," he says. "So you found that helpful?"

"I found it incredibly helpful. But that's not really the point."

"What's really the point?"

"The *point* is that the humiliation I feel as a psychologist for not being able to figure this out myself is much stronger than any helpfulness I feel from Gail."

From the den comes a shout. "Daddy!" Max yells. "Wanna see Dora the Explorer! Wanna see it now!"

"Maxie hitting me!" Sam shouts. "Maxie bad!"

Between bouts of shrieking can be heard my daughter's voice, trying desperately to play Mommy for me once more. "Guys, be good! You're best buddies, remember? No hitting! No hitting!" After a few more screams and a thudding noise, she yells for my husband (never me, no longer me). "*Joel!*"

Joel quickly stands up, patting me on the shoulder on the way out of the room. "This sounds more like a pride thing, sweetie. You're going to have to get over that quick if you want to get better. And we *need* you to get better."

As he walks into the den, I can hear my husband advising Meg to be Sammy's corner man, while he deals with Max. I put my head on the table and begin banging it, hoping to find the satisfaction that bonking so clearly seems to bring.

Section Four Guilt

CHAPTER 10

With endless time on my hands, I find myself pulling out all of the former choices I've made in my life and painstakingly examining each for holes. Why did I choose to go into Psychology in the first place? Given my love of reading and writing, why didn't I pick English as a major? And once I decided on Psych, what made me think that *Clinical* Psychology was the best way to go? How in the hell did that field fit with private, introverted me? Why couldn't I have decided to do something less hands-on and messy, like Social Psychology or even better, Experimental? I could be working with rats or pigeons right now, rather than obsessive-compulsive, possibly suicidal eighteen-year-olds. Why did I choose this stupid path, and why didn't anyone try to stop me?

The knowledge, when it comes, fills up my pores so gradually that I'm not aware of its weight until I am sodden with it: *I can't be a psychologist anymore.* After four years of undergraduate training, six years of graduate school, two years of jumping over, under, and through professional qualifying hurdles, and many, many more years spent actually working in the field, I've had it. I am done. Now even the thought of returning to the work I once found satisfying exhausts me. Having to meet and greet each new client and present them with a gift of hope that I have carefully boxed and wrapped, has become too much. Every single thing about the job has become too much—having my days sliced into fifty-minute increments (otherwise known as the therapy "hour"), having certain clients challenge me with their unblinking stares to fix them, while others place all of their trust into my only somewhat competent hands after having just been introduced. *Wait! Please don't give me that! It's too valuable! What if I drop it?*

It suddenly strikes me that in order to be good at the job, I have to deeply care about each and every person, to want to put in the energy and effort required in order to actually help them. The clients who come and sit across from me aren't there because they are in awe of the schooling I've completed, or of that nicely framed degree on my wall, or of the fact that fifteen years ago I got into a competitive graduate school program. Hell, most of the time they aren't even aware that I'm not a social worker or that I have more than a Bachelor's degree, and what's more, they really don't care. What is going on in their heads and their hearts is what they care about, why they are coming to see me, why they *need* to see me. And so I'd better be ready when they arrive. Ready to help pick up their burden as they drop it at my feet, like a giant sack of flour that they've been lugging around for weeks at a time. Because that is basically what they've been doing, lugging around way too much weight for any one person. So I'd better have more than my ego and my degree and a bright, shiny office ready when I greet them. I'd better be prepared to get dirty, to get into the trenches, to meet their heads and hearts with my head and heart. Because if I'm not? If I'm not, I need to get the hell out of that bright and shiny office as quickly as possible.

It doesn't take a genius to figure out that my recent increased disillusionment in all things psychological has neatly coincided with learning that Max has Autism. The one thing more humbling as a psychologist than developing a psychological or emotional problem yourself is learning that your child has a psychological or emotional problem, and knowing that ultimately there isn't a damn thing you can do. *There is not a damn thing I can do to stop this*. When Maxie is in the throes of a meltdown or in the grips of an episode of uncontrollable silliness, I'm struck by just how useless having a shiny Ph.D. to hang on my wall really is. While I've been told too many times to count that being a psychologist is not what matters here, that being the *mother* is what truly matters, I find myself incapable of extricating the one from the other. When time and again I see that my skills are so limited and so lacking, more like a bailing bucket against a tsunami than anything of true use, I can't help but hate my profession. Beyond the stress and the commute, beyond the balancing home and work, and all that entails, at the core of my current emotional paralysis is this —how can I possibly be expected to go back into those trenches once again and actually help people when I can't even help my son?

* * * * * *

I'm up early with Max and the rest of the house is quiet. He'd called out to me in the dark and I'd brought him downstairs to *his* spot on the sofa. We cuddle together under a blanket, one of my favourite things to do with my little boy. He rests his head against mine and sighs, his entire body relaxed. I make a mental note to try and have as many of these slow wake-ups as possible. *This is what will help with the storms, this is what he needs.*

After a few minutes of snuggling, Max wakes up a bit more. "Mommy? What is that on the cars?"

"The white stuff?"

"Yeah."

"That's frost, Maxie."

"What's frost?"

"It's kind of like snow. It's what happens when it gets really cold at night and dew freezes."

"Oh."

We snuggle again, our breathing in sync. Max then sits up, a thoughtful look on his face. "Why did we get a new futon cover, Mommy?"

"Um..." I look at the current cover, which has been on the sofa for about a year. "Well, I think it was because the old one got dirty and had lots of stains on it from the cat and the baby."

Suddenly, the ground breaks open and out erupts a scream. "NO!!!!!!" Max sits up straight, his body beginning to tremble. "Tell me why we got a futon cover!"

"Um..." Suddenly, I'm straddling the other side, my son lost to me across an abyss. My heart starts to race and my eyes begin to tear. I blink away my sadness--I *cannot* make this moment about me. "What's wrong, Maxie?"

"Tell me!" He shrieks louder and louder, now kneeling in front of me on the futon. "TELL ME!"

"Honey..."

"I'M NOT HONEY! I'M MAXWELL! TELL ME! TELL ME WHY WE GOT A NEW FUTON COVER!!! TELL ME WHY! TELL ME WHY! TELL ME!!" Tears and snot flow down his face, a face that had reflected pure contentment just minutes before. *How did we get here?*

I reach out to try and comfort my little one across the gulf, to somehow try and soothe him, but Max shrugs me off. I pick up a nearby book to read to him and he throws it.

"Maxie," I say, trying to keep my voice low and neutral, "what do you want me to tell you?"

"TELL ME!!!!"

"Maxie," I try again. "What do you want me to tell you?"

Max stops screaming for a moment and puts his chin against his chest. He mutters something but I can't decipher it.

"What, Maxie?"

He looks up momentarily, then down again. "Holes," he whispers, his chest still heaving.

"Oh! Of course! You're right, Maxie! The old futon cover had holes in it! That's why we replaced it! Because of the holes!"

"Yeah," he nods. He climbs back onto my lap, wrapping a strand of my hair around his finger. He sighs against me and is content once more, his despair instantly forgotten. *But not by me, not so easily by me*.

******

Upon hearing this story, my mother points out what to her is most significant—the fact that when Max was beginning to rev up like the Warner Brothers' Tasmanian Devil, I was somehow able to make a direct connection and calm him down.

"You got through to him, honey," she says, looking at me in that wise way of hers. "I know it's upsetting when Maxwell has a meltdown, but you mustn't forget that *you got through to him*."

I nod back at my mother, who gives me a quick hug before going on her way. After I shut the door behind her, I think about what my mother just said, a point that I know on some level is true. Unfortunately, it's not my main point. Unlike my mother, I'm not an expert at finding the diamond in the rough. It's not so much that I'm a pessimist (although an argument could definitely be made in this direction). It's more that for me, what is most important, what is the *point*, is how I feel in an experience. And how I felt as Max began screaming on my lap and hitting at me with his little fists was defeated. Whether or not I was able to ultimately *connect* makes little difference to me, as I was clearly so woefully incapable of being able to *prevent*.

CHAPTER 11

It's Remembrance Day and I'm in the front hallway with my mother, who arrived at the house about an hour ago with my father in order to watch Max and Sam and thus allow me to go to Meghan's school assembly. Since they've arrived, I've been joking around with them, conscious of the importance of at least attempting to maintain some semblance of normality. Sure, I've clearly lost some weight (about eight pounds at this point) and there are dark, deep circles under my eyes, but at least I still have a sense of humour and can make light of almost any situation. At least I still have *that*. If nothing else, I don't want to give my parents *one more thing* to have to worry about. I turn away from my mother to grab my coat off its hook and when I turn back, she suddenly reaches over to put a hand against each side of my face.

"I've been through this before with you, Alicia," she says, tears in her eyes. "You got through this when you were seventeen and you will get through this now. You are strong, my daughter. Remember that. You are much stronger than you think."

I nod, pulling away from her hold. I smile at her then rush out the door, coat still not on. This moment, so unexpected, sends my mood tumbling further down. The fact my mother felt it necessary to remind me of my strength makes me realize I'm much worse off than I initially thought, and that I may in fact be heading up the proverbial creek without a paddle.

******

Despite being considered the "common cold" of mental health, this whole depression thing is nothing to sneeze at. When in its clutches you are more likely to feel like you have a slowly encroaching brain tumour or perhaps a terminal illness rather than a simple bout of the sniffles. Depression can be felt in every muscle and joint, its heaviness making even your eyeballs ache. It affects every aspect of your being—how you think (or how you no longer seem capable of thinking), how you feel, how you behave. Basic things you used to take for granted are suddenly gone, like your appetite, your ability to concentrate and actually process information, the way you can always slide into a deep, peaceful sleep. Depression takes away all peace, even when you are unconscious.

What I find perhaps the most difficult is the unbearable sameness of depression, the unrelenting, dull monotony of despair. It's not until I am in depression's clutches that I realize how much I actually depend upon normal fluctuations in mood to give my life meaning—feelings of joy, surprise, fear, sadness, even anger are better than this steady, seemingly endless ennui. I find myself wanting to be anywhere but here, while at the same time filled with a restless panic whenever I actually venture away from my house or my family and am left to my own devices. I want to be here yet not here, there but not there. In other words, I am fucked.

Many people describe depression visually. It's a darkness, a blackness, a place devoid of light. For me, the best way to capture its essence is in terms of sound. Depression is like being lost in a white noise machine, its volume cranked up to ten. When surrounded by such sound, the mundane conversations of others fall into the background, incomprehensible, lost. I've always related to Munch's "The Scream". The utter horror on the face, hands to the ears. For me, nothing is more terrifying or deafening than the experience of depression.

As I begin my slide down, I put all of my energy and focus upon still hearing the words that come out of the mouths of my family and of the professionals involved in Max's care. What my parents and in-laws say, what Joel says, what the children talk about, all of these utterances I make a concerted effort at grabbing at, in order to make sense of what the hell was just said. But what about the voices of those who form a circle around my family, the voices of my close friends? These I start to shut out—the noise is just too much.

In the months following Max's diagnosis and my own fall into depression, I keep in touch with most friends and extended family through Facebook. Facebook allows me to get support without actually having to put in any true effort of talking to people, of telling my story for the umpteenth time. Facebook gives me the chance of appearing to still have a social life, when none in fact exists. With Facebook, you can still communicate without any sound.

Despite this, two of my closest friends push their voices through and force me to keep listening to them. Both call me regularly on the telephone, one leaving messages that are brief but loving, the other almost soliloquizing through the phone lines (as I used to do for her). Each friend also pushes their way into my house, making sure to see me and talk to me in the flesh.

"I'm coming over," Alisa announces, "and I'm bringing coffee. If you want to talk, I'll listen. If you don't, we'll just enjoy the coffee."

Alisa's visits are fairly infrequent (as a full-time working mom who lives in another city, how could they be otherwise?), but they still serve the purpose they were designed for. A friend since childhood, the mere presence of Alisa helps to turn down the volume on my despair. She watched me go through hell as a teen, and then come through to the other side. This fact, this fundamental fact, allows me to believe her when she says I'll get through this, too.

With Patty, the noise gets ramped up during her more frequent visits, with the channel of the radio changed. Patty, with her fast, yet gentle way of speaking and the lyrical lilt to her laughter, brings the feel of music to my ears. No matter how low I get, Patty can somehow edge her way underneath all of my navel-gazing and despondency and use her spirit to push me up.

"It's been too long between visits," Patty will say during one of her four-minute voice messages. "I know Joel's out of town for the weekend, so I'm coming over for a girl's night, and bringing a DVD. Scary or funny, it's your choice. Unless having me staying over is too much right now. If it is, then no worries! I can just come for lunch, which I'll bring with me. Sandwich stuff, chips, dessert, fruit, the usual. Just tell me the time and I'm there!"

And so, I do, and so, she comes, her presence triggering laughing fits in me where apathy had sat just hours before. During her visits, Patty regales me with her own tales of woe from life in the dating world. Some of these stories are humorous, some are more vulnerable or painful. Either way, they pull me out of my own brain and my own noise and let me focus on someone else's experiences for a while.

"How does she do it?" Joel asks me following a recent Patty visit.

"Do what?"

"How does she make you feel so good, when I'm clearly so incapable of it?"

I look at my husband and sigh. "Because you're in this with me. Patty isn't. She's cheering from the sidelines."

"I can cheer too, you know."

"You, cheer? All you do is kvetch!"

"Why did you marry me, then, if I can't even make you laugh the way Patty so obviously can?"

"I don't know why. Patty's like my other half."

"But I should be your other half!" Joel says. "Don't you even want me to be?"

I look down at the floor, unable to answer. What I want to tell my husband is that even the mere idea of him being my other half is laughable, given how incredibly different we are. What I want to explain is that what he means to me is both different and yet somehow *more* than being my other half, that his role in my life is so damn vital for the very reason that he is *not* even remotely like me. Instead, I stay mute, knowing that I don't possess the words to explain this in any way that will make sense. Patty is Patty, Alisa is Alisa, Joel is Joel, and I am me. To try and somehow take any of us apart to replace one with the other is impossible. Just like with Max—we are who we are.

******

On the days when Patty and Alisa are not here (and that would be most days, given my recent hermit-like ways), I feel like I'm on a carousel that's gone haywire—much like the one during the disturbing end sequence of Hitchcock's *Strangers on a Train*. I'm hanging on for dear life, not knowing if or when this damn merry-go-round will slow down enough to let me off. The way I see it, I have an underlying vulnerability to depression that was triggered in part by the reality of Max's Autism. My worsened mood and increased stress level has meant that I'm less capable (to put it mildly) of remaining calm and coping appropriately with family life, which in turn likely triggers Max's meltdowns, which then influence my mood. Round and round and round my little son and I go, where we'll stop, nobody knows.

Please don't mistake this somewhat flippant description of what is happening at my house for glib feelings about my role in Max's meltdowns. The knowledge that my low, often irritable mood may be triggering for Max overwhelms me with guilt and despair, feelings which make me extremely angry at myself and remind me of why I turned to cutting so many years ago. How can I be so selfish right now to make *any of this* about me? Why can't I just deal, as Joel seems better able to do? Why can't I just be thankful that my child is so high-functioning and that we have such supportive friends and family in our life? Why can't I put all my energy into learning about how to best help Max, rather than crying in the bathtub, the one place I feel safe enough to actually let go in. But even there more often or not, Max will begin rattling the doorknob, his voice becoming increasingly agitated as he realizes that I have locked myself in and thus him out.

"Mommy?" he calls as tears slide down my face and into the bath water. "Mommy! Mommy! Mommy!"

"Just a minute, honey!" I call back, submerging myself up to the chin. *A hot bath can reduce stress and improve mood. A hot bath can reduce stress and improve mood. A hot bath...*

"I'm *not* honey! I'm not a sweet food!" he yells, rattling the door knob again. "I'm Maxwell Thomas! Mommy! Mommy!" *Where the hell is my husband?* And so the carousel continues, going faster and faster until both Max and I almost fall over with dizziness.

While I try to reassure my two oldest children that I am merely off work for "stress" and life will return to normal soon, I occasionally catch each of them giving me the shifty eye, as if not certain whether or not I will turn into a raving lunatic if they don't remain vigilant. My awareness in the effect my mood is having on *all* of my children (including toddler Sammy, who seems oblivious but clearly cannot be) depresses me more. Ever since becoming a parent for the first time over fifteen years ago, my biggest priority has been to be a good mother. Not a perfect mother, but at the very least what the powers-that-be blithely refer to as a *good enough mother*. During the last few months I feel as if I haven't even hit this mark and that is absolutely unacceptable to me. I find myself putting all of my energy and focus into maintaining a cheerful front for the children, but even in this I fail miserably, as the front can quickly be replaced by tears if I perceive my husband's words to be a tad too sharp or Max's fists to be a bit too hard. *Mom has to leave the supper table to go to the bathroom for a minute* becomes euphemistic for *Mom is having another mini-breakdown in the downstairs' lavatory.* Either way, the children and my husband are expected to continuing talking amongst themselves and ignore the crazy woman who ultimately may need to be locked in the attic a la the original Mrs. Rochester.

At this point, I see my only true hope as coming in pill form. Whether or not it turns out to be a miracle cure or mere snake oil, I'm placing all my bets on Celexa and am just biding my time until it begins to work its wonders.

CHAPTER 12

I feel like I'm in the middle of a treasure hunt, with few clues to go on. Should I turn left? Should I go right? It's like I'm lost in the wilderness and the only one who has a map doesn't know how to read it. During the last several weeks on the three days that Max goes to preschool, he has woken up upset. Max being upset in the morning because he just woke up isn't unusual, but Max with his eyes still shut shouting *"NO SCHOOL! NO SCHOOL!"* is. Before he's had the chance to even get out of bed and face the day, my son is distressed.

Usually such distress presents as a more extreme version of his typical hurricane meltdowns, involving screaming, shouting angry ultimatums at his parents (*"You go to work!"*, *"You run away, now, bad woman!"*), not to mention physical aggression (head-putting, pushing, smacking). As I always do, I attempt to make breakfast for my other three as Maxie pulls on my shirt, yelling to be held. When I stop what I'm doing and try to hold him, he becomes out-of-his-head distraught, hand-flapping and wailing.

Joel and I will take turns trying to soothe Max, gently encouraging him to go with us to the "quiet spot" (just a corner of our dining room filled with pillows and blankets, but at least away from the fray), as recommended by the OT. We've been instructed to give him a deep pressure hug, to rock him if possible, to give him hand or leg hugs. Anything to help physically calm down our little boy when he cannot calm himself. When he allows us to grab him and use pressure, it often works wonders. Unfortunately, more often than not, Max will absolutely refuse our touch, clawing and screaming if approached ("You're hurting me! Stop hurting me, man!"). It's at those times that we hold up our white flags, remove any breakable or dangerous objects from his reach, and wait for the meltdown to run its course.

Daniel and Meg are now so used to this little scene being played out most mornings that they continue eating their breakfast and try to have a conversation with me in the midst of the meltdown. The fact that the screaming has now become normal for them can pull me down like stones in my pockets if I let it. Sammy varies from also ignoring the commotion to being concerned about it.

"I worried," Sammy confided in me this morning, his toddler forehead furrowed. "Maxie sad. I sad, too."

I found myself scrambling to reassure my baby and somehow explain Autism to him in a way that makes sense, telling him that Max sometimes finds it hard to feel "big" feelings and that Mommy and Daddy are trying to help him, not hurt him, as we use quarterback tactics to tackle him to the ground. He looks at me wide-eyed, clearly not understanding a word I've spoken. All this said as Max threw his plate off the table, his peanut butter and jelly sandwich cut incorrectly.

After about forty-five minutes, a break may occur between the first meltdown and the second. Suddenly Max is a different child altogether, reachable and affectionate, at the table while he munches on his breakfast (that same sandwich cut *wrong* now inexplicably *right*). And so it goes. I dress Max and Sammy for preschool while they watch TV, my third child now sweet-natured and gentle, often getting his little brother's hat or mitts for him. Joel leaves the house with the two little boys in tow and they all wave goodbye to me. Bye, bye, see you soon! We personify "Happy Families" (*if you haven't seen this British card game from the 1970s, I urge you to go hunt it down on Ebay as soon as possible; you will not be disappointed*). Each time as Max gives me that one last hug (ending with a nose rub), I hold out hope. Maybe today the drop-off will go fine at daycare. Maybe...

Except that during the last several weeks, it has not. Despite seeming like a happy little boy in the car, despite following the same school morning routine that he has always followed, once Max is dropped off at the preschool he breaks down once more. *Meltdown number two.* This one, however, lacks any of its predecessor's aggression or "bossy" nature, and is instead pure despair. According to my husband, Max clings to him like one of those poor orphaned monkeys holding onto their wire mesh mothers and wails, absolutely inconsolable. No matter how much we attempt to prepare him for going to preschool, no matter how routine this is for him, it is as if Max believes his father is leaving him forever, abandoned.

This second meltdown is not normal for our Max, who previously would run over to the toys in the playground when dropped off or eagerly find his mat for circle time. No tears, no clinging, no utter, heart-rending despair. Something is wrong and Max doesn't have the words to tell us.

Joel and I have racked our brains, trying to figure out what is going on. There have been no changes at our house. Max's life here is the same as always, the routine strictly adhered to. We've spoken to the daycare teachers, to the manager of the preschool. Have there been any changes there? Has any child been cruel to him? We trust the daycare and thus believe them when they say that other than the addition of a few more children to his classroom (could *that* be it?), everything has remained the same. We also believe them when they tell us that Max calms down soon after Joel leaves and is once again a happy little boy. Knowing that the meltdown ends is reassuring, but it is not enough.

Last night after his bath (also calming), I reminded a sleepy, relaxed Max that he would be going to school the next morning.

He shook his head. "No school," he said.

I decided to try and find clues, knowing that I needed to tread lightly and not put any words into my child's mouth.

"I thought you liked school, Maxie," I said. "Remember the craft you're making? It sounded like fun!"

"No school," he said, louder.

"I thought you liked circle-time, and snack, and playing with the cars."

"NO SCHOOL!"

"Did anything happen at school, Maxie?" I asked, picking my words so carefully. "Has anyone said something that...hurt your feelings?"

"Yes," he said. "I hurt."

"You hurt?" My throat grew tight. "Did one of your friends...hurt you, Max?"

Max pointed at his head. *A clue?*

"Did one of your friends hurt your head?" I asked.

"Yes."

"Who? Who hurt your head?"

"Jessie," he whispered.

"Jessie hurt your head? Is that a little girl in your class?"

"Jessie the cat," he said. "She scratched me. She scratched me when Sammy pulled her tail and I tried to pet her and she scratched me on the couch and it was in the den and I turned the light off and then Sammy yelled and it was too loud..." Max continued, suddenly remembering with razor sharp precision an "ouchie" from our pet cat that happened over a month ago.

"But what about at school?" I persisted. I tried to look Max full in the face, but he was already gone. "Did another child...hurt you?"

"I wanna go watch a video before bed! I pick first and then Sammy and then Daddy. I wanna pick first!'

And that was that. I was left clutching...nothing, knowing that when we woke up this morning, another extreme meltdown would likely strike (and strike it did, with almost an hour of hitting, screaming, and hand-flapping, until a calmer Max sat down to eat, a happy little boy once more until he reached the preschool parking lot). And while my husband and I will continue asking the questions and searching for answers (is it even possible that nothing has happened other than Max's mind has fixed on preschool being "bad", like cutting his toast or touching his hair are now bad?), my fear is that we will never find out what is upsetting our beloved child so. For when it comes to this particular treasure hunt and being given actual clues to follow, Autism refuses to play by the rules.

Section Five Depression

CHAPTER 13

During my second visit to the River Glen Centre I find myself less judgemental of my surroundings. Without Halloween as a distraction, I notice that the building is actually well laid out for its elderly residents, with large windows, inviting lounges, and bright lighting. If one had to be in some sort of long-term facility (if that is what this is), then such environs probably wouldn't come more attractive than this. I also notice that the staff is much more inviting than I remember.

I sit idly waiting for Gail by the front desk and listen to the conversation taking place between the receptionist and a staff member in an apron.

"I'd better head back to the kitchen," the apron-clad woman says. "It's almost time for lunch."

As she starts to move away, I observe a quite elderly woman start to walk over towards the reception desk. When I say walk, what I really mean is wander, for it is clear to me that the woman in question doesn't really know where she is. Dressed in her pyjamas and a housecoat (this despite it being mid-day), she seems even more disoriented than I felt during my first visit, unsure of anything other than the need to keep moving forward. Her blatant vulnerability makes me want to look away. Very quickly both the receptionist and an apron-clad staff member walk over to her, speaking gently.

"Hi Agnes, I just got a call from your nurse," said the receptionist. "She didn't know where you were."

The elderly woman moves her head slightly from side to side, a look of confusion painted across it.

"Your alarm is going off," the receptionist says. "May I check to see if it's around your neck, to turn it off for you?" She waits for a moment for the elderly woman to answer, but no response comes. The receptionist then very carefully reaches towards the other woman's neck and lifts a chain that's around it. "I see that keys are here, but no alarm. Agnes, do you know where your alarm might be?" Again, no response.

"Do you know why you came down?" the woman with the apron asks, also in a gentle tone. "Was there something you wanted to ask someone or anything that you needed?"

Silence once more from the elderly woman.

"Why don't I help you back to your room?" suggests the woman with the apron. "If you take my arm, it might make it easier for you to get back."

The elderly woman says nothing, but suddenly reaches out her hand to grab hold of the arm that is extended to her. The woman with the apron smiles and nods gently. I watch as together they begin to move down the hallway, their steps slow and in tandem, as if the woman with the apron has all the time in the world and isn't really needed back at the kitchen, after all. This brief interaction, an interaction clearly not meant for my eyes, makes me want to weep. In sharp contrast to the lollipop incident I remember from my last visit to the River Glen Centre, what I observe today exemplifies human dignity and the power of simple respect.

******

After my appointment I begin my drive back home, but take a sudden detour before heading on the highway. I decide to drive through my old neighbourhood, the one I lived in a lifetime ago, as a single mother with two young children. I have all the time in the world today, after all, one of the unexpected benefits of being on stress leave. Besides, I know that driving on those familiar streets may make me feel better, more grounded once more. It is a place filled with such lightness and joy, coloured as it is by the happy, carefree memories of my eldest two's childhoods. As I pass by Daniel and Meghan's old school, memories flood my mind. Here is where I used to stand every day with my son, who until grade three, insisted that I stay until the bell rang. And here is where I used to wave goodbye to my daughter who began insisting I not stick around once she was in grade one. I drive down my old street, slowing somewhat as I pass my former house, now seeming so small but at the time perfect in size. The right side of a duplex, you could hear the sounds of another busy family through the walls. I smile to myself, a wave of happiness lapping against me for the first time in weeks. It recedes as quickly as it came, leaving in its wake the detritus of sadness and guilt, remorse and shame. Shame because as I stare at my old house, my former life, the yearning to be back there once more is so great that I almost choke on it. Gripping the steering wheel tightly, tears begin to blur my vision as I start to cry. I consider pulling over to the side of the street but want to get away from this neighbourhood as soon as possible, my presence here proof of my failings as a mother. I'm also afraid that if I pull over I will never want to leave this place. Why did I come back? Am I trying to relive a time before Max existed, a time where Autism was a nonexistent part of my daily world? *What kind of shitty mother am I?*

* * * * * *

It's hard to describe how ultimately humiliating it feels as a psychologist to become the patient. Until now, a professional shield of sorts has surrounded me. Upon hearing my title and credentials, people have tended to treat me with a certain type of courtesy and respect that I've come to perceive as the norm and have even begun to depend on. In what may have been my biggest mistake, I've actually come to believe that it is me as a person, rather than the title that I pin to my chest that makes me *special* and garners the most respect. For some inexplicable reason I've come to forget that without the title of "Psychologist" I'm just like everyone else—simply human.

Almost every interaction with other health professionals now brings with it feelings of vulnerability, a sense of nakedness, and even shame. It's like layer after layer of what may have been puffed-up pride is being sloughed off in this recovery process. When I see Gail for the first time and have to describe personal, often embarrassing details about myself to a mere stranger—there goes a layer. I get informed by my workplace that I must fill out long-term disability forms for the insurance company, just in case I remain completely incapacitated (this despite still having months and months of sick leave left before LTD would even kick in, months which I can't imagine needing to use up). I admit to my physician that the antidepressant isn't doing its job quite yet and he indicates he's going to seek advice from a colleague who happens to be a psychiatrist, a professional who, in my very recent past life, may have been *my* colleague to consult with about difficult cases as well. There goes another layer. My physician's office calls me a few days later to indicate that Dr. Seidler not only consulted with the psychiatrist about me but has decided to refer me to see him (a decision I recognize as one that is meant to serve my best interests, but a humbling one nonetheless). I bring my prescription for a sleeping aid (Clonazepam) to the local drugstore and am politely asked by the person across the counter to please give them my health card to copy, as well as a photo ID, as the medication is a "controlled substance" and god forbid I turn out to be one of those shit-faced, doctor-shopping addicts or else someone who tries to sell it on the street for others to crush and snort. As I sheepishly hand over my identification, I notice a few more layers of pride and self-respect being shed. I walk out of the pharmacy with my head down, my proverbial tail between my legs. By the time this process is over, will there be any of *me* left?

******

It turns out that there were a few layers of dignity left, as they get torn away by a phone call I receive few weeks later during Max and Sam's nap time, while my parents are at my house. When I answer the phone I'm informed by the voice on the other end that her name is Jenny, that she is calling from my employer's insurance company, and that if I have a few minutes, she would like to review my claim.

"Review my claim?" I ask. "What claim exactly are we talking about?" *Did I fill out the forms I submitted for Max's recent OT sessions incorrectly?*

"Your claim for long-term disability," answers Jenny.

"Um, but I don't understand. I thought my work had something like one hundred and twenty days of sick leave to use up before long-term disability would even kick in."

"This is part of the early referral process," Jenny informs me. "I am calling to review your application now. I have some questions I would like to ask."

"Okay," I say. I sit down at the kitchen table, a sense of foreboding coming over me.

And so the process begins, one question after another shot through the phone in rapid fire, the next one coming from Jenny's officious voice before I've had a chance to fully understand the last. "It says here that you went off work due to symptoms of depression and anxiety. What were those symptoms exactly?"

"Um...well, I'd been having some problems with sleep for a while and appetite, but on the day I called my doctor I realized I couldn't concentrate on anything. I was trying to read an email and I couldn't understand the information."

"So your main symptom was a problem with concentration?"

"No! I had a lot of problems with mood and anxiety, but I tried to deal with them on my own. When I found I couldn't concentrate, I knew I needed help."

"And would you say that your son's diagnosis of Autism was the trigger for your depression?"

"The trigger?"

"Would you say that your son's diagnosis of Autism triggered your depression?"

"I can't say that. No one can say that. No one even knows what causes depression!"

"Would you say it was a triggering factor?"

"Um, okay, yes, I would say that it may have contributed to me getting depressed. But not that it caused it!"

"You went off work in mid-October. When was your son diagnosed?"

"Um, in September."

"And how long before you went off work did you begin to experience symptoms?"

"Um, I'm not really sure. They kind of came on gradually. Maybe weeks? Um, I'm not really sure..."

"Your physician wrote on your claim that he anticipates you being off from work anywhere from January to March. Do you agree with this?"

"Um...I can't really say..."

"Do you anticipate that you will require a leave of absence for your symptoms until March?"

"Um, I hope not! I mean, I can't see returning in January, with how I am doing. But I have faith in my doctor and my therapist. March seems so far away. But I can't really predict what I'll be experiencing..."

More questions are fired at me, each more personal than the next. Questions about whether my therapist is a registered psychologist or not and what her name is. At some point, my awareness that Jenny has never even mentioned anything about privacy or the protection of personal information wakes up the dormant psychologist in me.

"The name of my therapist is confidential information," I say, finally annoyed.

"I need this information in order to successfully evaluate your claim," says Jenny, in an equally irritated tone. Clearly she has dealt with belligerent claimants before.

"But..."

"I need this information in order to successfully evaluate your claim," she repeats.

My brief burst of defiance over, I answer each question that follows, including what my current dosage of Celexa is, the fact that it has been increased, how I am functioning at home, and finally whether or not I'd be willing to meet with a psychiatrist of the insurance company's choosing, for an independent evaluation.

"Um, but why would I need that?" I ask, my voice a mere squeak.

"It will depend upon what medical personnel say, after I consult with them. But if they *do* recommend an independent evaluation, it would be in order for us to find out if there are additional means of helping you."

"Additional means of helping me?" Given that I am already off work, taking psychotropic medication, seeing a psychotherapist on a weekly basis, and walking an hour a day as prescribed by my physician, what other means of helping could there be? *Electroconvulsive therapy, perhaps? A lobotomy?*

"Should you undergo an independent evaluation, a report will be sent to your physician, perhaps with recommendations for the appropriate medication," Jenny answers, her voice increasingly distant. I can almost see her glancing at her watch, relieved that she can soon check yet another phone call off her list.

"Okay," I say.

"I will contact you if a referral to a psychiatrist is going to take place," Jenny says, before ending the conversation.

I sit at the kitchen table for a few more minutes, holding the phone. As I sit, I can't shake the feeling that I have just been interrogated by someone who I highly doubt is a health professional in any form, and whose job seems to be to prove that I am somehow a liar, that I am trying to milk the system for what it's worth. How absurd this world is that a physician's diagnosis would be considered so suspect that an insurance company would even consider demanding a second opinion? And how absurd that rather than focus on recovery and *not* being depressed I may be required to drag my sorry-assed self over to a psychiatrist to actually *defend* my depression! A psychiatrist, I might add, who I have every reason to assume is a highly ethical professional, but who I also know will have been hired by the insurance company not necessarily to *help* me, but to put me under the microscope, as it were, to ensure that I am not malingering (a "clinical" word for trying to bullshit someone). Would someone who is off on sick leave due to colon cancer have to defend their illness in the same way?

I know that if Gail were here she would put a positive spin on my current anger and point out that me being indignant and pissed off is actually a *good* thing, that it is much better than flat-lining in terms of mood, and that it indicates that some of my former spunk is returning. At this moment, however, it does not feel like such a good thing. In fact, if feels like a pretty crappy, horrible thing. Eventually I walk into the living room where my parents are reading, sit down next to my mother, and burst into tears. Tears of humiliation, degradation, and shame. So much shame. Never have I felt so useless and exposed, so vulnerable and worthless. Never have I felt so much like garbage. *So this is what it's like to be on the other side of the mental health divide, this.*

CHAPTER 14

Joel slams a magazine article down in front of me on the kitchen table. "Look at this."

"What am I looking at?"

"This." He points his finger at an opinion piece. "It says here that 80% of parents who have an autistic child end up divorcing."

I pick up the paper. "Where's the study? Who wrote this?"

"I'm not going to quibble about statistics, Alicia. This is serious."

"Statistics *are* serious!"

Joel sits down across from me. "Maybe I shouldn't be bringing this up right now, given your mood stuff, but in case you haven't noticed, our marriage isn't exactly the strongest right now." He sighs. "We barely spend any time with each other, and our main communication is by email."

"But you're the one who's obsessed with the emailing! Didn't you once tell me that it's what writers are meant to do?"

"I only email you so much because you refuse to actually *talk* about how you feel."

"That's not fair. You know it's hard for me."

"Okay. So it's hard for you. But communication is kind of vital for a marriage to work!"

"Fine." I look at my hands.

"And I can't even remember the last time we were physical."

"Physical?" I look up at Joel. "As in 'Let's Get Physical'? Are you seriously going to use '80s pop hits to try and woo me?"

"I'm not trying to 'woo you'," Joel says. "I'm worried about *us*, okay? And this 80% finding shows me I have good reason to be."

"Do you know the statistic for second marriages? Supposedly 67% of them end in divorce," I say. "I failed with Steven, as you well know. Who's to say I won't fail with you, too, right?"

"That's not what I was trying to say."

"No, no," I say, holding up my hand. "If we're going to take percentages, we've got to get it right. So let's use the 67% as our starting point, as you did take a huge risk in marrying a divorcee! Now, that gives us a 33% chance of success to begin with." I grab a nearby pen and start scribbling calculations on the top of the article. "So if you take 80% out of that remaining 33%, you're left with, what? A mere 6.6% chance of having our marriage succeed. You definitely shouldn't have married a shiksa, Joel. Based on these odds, I'd say we're doomed." I slam the magazine shut and push back my chair. *Take that!*

Joel sighs again. "I'm serious, Alicia. We can't let this distance us. We have to stick together."

"And by 'this' are you referring to my *Snake Pit* depression or to our autistic son?"

Another sigh. "That's not what I meant and you know it. What I'm saying is that we have to make this work, for Max's sake. For all of their sakes!"

"Okay."

"Just okay? Are you going to say anything else?"

"What do you want me to say?"

Joel reaches out to touch my hand, his voice gentler. "I can't do this all on my own. I need to know you're committed to actually working on things, to spending time together as a couple. I need to know."

I snort. I don't mean to (I swear I don't mean to), but it comes out, childish derision an easy disguise for all of my loneliness and fear.

Joel draws his hand away. "I need you to verbally commit, Alicia."

"I need to verbally commit? And what if I say I can't right now? What if instead I say you'll just have to live with it?"

Joel blinks. "Just live with it?"

"Yes! For now! *Just live with it!*"

"I can't believe you just said that."

I sigh. "Do you remember the cup?"

"What?"

"The cup! Don't you remember what Gail once told me about the cup?"

"About it needing to be refilled? Yes, I vaguely remember."

I nod my head vigorously. "Well, mine's goddamn empty right now and likely will be for the foreseeable future, so yes, you're going to have to live with it!"

In response, my husband pushes back his chair, then strides out of the room, leaving me with the article and my furiously scribbled calculations. *What does he expect from me? What?*

******

At Gail's request, Joel comes to my next therapy session. It seems that during the last few appointments I've been rambling on about my husband, my marriage, and about how its mere existence is statistical suicide. Clearly, an intervention seems warranted. Joel and I sit in comfortable chairs beside each other, a tiny side table between us. It's the middle of the session, and I'm feeling increasingly anxious. I have the sudden urge to feel my husband's touch, to have physical proof of his caring. If I wanted to, I could reach across and take his hand, hold it in mine, and hope that he gives my fingers a reassuring squeeze. But of course I don't do this. What kind of WASP would I be if I made the first move, if I actually was more demonstrative with my affection, especially in public? Instead I focus on keeping my spine straight and my hands neatly folded together in my lap.

"I wasn't blaming you for anything, Alicia," Joel says. "Just trying to explain to Gail how it is from my perspective. How tough all this has been lately..."

"But hearing you say how hard it's been just makes me feel worse." I pause, looking at my lap. "Don't you think I realize how hard it's been for you? How much has been put on your shoulders?"

"That isn't what I was saying..."

I start to cry. "Don't you think I know that you might say you've had enough at some point, that you might leave?" I begin to sob into my hands.

"How am I supposed to respond to that?" Joel asks, clearly exasperated. "I try to reassure her that I'd never leave, that with Max having Autism we're stuck with each other..."

I lift my face from my hands, still crying. "Stuck with each other! If that's how you feel, why don't you leave me already? If that's what 80% of people do, no one would be surprised!"

Gail intervenes. "Now, Alicia, I don't think that's what Joel was saying. I think the depression is influencing how you're interpreting things."

"That's what I'm always trying to tell her," Joel says. *What do you want? A gold star?*

Gail holds up a hand. "And Joel, in listening to you, I can tell that you love Alicia dearly..."

Joel interrupts. "Did you hear that, Alicia? Did you? She said dearly!"

Again Gail holds up her hand. "I also can tell that you may have a bit of a harsh way of talking at times. That you love Alicia but that your words might not always convey how you feel. Would you agree, Alicia?"

I nod and stare at the wall across from me.

"What's it like for you when you perceive Joel to be harsh?"

"I just feel so alone in all of this sometimes!"

"And what would make you feel less alone?" the therapist asks.

"If Joel hugged me more. If he came to bed when I go sleep. I always go to bed alone!"

"That's because I'm a night owl," Joel says. "You *knew* that when you married me! You've got to know how much I love you..."

Gail leans over and gently touches Joel on the leg. He instantly shuts up. "Alicia has often spoken to me about her fear that you'll leave. Yes, the fear might be totally unrealistic, but it's where she's at with her mood." The therapist pauses. "When someone's depressed, they need words and gestures of love to be more blatant, obvious. Extra hugs, extra words of encouragement." Another pause. "Do you think you could do that?"

I stop crying to let out a snort. *Can pigs fly*?

Joel politely ignores the grunt and turns to look at me. "Do you think that would help you? I mean, really?"

I nod and turn my head ever-so-slightly towards my husband. My hands back in my lap, Joel reaches out and takes my fingers in his, squeezing them. The squeeze is warm, soft. I keep my hand limp for a moment, then let myself go enough to squeeze back.

CHAPTER 15

Ever since Max was diagnosed with Autism, the reactions we've received have ranged from the expected to the surprising. Most family and friends have responded with love and support, seeking to understand what is happening with our little boy. A few have expressed surprise at the diagnosis, telling us, "But Max is just like any other normal kid. It's hard to believe that he has Autism at all!" I understand this reaction, and in fact I am pretty sure I've said something similar in a well-meaning way to other parents of other children in the past. I also recognize that it is *because* Max is so high-functioning that he can come across to people as just like "any other normal kid", and for that I am grateful.

What I don't understand is the intentions of the few people who have pushed it further, not wanting to let it go when I nod and say, "Yeah, it is hard to believe. But he does have Autism." These people (who have typically been acquaintances or even strangers) seem eager to pursue the issue, actually arguing with me or my husband that Max *couldn't* possibly have Autism, because he does this or does that and Autistic kids can't possibly do this or that. To put it mildly, this is the least helpful of any reaction and is the one that I find the most exhausting.

Unlike Joel, who is able to nod and walk away, conversation over, I end up wasting time explaining at length why Max has the diagnosis he was given. Typically, I become involved in a peculiar, topsy-turvy debate, with me arguing *for* my son's psychological difficulties. Is it so hard to believe that a sweet-natured, intelligent, curious child may also struggle with his behaviour and emotions? Are we really all so black-and-white? Having someone question the diagnosis in such a strident way makes me feel incredibly isolated as a parent, as if Max and I will get sucked into our own little vortex the next time a "non-normal" behaviour occurs.

In contrast, perhaps the most helpful reaction to Max's diagnosis occurred just last week, and came from a stranger. It was a typical Thursday morning, and so I did what I normally do on such mornings: I took Max and Sam to the local library. Because I find the main library too overwhelming with a highly energetic Sammy in tow, we headed to the small branch. This branch is located in a nearby strip mall and has a lovely, small children's section, Sammy-sized. The visit to the library went wonderfully, even better than normal. There were no other children in the room, which made Max happy. He quickly found the toy truck he loves and played contently with it for half an hour. He then helped me pick out books we planned to read once we got home, while Sam moved chairs around the room and then sat on each one in turn like a little king.

The library visit over, I walked outside with a bag filled with books in one hand, Sammy's little paw in the other. Max was skipping beside me, singing a made-up song.

"Anybody can be anything," he sang in a sweet, off-key voice. "You can be a tree or a library or even a car, too…" The song continued, with every object he saw added to it. I walked towards where the minivan was parked and let go of Sam's hand, telling him to hold onto my leg instead, and then reached into my pocket for my keys. Suddenly, inexplicably, Max bolted into the parking lot, almost getting hit by a car. His happy song had been replaced by hysterical laughter, reminiscent of zoo monkeys in heat.

I dropped the keys on the ground and quickly picked up Sam, then rushed us both into the parking lot. I somehow managed to catch Max by the sleeve of his jacket. He began to swing at me, screaming. He twisted out of my grip and darted once more. I shifted Sam onto my hip and managed to grab Max's sleeve again, as a car honked at us and the driver gave me the finger. I dragged a shrieking, punching Max onto the curb and tried to catch my breath.

"Back off, man! Just back off!" Max screamed, writhing in my hold.

"No, Maxwell! No!" I realized I was shouting at my child, but at this point I really didn't care.

I shifted Sammy on my hip again, while holding onto Max's sleeve. I looked at my keys, still lying on the ground by the minivan. Just a few feet away, their close proximity teased me, taunting me as a mother. Just try and get us, they seemed to smirk in their shiny, asshole way. Go ahead and try it.

I turned back to Max. "Please, Maxie! We'll read the books once we get home and you can even have a juice box!"

Max twisted his face towards my hand and gave it a bite. I flinched but forced myself to keep holding onto my son.

At this point, a confused little Sammy began to cry. "No, Maxie, no! Maxie bad. Maxie naw-tee!"

Again more screaming and punching. "No! No! Back off, man! Back off!"

About twenty feet away, a neatly dressed woman in her early seventies got into her car and turned on the ignition. After a few moments it became obvious that she wasn't going to drive away. Instead, she turned off her car and got out again, walking towards my little triumvirate of wills.

Just as Max gave me another bite, the woman began to speak. "Let me help. Which one should I hold?"

I pushed Sam at her, not caring if she was the distant cousin of Mussolini or Jack the Ripper. He instantly stopped crying and reached out to touch the woman's face, giving her his dimpled grin.

"I'm Sammy. Sammy David."

With both arms now free, I picked up a shrieking Max and held him firmly in my arms. He tried to slap at my face, but I jerked my head away. While still holding him, I bent down towards those damn keys (*gotcha!*) and opened up the minivan. I tried to force Max into his car seat without actually causing him bodily harm, but he was having none of it. He made his arms and legs like pieces of steel, rigid and unbendable. As I felt his strength build against me, I noticed my own start to dribble away. *I can't do this!*

"He has Autism," I called out to the woman. I knew there were tears in my voice, but I didn't care. I wanted this stranger to know, no, I *needed* this stranger to know that the scene she was witnessing wasn't totally a reflection of my ineptitude as a mother.

"It must be hard," she called back.

When I heard those words, those four simple, yet so validating words, I was suddenly able to push my child's flailing limbs into position and snap, snap, buckle up his seat belt. I then turned back to the curb to go get Sam from the woman and to thank her for her help.

Before I could say anything, she smiled at me and nodded towards my toddler. "Your Sam has beautiful long eyelashes, just like his mommy." She then smiled again and walked back to her car and drove off. And that was that.

For me, that entire morning, from when we first left our car to go into the library until we finally drove off again is what I wish anyone who meets Max (or meets any child with special needs for that matter) could experience. To me, that morning represents it all: Yes, Max can be such a joy, and yes, it can be difficult to believe that he has Autism, and yes, the hard times can be so *damn* hard, and yes, sometimes an offer of help or of understanding or of just *getting it* makes all the difference in the world. Yes, yes, yes, and yes.

CHAPTER 16

Another meltdown has erupted in the house, but this time Max is not the volcano in question. No. This time the source of the eruption is his eleven-year-old sister, Meghan. In the last few weeks she has been a whirling dervish of slammed doors, yelled non sequiturs, and tearful outbursts. It seems that when no one was looking, puberty has created a nest in our house and has decided to stay for a while. In the last few months my lithe, graceful daughter has shot up at least three inches, suddenly becoming a jumble of elbows and knees, large, ungainly feet, and skinny hips. With this growth her attitude seems to have expanded, too. While her stepfather has been the target of the occasional pouty mood for months, I have been immune to most moments of sulkiness from my daughter. I have felt proud of our relationship over the years. While I've always enjoyed a deep, loving bond with my eldest son Daniel, there is something unique about the relationship between a mother and her daughter.

When Meghan was younger she was my mascot of sorts, cheerfully skipping beside me on whatever errand or chore needed doing, chirping happily away all the while. A trip to the grocery store seemed to trigger as much joy in my little girl as a stop at the video store. As long as it was Mommy-Meghan time, life was good. I made a point of creating time just for her, reading her stories every night in my past life as a single mother and, ever since my marriage to Joel, continuing to keep the hour before her bedtime as a sacrosanct time sliced out of the day just for us. I remember how not that long ago we made the point of dressing up to root for our favourite contestant on American Idol and how I'd make sure to brush her long, silky hair every night, checking for knots.

But while we continue to watch TV together every night between the hours of eight and nine, much of that time is spent sitting side by side with crossed arms and sticky silence. *What has happened to my little girl and how do I get her back*? Any mother who is reading this will undoubtedly shake her head and give a rueful smile. How can I be surprised that the onslaught of puberty brings with it a new dynamic between mothers and daughters? This tension has likely occurred since the beginning of time. Where is my shock coming from? My dismay?

I think part of it arises from the guilty knowledge that in the last six months most of my energy and focus has been spent upon Max and his behaviour. Yes, I've kept that one hour each evening just for Meghan, but what about the other hours in the day? What about the many times that she has come up to me eager to chat about a new crush or to get advice about a drama going on between friends at school and I have shooed her away, promising to talk about it later, when Max isn't screaming/kicking/biting/throwing toys/needing all of my energy to be calmed down. *Later, Meggy, but not now (never now). And if you don't mind, could you please leave the room? I think you being in here is triggering Max right now.* Suddenly my resemblance to the clueless protagonist in The Cat and the Cradle is a little too much for my liking. Has Meg reached a point where she's sick and tired of my empty promises and my seeming inability to just stop for a minute and pay attention to one of my other children for once? To just stop, please Mommy, just stop and *listen*?

I attempt to make it up to my daughter now, without bribery or placation. At first I try to talk to her about Max, having answers all prepared for her hypothetical questions. I print out a "Sibling's Guide To Autism" package off a respected internet site and search out a local group of children with siblings on the spectrum. When I try to present such information to Meghan, however, I'm met with a quick dismissal.

"Why would I want to go to a stupid group like that?" she asks, continuing to play a computer game.

"Because it might help you to…have a place to talk about your feelings and to be with other kids who know what you're going through."

"My feelings?" she snorts. "What feelings?"

"Feelings you might have about Max."

"I love Max. Why wouldn't I love Max? He's my little brother." She starts typing something faster on the keyboard, picking different outfits for a slutty cartoon fashion diva with dimensions that would make Barbie blush.

"Meghan, can you please look at me for a minute."

"I'm playing a game."

"Turn away from that screen and look at me!"

My daughter sighs dramatically, then slowly lifts her hands off the keyboard and faces me, the effort this requires clearly obvious.

I take a deep breath. "I know that you love your brother, honey, I just thought you might have some…feelings about how Max has been getting so much attention from me and Joel."

"I don't care," she shrugs. "Why would I be jealous of a three-year-old? *God!*"

"Well, then it might be good to get information about what Autism is. To find out what it's all about. You might learn some tips for what to do when Max is acting out or upsetting you."

Another shrug. "I already know enough." She glances at the computer screen. "My turn is almost over! Can we please be done talking about this?"

"Yes, honey, we're done for now." I reach over to touch her hair, but she shakes me away. "I'm going to talk to you about this more later, okay?"

"Fine. Whatever," she answers.

Next I attempt to bond with Meghan my tried and true way—over television shows. That night as we sit at opposite ends of the sofa, I chatter about story lines as we watch Glee. A few days later, I talk excitedly about which team should win as we watch The Amazing Race. I even agree to sit through nauseating tween shows on the Family Channel, shows that make me want to stick my head in the oven. *You call this intelligent entertainment? This*? During commercials I make a point of talking about the superficiality and materialism of the cosmetic and diet industries and the disturbing underlying messages found in the different ads we see. In response, Meghan rolls her eyes and crosses her arms tightly.

"Can we please just watch TV quietly for once, without you turning every single thing into a little lesson?" she asks.

"I can't help it, I'm your mother," I retort, my tone sharper than I had intended. I am your mother, dammit, your mother. In the maelstrom that is Autism it may have seemed like I forgot that for a while, but now that I've remembered I'm going to keep this fact front and centre, regardless of meltdowns from you, Max, or your other brothers, so you'd better get used to it, Little Missie, because it's never going to change: *I am your mother.*

******

Within the bedlam that has become my home toddles a carefree little boy who seems confident in his sense of self, despite being not quite two. Sammy is probably my simplest, yet most physically exhausting child, a fact that remains true the bigger he grows. He is like a mountaineer without a map, boldly exploring each and every new territory he finds just because it's there. Turn your back for a moment and he's washing toys in the toilet bowl. Turn away once more and he's climbing onto the train table, attempting to pirouette off its side. Bend down to tie your shoe and there he goes, zooming down the aisles of the library, nearly chirruping with joy. He's a mix of fearless and tender, bold and gentle, one minute dumping his sippy cup onto the floor on purpose and the next getting a towel to mop up the mess, followed by trotting over to me to look up with wide, unblinking eyes and ask, "Are you sad, Mommy? Are happy now, Mommy? I sor-wee." It is Sam who has fallen in love with not one, not two, but twelve stuffed animals, toys that he has named himself ("Bunny", "Udder Bunny", "Kitty", "Udder Kitty"), and that line the perimeter of his crib each night, forming a wall of security as he drifts off to sleep. It is Sam who treats Max as if he were any other child, pestering him like any little brother would, and in so doing, reminding us that our autistic son may not need to be treated with kid gloves, after all.

Finally, it is Sam who, in the midst of my introverted, navel-gazing depression, made me laugh for the first time in weeks. Despite the fact that my family uses the proper terms for all our body parts, Sam has named his diapered area his "Nee Nee". One recent afternoon while Max, Sam, and I were sitting together on the den floor, and I was trying to convince myself that I could somehow make it through the mind-numbing hours until dinner and then bed, my youngest child announced that it was time for a sing-song. And, after a few rousing rounds of Ring Around the Rosie, Sam decided to choose another familiar, well-loved ditty, one that required even more actions. My toddler solemnly stood up, carefully linking words and gestures together, just like he'd seen his daycare teachers do. This time, however, he gave the song his own personal stamp.

As Max and I placed our hands on our heads and waited, Sammy began to sing: "Head and shoulders, nee-nee, toes..."

As he pointed to that third body part, a laugh of pure glee burst out of me, shocking me into a moment of sudden happiness. Sammy immediately stopped singing to look at me, but rather than cry, he began to laugh, too. While he clearly didn't understand what the joke was, he knew that I wasn't making fun of him, but rather had found something he said (or sang) to be funny, and that was good enough for him. And for the next few hours, I felt something heavy lift, if just a bit, and that was good enough for me, too.

CHAPTER 17

After several weeks on Celexa, my concentration improves, but my mood remains low. *Not such a wonder drug, after all*. Along with a low mood comes an increasingly low weight. One morning after showering I stare at my naked self in the mirror, something I have avoided doing for a while. To my disgust, I notice that not only does my collarbone jut out, but so does the plate of bone below it. What little breasts I had (and as a card-carrying member of the Itty Bitty Titty Committee, let's just say there wasn't much going in that department to begin with), have now turned into sad, empty sacks of nothing. When I turn to the side I can see all of my ribs and notice that my bum has deflated in an unflattering manner. As I stare at my forty-year-old, now-pinched face, the image of my former adolescent self transposes itself on me and I feel nauseous. *So, we meet again*. Looking emaciated and possibly anorexic at seventeen can be viewed as tragic. Looking the same as a middle-aged woman cannot be perceived as anything other than somewhat unseemly and even unforgivable. *Good God, woman, you're a mother! Can't you get your act together?*

The thing is, I'm not and never was anorexic, not in the true sense. At seventeen I didn't view myself as even remotely fat nor did I feel the need to look thinner. Weight loss was intricately woven into my depression, with normal eating not occurring until my despair began to lift. To eat was to admit you wanted to live, so how can you force yourself to consistently take food in when you are straddling the line with death? While I'm thankfully not close to that line this time around, I do feel a weird disconnection from food. The very act of chewing makes me nauseous, reminding me of a cow after it's regurgitated its cud.

When my mood diminished so did my appetite and it has yet to return. As an adult and as a mother I know enough to make sure I don't lose too much weight. If nothing else, I have a vulnerable daughter watching my every step. I can't let her think that emaciation or heroin chic is the way to go. Since my weight has begun plummeting I've taken to writing down reminder notes to myself to "have a snack at 10 am" or "make sure to eat lunch". It seems that my memory lapses extend to nourishment, as well.

After seeing my naked, skinny self in the mirror for a minute longer, I hear the front door open and race down the stairs to my husband.

"Joel!" I call, still dripping from the shower. "I know this sounds odd, but can you please look me over and tell me if I look disgusting? I know I've lost about ten pounds by now and you're the only person who ever sees my body."

My husband looks at me startled. "You're naked, Alicia!"

"I know, I know. It's okay, the kids left for school a while ago. No one else is here."

"But the neighbours might see!" he glances behind him at the window.

I shrug. "I really don't care at this moment," I say.

"But...I have to get to work. I just came back to pick up something."

"Please just tell me how I look! Please!" I do a little turn around on the floor, letting Joel see all of me, each and every bony bit of me. "Too skinny?" I can feel panic begin to clog my throat. Am I going to inevitably go down the same road I went as a teenager? Is there any way to choose another path this time?

"You *do* look skinny, I wouldn't lose any more weight, but ten pounds isn't thirty. You need to try not to get too freaked out."

"But I am freaked out! I don't want the same thing to happen that happened when I was seventeen!"

My husband looks at me. "Sweetie, you're not seventeen."

"But still!"

"Repeat after me, 'I'm not seventeen.'"

"Joel...that's stupid."

"Just say it."

"Fine," I say, rolling my eyes and attempting to look as jaded as possible, not an easy feat when standing in the front hall buck-naked. "I am not seventeen. I, Alicia Hendley, am not seventeen. In fact, I am almost forty-one, with a saggy butt, so there you go." I look at my husband. "Happy?"

Joel doesn't say anything, but instead reaches out across the void that has grown between us since Max's diagnosis to touch me. And in the hour that follows, it turns out that my affection-starved husband doesn't find me too skinny, after all, and that, for a few moments at least, I manage to reconnect with my body once more.

******

I'm sitting shotgun in my father's car as he drives me to the home of some random psychiatrist, in order to undergo my Independent Assessment. I was sent a letter about it by the ever-lovely Jenny, who informed me that if I did not show for the appointment or cancel with at least five days' notice, I would be charged $1500. After receiving this correspondence, I began to hope against hope that Sammy or Max would develop a highly contagious, vomit-inducing virus a few days before the appointment and that I would be forced to bring them with me ("*I'm so sorry there's diarrhoea on your Persian rug, Dr. So-and-So, but because my son became ill only two days before the appointment, my hands were clearly tied. Too bad, so sad.*"). Unfortunately for me, my household has remained healthy, so here I sit, next to my dear old Dad, without a puking kid in tow.

Throughout the forty minute drive (*Did I happen to mention that the psychiatrist I've been referred to does not live in my city and in fact resides somewhere in the country, away from direct bus routes? What if I was some poor sod with no transportation?*), my father tries to entertain me with as many sarcastic comments as possible. Luckily, it works, and I arrive at my designated appointment feeling relatively anxiety-free.

I walk up the long driveway as my father watches from the car, and ring the front doorbell. It feels odd that I'm having my Independent Medical Evaluation conducted at someone's house, but then again, the last six months have been odd, so who am I to complain? A woman opens the door, a large dog at her side. It eyes me warily.

"Are you Alicia?" the woman asks. Her voice sounds kind. *Dammit. I might have to like her.*

I nod.

The woman puts out her hand and I shake it. "I'm Dr. Rees and I'll be doing your evaluation today. Nice to meet you."

"Nice to meet you, too." I turn back to look at my father, still in his parked car, and wave him away, feeling about fifteen again.

"This here is Angus. He's a nosey thing and loves to be a part of the action. Do you mind if he is in the room with us?"

I nod, then start to grin despite myself, as I find this request more than a tad bizarre. *A dog in a professional appointment? If I ever return to work, maybe I should suggest having ferrets perched on our desks during client sessions.* I think I like this woman more and more.

"If you'll come with me to my office," she says. Angus and I follow Dr. Rees through a wide, airy hallway, past a beautiful kitchen, and through a living room. Dr. Rees opens a door and gestures for me to come inside. I sit down in the chair she points to, and Angus soon follows. I make the mistake of not crossing my legs immediately, and Angus proceeds to sniff at my crotch. Due to his enormous teeth and the sheer number of them, I find myself unable to do anything and wait for Dr. Rees to notice. Eventually the damn dog gets bored with my private parts and heads over to a gigantic pillow, where it circles several times before lying down.

The first hour of the evaluation involves me talking about my past and present mood problems. I find myself often rambling this way or that, with tears flowing at the oddest moments. Dr. Rees remains kind but removed. After I've shared all the nasty bits of my life with this stranger, she begins to test my basic cognitive skills. I perk up during this portion of the evaluation, as I've conducted thousands (okay, maybe more like sixty) similar assessments before. I just happen to be on the other side of the desk this time, a minor, hardly noticeable difference.

As I lean towards the psychiatrist, eager to impress her with my sheer brilliance, she asks me to remember five words. Five words, ha! After a few minutes, she asks me to tell her the words back. I remember four. After a few more minutes, she asks for the words again. This time I can recall three (*stupid fucking test*). Towards the end of the session, Dr. Rees asks me to count backwards from ninety by sevens. I lean forward once more. *I've got this, I've got it! I didn't take multivariate statistics in graduate school for nothing, by George!*

The brilliant recesses of my mind are a blank. I stare at Dr. Rees. I blink. "Um, could you repeat the question?"

She smiles kindly (did I mention that she was kind?), then nods. "Of course. Please count backwards from ninety by sevens. Take your time if you need it."

I look back at the psychiatrist, watching as she begins to jot something down on her giant pad of paper. The clock in the corner begins to tick loudly and I can hear that damn dog start to snore. I hit my forehead with the palm of my head, hoping to shake some brilliance back in.

"Of course I know this! I have a Ph.D., you know! Just give me a minute here. You said count back from ninety by sevens, right?"

Dr. Rees nods her head again and continues to write on the

note pad.

"Okay, okay, I've got this. Of course I've got this! Just give me a second!"

I start to mumble numbers under my breath and force myself not to smell my fingers. *Now is not the time to appear clinically insane.* I'm acutely aware of the kind psychiatrist's eyes boring down on me. *Give me a minute here! Just give me a fucking minute!*

Despite myself, I giggle. "This is really embarrassing! Take back that Ph.D., somebody, because I clearly don't deserve it! Ha!"

"Just try your best."

"Okay, okay. Count back by sevens? I know this. Of course I do! It's just that there's this weird blank in my head to get the stupid thing started, you know? Once I start, I'll be fine. I just need to get it started."

Angus lets out a low growling noise and I cross my legs tightly.

"Okay! Here goes! Ninety minus seven is eighty-two, which means that eighty-two minus seven is seventy-five. Seventy-five minus seven is sixty-one. Sixty-one minus seven is fifty-four…"

"Thank you so much, Alicia. You may stop now."

I laugh nervously. "How did I do? Am I too crazy for you, or did I come across okay?"

"Alicia, as I mentioned at the beginning of the evaluation, I work for Northern Life Insurance, so I cannot disclose any of your results directly to you. Please know that I will be sending a copy of my report and my recommendations to your physician, who can share those with you."

I throw in the towel and have a field day sniffing at my hand. "Recommendations?"

"Yes." Dr. Rees says, rising from her chair and gesturing at me to do the same. "I know today was particularly tiring for you. I'd suggest that you do nothing strenuous for the rest of the day. Just try and take it easy, all right?"

"Okay."

I follow the psychiatrist out of her office and through her beautiful house, Angus's toenails clicking close behind me. I walk outside and see my father's car waiting for me in the driveway. Again, I feel like fifteen rather than forty, and this time that's a good thing. *Thanks, Daddy, thanks.*

CHAPTER 18

What I find the most difficult is not the here-and-now so much as imaging Max's life in the future. It's a bit of an addictive game, such imagining, a game that can lead me to dark places I have no business entering. What if he never has a true friend? What if he's teased by his peers throughout school? What if he never knows what it's like to be in love, really in love? What if he remains isolated into middle age, with no true connections to anyone outside of his family? What if? What if? What if? Such thoughts are weighted down with the knowledge that my husband and I are not spring chickens. I had Max at thirty-seven, while Joel was almost forty-eight. Fast-forward to my little son at forty-five or so. Will he still need his parents to help guide him in some way? And if so, will we even be around?

Whenever I've spoken such thoughts aloud others have tried to reassure me that Max already has a large, loving safety net created of family and friends, including three siblings who will surely not let him fall. While this gives me some solace, it does not help with my thoughts of him being rejected or ignored by his peers when he leaves the relative security of daycare for the no-man's land of elementary school. After many sleepless nights dwelling on what I hope Max will experience in the world as he grows, I've come to realize what I don't want for him—tolerance. Don't get me wrong, I would much prefer that the people Max comes into contact with express tolerance towards his differences, rather than aggression or bullying. It's more that I see tolerance as merely the first step in a long journey towards acceptance and not as the end destination itself.

To better illustrate what I mean: When I was in elementary school, there was a boy in my class who I'll call "Michael". Michael was a child who was clearly different from the rest of us. I'm not sure what his actual diagnosis was, but I do know that he had hydrocephaly, that he required a shunt, and that he didn't always act "normal". I also remember that Michael didn't seem to have any true friends.

In grade five, our teacher (Mr. H.) would often select one of the more goody-goody kids to be "in charge" whenever he had to leave the room unexpectedly (naturally, I was chosen more than once). Being in charge basically meant keeping a list of every child who started talking and fooling around, when they were supposed to be quietly working. For reasons that now make me cringe, I seemed to revel in this role.

On one particular occasion, I remember putting all of my energy into creating a perfect list to give the teacher upon his return. As soon as Mr. H. sat back down at his desk, I rushed over, saying loudly, "Here are all the kids who talked. It says that Allan talked eight times, but Michael actually talked the most, at least ten times! I didn't put his name down, though, because I know he can't help it."

I remember Mr. H. giving me a "look", and me not understanding what message he was trying to convey exactly.

"But I wasn't supposed to write Michael's name down on the list, right? Because he has problems with his brain and stuff, right?"

"Thank you, Alicia. Now please return to your seat."

I remember feeling confused by Mr. H.'s brusque response and totally oblivious to Michael, who was sitting in the front row at the time, and had likely heard every sanctimonious word out of my mouth.

Other Michael stories arise. I can remember noticing boys teasing him one afternoon at recess and running up to them yelling, "You leave him alone!". I can remember the wonderful, warm feeling that coursed through my veins at having done such a good deed for someone, without even expecting anything in return! Only now my memory goes further, to a less warm place. I'm now reminded of how quickly I left Michael on the playground by himself so that I could go and play once more with my friends. Did I invite Michael to come play with us, too? Of course not! Because my standing up to bullies wasn't for Michael's sake, not really. It was for my own, to feel good about myself, not to make friends with someone who seemed so...strange.

Fast-forward a few decades. When Daniel was in grade two or three, I used to wait with him on the school tarmac before the bell rang each day. One morning I noticed a little boy about my son's age who was standing against the brick wall by himself, his knapsack still on. I remember thinking that he had a lost, forlorn look about him, like he didn't know quite what to do or how to be. I remember feeling relieved the next morning, when I saw the little boy's mother holding his hand and waiting with him for the bell. Each morning that followed she was there and I soon forgot all about the lost look.

A few months later, I met with Daniel's teacher for the annual parent-teacher interview. "That son of yours made me cry the other day," she told me once I had sat down.

"Daniel made you cry?" I asked, startled. "I'm so sorry! What did he do?"

"No, no," she said, smiling. "He made me cry in a good way!"

"He did?" Now I was even more confused.

"There is a little boy in our class who is mildly autistic," she confided. "We've talked to the other children and made sure that no one bullies him, but we can't force them to play with him. Each recess he's stood all by himself, no one noticing he's even there. Until last week, when Daniel asked him if he wanted to go play on the climbers." She paused. "That's all it took. Ever since they've been playing together every day!"

At supper that night I brought up the topic to Daniel. "Do you notice anything different about your friend?" I asked gently.

My eight-year-old shrugged. "Well...he jumps up and down a lot and talks in a kind of funny voice when he's excited, I guess."

"And what do you like about him?"

Daniel shrugged again. "He likes to play Star Wars with me and he's fun. Plus he wants to be my friend, too."

And that was that. For the next several years until we moved away, Daniel and the little boy with the lost look were best friends. Not because Daniel *tolerated* him, but because Daniel *liked* him for the child that he was, with being fun more important than having a funny voice or jumping up and down.

That's acceptance. And that's what I hope more than anything for my own lost little boy.

CHAPTER 19

While OT is clearly not be the be all and end all when it comes to Max, Autism, and intervention, the techniques that Joel and I learn help to give us at least a modicum of control back as parents and that in itself is therapeutic. No longer completely helpless in the face of off-the-chart meltdowns, we now know at least some of Max's triggers and how to avoid/reduce them, as well as what the early warning signs are that a storm may be brewing. More strategies are also learned thanks to Janice, a preschool resource teacher whose job typically entails going into various day cares in the city to help teach the caregivers how to work with children struggling with various difficulties. Although ostensibly only meant to help Max at his daycare, Janice clearly feels concerned enough about our family to step out of her job's parameters and do some hands-on training with us at home. I don't know whether to take her level of concern as a good thing or not, but ultimately realize that at this point, any professional help is welcomed.

For her first visit, Janice arrives just as I'm trying to cook supper. It's a typical evening, with all chaos breaking loose in the house. Meghan is running from room to room, unable to find her homework binder, Daniel is blasting music in his room, and Sam and Joel are play wrestling in the "quiet" spot. And where, pray tell, is Max? He's clawing at my leg while I'm trying to prepare the evening meal, almost knocking me over each time I cross the room from the stove to the refrigerator and back. *Carol Brady I am not.* I notice Janice watching me, her facial expression unreadable, and my anxiety starts to rise.

"Maxie!" I plead, leaning down. "Why don't you go find Daddy? I think he's having a lot of fun with Sammy in the quiet spot!"

"No! Stay with Mommy!"

"Mommy would love to be with you, but I have to make supper right now. Why don't you go to Daddy and then I'll play with you right after we're done eating. We could play with the trains!"

"No!" he yells. He grabs my waist with both hands and begins banging his upper chest against me.

"Maxie," I beg.

"I hurt! I hurt!" he shouts, still banging.

I turn to look at Janice. "When he says 'I hurt' he really doesn't mean it. It's kind of his code words for wanting something else."

"It's a great way to get an adult's attention, though, isn't it?" she asks.

"I hurt!" he screams, the bangs now full-body thrusts.

I bend down and pull my son into a tight hug, using the deep pressure the OT has recommended whenever a meltdown is starting. "Do you want to go do a squishy?" I ask.

Max doesn't say anything, but stops banging. I carry him into the den and sit down with him still in my arms. I rearrange his body until his long legs are straddling me, with his chest pushed against mine. I hold him as tightly as I can without harming him and slowly rock back and forth, back and forth. Eventually I can feel his muscles loosen and the meltdown moving away from us, like a storm cloud that has decided not to stay, after all.

"Do you want to watch a show?" I ask softly.

"Yeah," Max says into my shoulder.

I lift him off me and carefully put him on the sofa against a few pillows, then tuck his favourite blanket around his legs. I turn on the TV and am relieved to see Thomas the Tank Engine fill the screen.

"Three black pillows," Max says. I can hear the revving up in his voice. "Why did you do two? *Three* black pillows!"

Knowing that Janice is watching this entire little scene unfold, knowing that I'm not supposed to feed into my son's endless demands and rituals, but also knowing that the pasta on the stove has gone from al dente to soupy by now, I quickly grab a third black pillow and shove it behind Max's back.

"There you go, Maxie! Mommy just forgot! Sometimes Mommy's brain is a little silly!"

Max ignores me, but is calm once more, his eyes on the TV screen and his hand in his thick, brown hair, twirling strands around his fingers.

I head back into the kitchen, my face shiny with sweat and embarrassment, and Janice follows close behind. I want to tell her to please go away, to please go far, far away, but I also want her to stay here forever, to wave a magic wand and make us all live happily ever after. I finish preparing the meal in no time flat and then call the rest of the family to the table.

Half an hour later, supper is over and I'm still in the kitchen, this time doing the clean-up while Joel plays with both little boys in the den and the bigger kids do their homework. For some reason, Max is almost always overjoyed to spend time with his father after supper, but rarely before. The reason doesn't really matter, at this point, as long as I can have a bit of peace and quiet to clean up this damn kitchen and get the day over with already.

"I hope you don't take this as a criticism," Janice says, watching me as I rinse off a dirty plate, "but I've noticed that when you're preparing the meal there's a lot of noise and cross-talking going on, which may be triggering for Max."

"Cross-talking?" I ask, as I put the plate into the dishwasher. I've never had someone watching my every move before and I feel my anxiety level rise even higher. I glance at the clock, aware that I can't take the damn Clonazepam for another few hours.

"You know, talking across rooms. You were in the kitchen and calling to your husband, who was in another room with Sam. Your daughter was talking to you from the den, while Max was also trying to get your attention here in the kitchen. And once the meal was on the table you shouted up the stairs to Daniel at least two times. Cross-talking."

"Oh, I guess maybe we do that. Big family and all," I say.

"Yes, it's totally normal and understandable, but with an autistic child all that noise can be...overwhelming. He seemed to be getting more and more agitated when it was going on."

"Really?" I close the dishwasher and turn to face the woman. "I never even noticed."

"Do you remember how he had a meltdown when you gave him apple juice instead of orange at supper?"

"Yes."

"Well, I think that's because his emotions were already up to here from over-stimulation," she gestures towards her chin. "That meant that it didn't take much for a meltdown to get triggered. He was too wound-up already." She pauses. "We want him to be down here, so that he can handle things like the *wrong* juice." She points to her knees.

"So what should we do instead?"

She smiles. "I know it's not easy with kids, but try and remind everyone to talk softly and to go to the room a person is in to have a conversation, rather than just shouting. Talking softly is probably the most important thing."

"So, use a library voice?" I ask, mentioning a term I use whenever I take Max and Sam to our local one to pick out books.

"Exactly," she nods. "Library voices." She smiles again. "One other thing—does he always try to climb on you as you're making dinner?"

"Usually," I say. "Joel tries to get him to go play a game or read stories in the other room, but he won't go." I sigh. "It makes dinner prep kind of stressful."

"Instead of ignoring him or trying to get him to leave the room, why don't you give him some activity to do in here with you?" Janice asks. "I mean, it's clear to me that after a day of preschool he really wants to be with his Mommy. Maybe let him use Play Dough at the table or even help you make the meal somehow. Just being allowed to be with you could help calm him down."

"Okay," I say.

Janice smiles at me and then reaches into the bag she's been carrying and pulls out a camera. "Do you mind if I go around your house and take some photos?"

"Take photos?" I ask. What's going on here? Am I suddenly on Candid Camera?

"I thought it would be a good idea to take a lot of photos of your typical evening routine, including pictures of each family member. I'll get them laminated for you and then you can use them as a visual story to show Max what to expect each night."

"But does he really need something like that? I mean, he's incredibly verbal."

"He might be incredibly verbal, but he also has Autism. Don't let his vocabulary fool you. Lots of kids on the spectrum are visual learners who can benefit from these visual cues. You can also draw story boards of activities for each day, if you want. I just like photos." She points to her camera. "But only if it's okay with you."

"No, no, please go ahead," I say, gesturing around the room.

"Great," she says, and begins snapping.

And with that single, albeit exhausting evening visit, many more practical strategies are learned. No cross-talking. Try to use library voices. Give Max an activity as I prepare supper rather than try to bat him away. Make use of pictures or photos to help him anticipate activities that I take for granted. The main lesson here is that if we consistently use these strategies plus those taught in OT sessions, we have reason to hope that the volume on the meltdowns may get turned down, at least a bit.

I quickly find that having such tools at my disposal makes the wait for other services such as ABA, speech therapy, or more advanced integrated social skills groups more manageable. Interestingly, I find that as Max's meltdowns lessen in frequency and intensity, his "silly" episodes increase so that my little son often seems like someone completely high on cocaine, rather than a three-year-old boy. It's as if his Autism knew its current ship was starting to go down, so it jumped onto a lifeboat instead. In a way, I can't help but respect such a formidable opponent.

******

The other day Max had one of his worst meltdowns in weeks and what I mainly felt was relief. It was during dinner (often a challenging time for my little one), and for no immediate reason that anyone could fathom, Max exploded. When I say exploded, I don't mean that Max became a little ticked off or cranky. I don't mean that he started to whine or even had a tantrum. What I mean is that he hit the roof, went ballistic, completely detonated. Yesterday during dinner Max suddenly exploded and he continued to explode for the next hour or so, his hands flapping wildly, his legs kicking blindly, his face bright red, and his voice a continuous shriek so loud and piercing that neighbours three doors down likely had to cover their ears.

So why on earth would I feel even an iota of relief that my little one had such an emotionally distressing meltdown that clearly exhausted both himself and his family? Let me explain. The linchpin here is that Max's meltdown didn't just occur in front of me, his father, and his siblings as it typically does, out of sight of friends or extended family. No. This meltdown took place in my parents' presence and for me that made all the difference in the world.

Why should that matter? Why should having my parents watch Max implode bring me relief? The relief comes from the fact that my mother and father have never observed this very upsetting but very common autistic behaviour from Max before. Like so many of my family and friends, when it comes to Max, they had never borne witness.

Sure, they had seen the weak beginnings of multiple meltdowns that my husband and I or even they themselves were adroit at extinguishing through distraction or various techniques learned in occupational therapy. My parents had also seen Max's inflexible adherence to seemingly nonsensical routines and rituals, such as needing to sit against *three* black pillows on *his* side of the sofa, while being handed a sippy cup full of milk that *he* helps to close after first looking carefully at the *bubbles*, while eating a specific snack from a *plastic bucket*, and while having a specific blanket (*no, not that one!*) tucked around his waist snugly and a children's television show on (*not too loud!*).

They had also observed how such routines and rituals seem to change on a moment's notice, often without rhyme or reason and how upset Max seems to get when those around him aren't immediately cognizant to such change. So yes, my parents were well versed in the quirky nature of their beloved grandson. But at the same time, they had also witnessed his affectionate side, his ability to be highly descriptive when speaking, his curiosity, his incredible, lovely sweetness. Witnessing such positives can sometimes make it challenging to truly *get* that the same child who is so lovely and so sweet also has Autism.

It's not that my parents are new to the world of Autism. Quite the opposite. In fact, they have been familiar with Autism for many years, my bright eleven-year-old nephew Jake having been diagnosed within the spectrum many years ago. But that's part of the issue, I think. My parents remember how Jake behaved at not quite four, and how different said behaviour was from Max's current actions. They have noticed that Max has strengths that Jake did not, and that Jake had (and has) strengths that Max doesn't currently exhibit.

How can two kids that are so incredibly different both be on the spectrum of Autism? Such a reality can be hard to wrap one's mind around until you realize that no two children with Autism are identical, because, just like any other two children in the world, they are each their unique selves, Autism or not.

So while my parents have been extremely supportive, helpful, and understanding in so many ways that I don't have room to list here, I don't think that my father at least (like most people who know and love Maxie) completely *got* it. Until yesterday's explosion, that is. Max, who had been keeping it together during the last few days, despite significant upheaval to his routine (my parents had been staying at our house following a brief illness of mine), by last night he had clearly had enough. The increase of noise and extra stimulation in the house, the reality of eight people living here instead of six, the strangeness of having Papa and Yaya sleeping on the downstairs' futon sofa when they *always* sleep in their own bedroom in their own house a town away, and the awareness that something had been wrong with Mommy, was just too much for this beautiful little boy to cope with and he let us all know, loud and clear.

It is what happened afterwards, after the meltdown had run its course, and a sleepy but calm Max had been put to bed, that meant the world to me.

It was the moment when my father turned to me on the couch and said, "Honey, I've always known Max's diagnosis must be accurate, but tonight is the first time that I really, truly *believe* it."

And that recognition, that acknowledgement from my father that despite his grandson's bright, sweet nature, Max *does* have Autism, an often highly overwhelming condition that he and his parents are working damn hard to cope with, was validation indeed. And for that, there is relief.

CHAPTER 20

I'm sitting on Dr. Seidler's examining table as I now do on a weekly basis, my legs dangling over the sides. As I watch Dr. Seidler examine my latest depression rating scale, I try to calculate how many hours I've been spending in professional's offices lately, including Max's appointments in my numbers. I find my brain unable to compute anything beyond three plus eight and have the sudden urge to rip the rating scale out of the physician's hands and change my answers. *Is there a correlation between suicidality and a person's new found stupidity?*

Dr. Seidler puts down the paper and looks at me. "We've had you on a relatively high dose of Celexa now for a few months. It's made an impact, but not enough."

"Oh. Sorry."

"No need to apologize!"

"Sorry about that," I say.

"As I was saying, the Celexa doesn't seem to be having a significant effect on your mood. I've consulted with the psychiatrist once more and we agree that you should try a related, but slightly different antidepressant." He pauses. "It's called Cipralex."

"I've never heard of it."

"Think of it as a close cousin to Celexa. The fact that you've had some improvement on Celexa makes us think that Cipralex may do the trick."

I shrug. "Sure, why not?"

"And as you know, I've referred you to see Dr. Kelly. His office will likely schedule an appointment with you shortly."

"See the psychiatrist?"

Dr. Seidler nods.

"Oh, yeah. HA!"

Dr. Seidler looks startled. "Did I say something funny?"

"No, it's just—I've never been in this place before. Having to take one antidepressant, and now another. First seeing a psychiatrist from the insurance company, and now seeing a second one. It's just very strange to me."

"But you did mention having been depressed before. Just that you never received the proper treatment."

The image enters my mind of me at age seventeen using a bent pop can to cut at my wrist for no other reason than I couldn't seem to get out from under a blanket of despair and hoped that a river of blood might help me float away. I look away from the doctor. "Yeah."

"Remember that even the best health professionals still become ill, they still need help."

"You're right, I know. I'll see him. It's fine."

"And you'll continue with your daily walks and seeing your counsellor?"

"Yes. I promise."

Dr. Seidler smiles at me while I try to get that image of my former forlorn self out of my head. *Out, damn spot, get the fuck out already!*

******

I'm sitting in yet another waiting room. The psychiatrist is only a few minutes late, but considering I showed up early, the wait has seemed endless. I smell my fingers on one hand, then pretend I was only scratching my face as I notice another patient giving me a repulsed look. Is this endless sitting on uncomfortable chairs penance for all the clients I've made wait? Eventually a door opens and the psychiatrist strides in. Dr. Kelly, a man in his late fifties who's sporting the most awesome Irish brogue I've ever had the privilege to hear. After a brief introduction, I follow him down a small hallway and into his office. His windows are large and let in light. There are a few photos of what must be grandchildren, judging by his age (my husband would be aghast by this assumption, given that he fathered our first child together as he was rounding fifty, but I'll let him be shocked). I sit down on a sofa across from him, my hands neatly folded in my lap.

"Very nice to finally meet you," he says. "Given that I've been advising Dr. Seidler about your medication for several weeks now, I feel like I know you already!" Dr. Kelly smiles broadly and then quickly glances at a folder he's holding. "So you've been struggling with depression for a few months at this point? First tried Celexa with only mild improvement and are now taking Cipralex?"

"Yes."

"And how are you finding the new medication?"

"It's working a bit better, I think. My concentration is almost normal now and I'm writing more."

126

"You like to write?"

"Yeah. I find it kind of therapeutic to, um, process my feelings that way."

Dr. Kelly jots something down. "And your appetite? Dr. Seidler mentioned that you have lost several pounds."

"I'm way too skinny, I know. But at least it's nothing like before!"

Dr. Kelly glances up from his notes. He puts the file down on a nearby table and leans forward. "Before?"

"Um, when I was sixteen and seventeen I think I experienced an episode of depression. I ended up running away from home, even though I had really good parents and nothing bad was happening there. I just wanted to get away from how badly I was feeling. I was a kid, I didn't know what to do! I ended up completely devastating my mom and dad!" A sob comes out like an unexpected hiccup and I cover my face with my arm.

"You ran away? Do you think you may have experienced any symptoms of mania or hypomania at the time?"

I shake my head, still crying. "I don't know. I don't think so. I never thought of it as anything but depression. Depression and total stupidity. I mean, can you imagine what I did to my parents?" I sob harder and find it difficult to catch my breath.

"I think that some of this guilt is a symptom of your current depression. I'd like to increase your Cipralex dosage and then see where that goes, okay?"

I slow down my breathing and nod. I grab a tissue from the box on the coffee table and blow my nose. At this point I'd do anything to feel better, anything.

CHAPTER 21

The thing with Autism is that most days it feels like one step forward, one step back. While movement is happening and positive changes are occurring, new "odd" behaviours and old, upsetting rituals are also popping up, usually when my husband and I least expect it. Max actually asks me for a drink and says "please" instead of merely whispering "juice, juice" into his chest—that's a big, giant step forward! Max once again pees on himself, soaking all of his clothes in the process and making a big puddle on the floor. This time, however, he decides to run his toy cars *through* the pee, chortling to himself as he spreads the liquid everywhere, laughing even more hysterically when I point out that this *isn't* an appropriate thing to do. A huge step backwards.

Max does very well during his assessment with the speech pathologist assigned to his daycare, impressing her with his decent vocabulary and good receptive language. What's more, because he's now functioning so well in terms of speech, he's being referred to the *Advanced* integrated social skills group, an intervention program where he and I will hopefully start to learn and practice the tools he so desperately needs in order to effectively interact with people outside of his family. Being referred to a group that deals with more complex interpersonal interactions seems like an enormous step forward!

Max screams in his grandmother's face when she says goodbye, makes a similar scream at his sister when she says good morning, and hits at me with his fists and his elbows (a new behaviour) when I gently touch his hair (an affectionate gesture he used to allow). Another step backward. Max suggests that we build a tunnel out of blocks together, rather than merely engage in solitary play. There's a step forward, right there! When I attempt to use a strategy I've recently learned called "intruding" and gently suggest that I be allowed to put a block where *I* want, rather than where Max orders me to place it, he reacts by shouting, hitting himself in the head, and throwing the blocks. Backward, folks, one more step backwards. Max stops "banging" my back with his upper chest for a week, but just as I'm about to declare it another step forward, the banging resumes, this time with more vigour than before.

Often the steps forward and back occur with such dizzying alacrity that it leads Max's dance partner to trip and stumble. My child will give me the most affectionate hug one moment but then laugh with what can only be called unbridled glee when he has his hands covering my nose and mouth and I shout out in panic that I can't breathe. He will be the perfect chef's helper during supper preparation, adding just the right amount of salt or flour when asked, yet will go into unreachable hysterics if I sing a song lyric incorrectly. Max will say the loveliest things imaginable, like "I miss you right here, Mommy", then yell at his father to "Run away, now!" because Joel had the audacity to suggest that they "go watch Michael Jackson's Black or White video", when the exact phrasing that Max had counted on hearing was that they "go watch Michael Jackson's Black or White video *from the beginning*". My child is someone who will shout at you for cutting his toast incorrectly but then not call out for help after vomiting all over himself in the night, choosing instead to point mutely at his wet, dirty pyjamas hours later when you go into his room to wake him. Max is perhaps the most delightful person I have ever met, and the most infuriating. He is the most affectionate, and yet the most distancing.

And so it goes. True gains are made, but other skills are lost. Learning occurs, but it can go in either direction. That, my friends, is Autism, at least when the person in question hasn't even turned four-years-old yet and would sometimes like to take a break from always having to *try* so damn hard. I think having me remain cognisant of the effort my little Max is making would be a big step forward in and of itself.

******

I'm back at Dr. Seidler's office, but this time it's to take Max, who may have a possible throat infection. While Max is in a good mood when we arrive to the doctor's office, and seems pleased his little brother is along for the ride, I know that when it comes to my autistic child, assuming what his future behaviour will be like is a stupid, even dangerous thing. While the three of us wait in the tiny examining room and Sam attempts to climb on everything in sight, the typical worries enter my mind. Will Max acknowledge Dr. Seidler's existence? Will he agree to do what the doctor asks so that he can actually be examined, opening his mouth at the required time? Will he instead start banging me with his head in agitation, or even worse, have a meltdown like he did during a previous visit? And if this happens, how will I handle a shrieking Max while also trying to keep a wild Sammy in line?

I'm so busy going through all the "What-ifs" that I almost miss seeing Max climb up onto the examining table by himself, and not only open his mouth when asked to do so, but say the loudest, clearest, most glorious-sounding "AHHHHH" that I have ever heard. An unexpected jewel, suddenly tossed my way.

"You've been such a good boy," Dr. Seidler says kindly, the examination now over. In response, Max looks him straight in the eye and gives a shy smile. A second jewel.

The visit over and Max diagnosed with a cold but infection-free, I gather up the coats and a wiggly Sammy, and prepare to go on our way. As I open the door to the parking lot, Max stops walking and begins to bounce on his heels.

"Maxie," I say. "We've got to keep walking to the car."

"Okay," he says. He starts walking again, but soon stops. More bouncing. *Shit.*

"Maxwell," I say. "You've got to keep walking!"

In response, the bouncing quickens. While still holding Sam in my arms, I bend down to Max's level. "Maxie? Can you please walk to the car for me?"

"Yeah," he says. He starts to bounce-walk by my side and hum.

As we reach the car, I open Sam's door first and buckle him in. I then turn to Max, who is continuing to bounce on his heels and hum. "Maxie?"

"I'm so happy for me!" he suddenly blurts out. "I wasn't scared and I said 'AHHH' and I'm so, so happy for me!"

And that, folks, is the biggest, brightest jewel that anyone could ever toss my way, something that I feel privileged to have been trusted enough to carry.

* * * * * *

After a few months of waiting (not bad, when it comes to Autism Spectrum Disorder interventions), Max's first session with the ABA preschool group arrives. Whimsically called "Playtime Pals", the intervention group takes place at the local community centre, in a room labelled The Clubhouse. ABA uses strategies based on scientific principles of behaviour to focus upon social communication, emotional regulation, and interpersonal skills, all areas of concern for my son. Given my own psychology background, ABA is a form of treatment that I feel able to trust, based upon solid research and measurable

130

outcomes. The official purpose of Max's several-week group is to "teach children skills that will assist them in beginning to navigate social interactions", but to my child, the main goal there seems to be just to have fun. While not wanting me to leave on the first day (this presents as Max clinging to me like a barnacle, only to then lie flat on the carpet with his face down, once one of the therapists manages to extricate him from my body), my little boy quickly comes to look forward to going to the new group each week, mainly for the fact that it is small (five or six kids, tops), with a lot of adult attention given to him, and shiny new toys to play with.

Both Joel and I are fine with the fact that Max is most excited about getting to play with new things, as we also know that, like the whole spoonful-of-sugar school of treatment, in the midst of all the shiny new toys the well-trained therapists are actually teaching the children important skills such as turn-taking, sharing, and initiating play. And not only teaching the children, but their eager-to-learn parents, too. A few caregiver education sessions are scheduled and multiple handouts are given. Through repetition and what are called social stories (stapled pages with colourful pictures on them, each detailing a specific step involved in completing an interaction), the children are taught how to engage in what seem like the most basic of interpersonal situations. In order to perform the skill of asking someone to play, for example, the following steps should be taken: 1) Look at the person's face; 2) Say their name to get their attention; 3) Wait until the person looks at you; 4) Say, "Can I play with you?"; 5) If the person says "Yes", then you get to play with the person!

Between sessions, Joel and I read these social stories with Max and practice what is taught. Role-playing becomes second nature in our household, with even little Sammy getting in on the action ("Ask me to pway, Max-Well!"). All of us our eager to have Maxie learn these strategies, to have the skills stick. Whenever Max successfully asks me to do an activity with him or even requests anything at all (such as actually asking me for a granola bar, rather than standing in front of the cupboard muttering "hungry, hungry"), I react like his personal cheerleader, praising him for actually letting me know what his needs and wants are.

On the last day of ABA, we're given Max's end-of-treatment report, which reiterates the fact that learning has occurred amid the shiny new toys. We're told that even without prompting from adults, Max is now able to request a turn much of the time, to respond to greetings made by others, and to sometimes even initiate the play process. We're also told that while Max performed well (very, very well!) throughout the program, we have the option of re-referring him to the waiting list and of having him go through all of the ABA sessions a second time. As I look over the report with Joel, I can feel my mood temporarily improving. *ABA worked! Our son is clearly one of their success stories, so there's definitely no need to go through the whole treatment rigmarole again! Things are going to be different from now on*!

Later, however, as I lay in bed next to a snoring Joel, I'm struck by the realization that, *oh my god*, ABA is now *over* and that once again Joel and I are left to try and paddle this leaky boat largely on our own. As this reality sinks into my brain, I start to feel my heart rate speed up and my skin sweat. Soon, my thoughts begin to ping-pong back and forth between optimism and doubt, the anxiety in me revving up. *Max learned so many wonderful new skills! He now looks people in the eye! He now tells them his name! Yes, but he also has started laughing at the social stories when they're read to him, ripping out certain pages, and throwing them in my face hysterically.* Back and forth, side to side. Rather than continue this internal debate, I get out of bed, take another sleeping pill/anxiety killer, and remind myself to call the ASD therapists in the morning to tell them that yes, we definitely want Max to be re-referred to the ABA waiting list. It turns out that I'm not so ready for ABA to be over, after all.

Section Six Hypomania
CHAPTER 22

It's been several few weeks since Cipralex first hit my bloodstream. My kindly psychiatrist started things off slowly with a low dose, then increased it by increments as its positive effects became apparent. While my husband and I haven't spoken much about how we feel about such improvement, I know that our thoughts must be in sync: *It's working! Finally, something is goddamn working*!

In the last few days, however, the drug's benefits seem to have kicked into overdrive. Not that I mind. How could I mind feeling so amazing? With this amazing feeling comes an all-consuming desire to dance my cares away whenever possible. In my living room, I sway back and forth to The Killers, my eyes scrunched tight. I twirl in circles, I hum, I flap my arms up and down, ready to take flight. As I move faster and faster, a realization laps at my ankles like the warm ripples in a whirlpool—I *am* the dancing queen. Over the music I hear the sound of small feet entering the room. I open an eye, just a bit. At knee level is a little boy, quite a little boy really, who just so happens to be looking pissed off at me in quite a big way.

"Hi, Maxie! Wanna dance?"

Max shakes his head and covers his ears. "Too loud!"

I ruffle his hair with a hand, then continue dancing. "I'll turn down the music after this one last song, okay? I just need it loud a bit longer."

"No!" Max shouts. "No dancing! Too loud!"

I try to talk to him while still dancing, but find it challenging, to say the least. The song has started to get faster in tempo and I'm trying hard to keep up with the beat. "Just the rest of this song, okay? It helps Mommy to dance a bit. You want to help Mommy, don't you?"

Max starts shrieking and hitting his ears. "No! No! No!"

Suddenly my husband is in the room. He heads to the stereo and shuts off the music, then turns to face me.

"What's going on?"

Max begins to bang his chest against Joel's legs. "Too loud! Too loud!"

I'm irritated by the sudden lack of music, but determined not to let that small speed-bump slow me down. I keep hopping from foot to foot, waving my arms up and down. "I just wanted to finish the song, that's all."

Joel bends down to pick up Max, then stands back up and faces me. I can't make out his facial expression, exactly, but I can tell that for some reason he ain't too pleased. "What the hell's the matter with you? Don't you realize how much loud music bothers Max?"

"It was just one last song. I really need to dance." I dance over to my husband and push myself against his chest. "Maybe we could do our own special dance later, if you know what I mean?" I purr. I try to stroke Joel's cheek and make a tiger noise. Max cries louder.

"What are you doing? Can't you see how upset our son is?"

"Can I help it if you're suddenly irresistible, you Jewish Adonis, you!"

Joel shakes his head, hugging Max tighter. "I was talking about the dancing and the loud music, although touching me constantly has become over the top, too."

"As I said, I need to dance!"

"Need to dance? What are you, fourteen?"

Max squirms out of his father's arms, now all calmness and logic. "It was too loud, Daddy. I said no and Mommy didn't listen."

"It's okay, Max. Let's go find your brother." Joel takes our son by the hand and leads him out of the room. I stick out my tongue in their direction, but wait until they're safely far away from me before heading to the stereo and turning the music back on. It takes a moment or two to find the beat, but I find it, and I'm there. Yes, I *am* the dancing queen.

******

Around the kitchen table sit Daniel, his best friend Josh, Meghan, and Sam. I have the radio on, but softly this time, so as not to offend anyone's delicate ears. I'm serving pancakes (*made from scratch*!), and dancing around the table as I drop them onto each plate. Once the pancakes are in their proper places, I toss a few cut strawberries on top, then stick the maple syrup in the exact centre of the table.

"Perfect," I say, then resume my dancing.

"Mom, can you maybe quit that?" Daniel asks.

"Why? Max isn't here tonight. He's out shopping with Joel, remember?"

"What's that have to do with anything?"

"The music! Even though I'm playing it low, I can turn it up as loud as we want without over-stimulating anybody!"

My son looks down at the table and mutters. "I think you might be over-stimulating yourself."

"Score!" Meg shouts. She reaches across the table to high-five her brother, then does the same to Josh. I stick out my tongue at them (my new favourite gesture), then keep dancing.

"You guys are just party-poopers. Sammy likes the dancing and the music, don't you, Sammy?"

Sam looks up at me, his mouth stuffed with pancake. "Too wow-d, Mommy. Too wow-d."

"Fine!" I shut off the radio, then go into the den and turn up the music there. *Where does a girl have to go to dance in peace?* "Satisfied, everybody?" I call out.

"Mom, can you be in here with us?" Meg asks.

I go back in and force myself to stop dancing. *When did my children become so lame?*

"Mom?" This time it's Daniel again. "Since when do you serve chocolate chip pancakes and ice cream for supper?"

"Are you kidding me, now? I thought you'd love them!"

"I like them, Mom," Meg says.

"I like dem," Sam echoes.

"Yeah. Really good, thanks," says the best friend.

Daniel shrugs. "I know they're good. It's just that you're normally Miss. Nutrition Lady. Whole wheat this, tofu that. It just seems weird."

"Je pense que tu es un spoil-sport," I say.

Josh laughs as he drinks some milk and it ends up coming out of his nose.

Daniel's face starts to redden. "Did you just talk in Pig-Latin or something?"

"Just a bit of French to liven up the atmosphere. You're becoming way too serious in your old age!"

In response, my son picks up his plate of half-eaten pancakes and puts it on the counter. He quickly drinks down his milk, then puts the glass next to his plate. He is nothing if not neat. Daniel then turns to Josh, who is stuffing down his own pancakes as quickly as possible.

"You ready to go?"

Josh takes a last swallow, then pushes back his chair. "Yeah."

As the boys walk out of the room, I turn the radio back on, and start to dance around. "They don't know how to have fun, right guys?"

"Das right!" Sam says.

"Sure Mom," says Meg. "Can I have Daniel's other pancake?" She holds out her plate and I dump the remains of my son's supper on it, before continuing my solo moves. *I knew I'd someday regret quitting ballet at twelve, I just knew it!*

******

Later, I'm typing rapidly on my laptop in the now clean kitchen. Otherwise the house is quiet, that kind of quiet you only get when a home is filled with sleeping children. Joel enters the room, rubbing at his eyes.

"Um, sweetie? Are you going to bed soon? It's almost two o'clock."

I don't look up, afraid to lose my train of thought. "Soon," I say. "I'm kind of busy here."

Instead of leaving, Joel remains in the doorway. "But it's really late for you and you've got the kids tomorrow. It's not a daycare day, remember?"

I lose where I was going in my story, but keep typing anyway, just to get the damn point across that I don't want to be disturbed. "Look, I'm writing this dystopian teen novel and I'm in the middle of a great action scene, so maybe you could go before I lose my flow?"

Joel sighs, the kind of patronizing sigh that only a spouse or parent can successfully do. I swear, that sigh is a work of art. "But I'm worried about your sleep," he says. "You used to be in bed by ten thirty."

"No offence, but maybe you should worry about your own sleep instead. I'm not tired and I need to write this. Just go!"

I wave my husband away as if he were a mosquito and wait for him to leave. Thankfully he does. I give my own long-suffering-spouse sigh, then resume typing once more, my train of thought caught again.

******

One week later, maybe two. I'm sitting on the floor of the den, cutting out long pieces of green construction paper and placing them into a pile. Once there's no more paper to be cut, I take each piece and staple it into a circle, then add another circle onto it. Pretty soon I have chain after chain of green paper, pure awesomeness. I pick up a stack

136

of perfectly made shamrocks and stand up, tape in hand. Within minutes the entire main floor of my house is decorated in green. I walk from room to room, staring at my interior decorating skills. I am so talented! I should be hired for one of those shows on TLC!

Joel stumbles into the living room, rubbing his eyes. "Alicia?"

I turn and give him a big smile. Maybe he could make a guest appearance as my faithful assistant? I smile broader. "Yes, sweetie?"

"Uh, do you know that it's six o'clock in the morning?"

I nod. "I know. Unbelievable, eh? I did all of this in only three hours!" I gesture grandly around the room. "It's going to be perfect for the kids. Just perfect!"

"Perfect for the kids? What the hell are you talking about?"

"For St. Patrick's Day, of course!" I notice a chain that is starting to fall off a wall and rush over to retape it. "I couldn't exactly use the red and yellow decorations I put up for Meg's twelfth birthday two weeks ago. That would be nutty!"

"Um," Joel scratches his head. "About that...I think Meghan might have been embarrassed by how much you decorated the house."

I stop cutting for a moment. "What do you mean?"

"Ah, well," my husband pauses. "Don't you think she's a bit too old to have matching napkins and paper plates, not to mention the helium balloons for each guest?"

Images of my daughter's recent sleepover-birthday whip through my mind, each one brighter and more positive than the next. The snacks, the rented DVDs, the cake and make-your-own sundaes! I so rocked as a hostess to tween girls! The only memory that gives me pause is the image of my darling girl refusing to let me crash her party, this despite the fact I had my own sleeping bag ready to go. No matter, it was still a success!

I look at my husband and laugh. "You're not a girl. How would you know, silly?" I then turn back to my cutting. "Anyway, today's St. Patrick's Day! Isn't this great? Think of how surprised they'll be when they come down and see all of this!"

Joel scratches his head again. I notice that his pj bottoms are starting to fall down on one side. *Adorable.* "It's six in the morning, Alicia," he repeats.

I nod. "Exactly!"

"And since when do we even celebrate St. Patrick's Day? The little guys are half-Jewish."

"And they're also about one fourth Irish, give or take a bit!

Anyway, wait 'till you see what I've got planned for Passover!"

"For Passover?" Joel scratches his head again. "It's six o'clock in the morning.."

"Um, you've said that three times now," I say. "Are you all right?"

"Am *I* all right? *Me?*"

I grab my silly husband by the hand and pull him into the kitchen. "I saved the best for last!!" I say. "Hurry up!" I pull him harder and he reluctantly follows. I point at a green loaf of bread.

"What the hell?"

"I know," I say. "Pretty amazing, isn't it? I used food colouring to make it look perfect. I plan to use it to make cinnamon toast. I know cinnamon might not be exactly Irish, but that's a minor…"

Joel interrupts. "You don't have the monitor turned on! What if one of the boys had been crying?" Joel heads over to the counter and flicks a switch. Immediately the sound of a child yelling can be heard. "See?"

"Oh! That's Sammy! Please don't let him see this floor until I'm done, okay?"

"But you were going to get them up and ready this morning, remember? I had to work late last night …"

"I don't want to ruin the surprise! Please!" I shove my husband out of the room and let out a small giggle. "Think of how excited they'll be! Just think!"

Joel sighs hugely and begins clomping back up the stairs. "You owe me one," he mutters. "You really owe me."

"Okay! Whatever! Just don't come down for another thirty minutes!" I blow a kiss towards my foolish husband and then grab a bag off the table and rip it open. *Time to blow up the green balloons.*

******

More time passes, but I'm oblivious to it. Or to put it more accurately, time has ceased to exist in a chronological, second-by-second way. To me, time has become like that cool Oobleck stuff fifth grade science teachers make to impress kids (you know that stuff—sometimes a solid, sometimes a liquid…Oobleck!). All I care about right now is the fact that I'm about to have a delightful lunch at the Golden Griddle with my parents, Meghan, and the little boys. The fact that a mere fifteen minutes ago I forgot to buckle my two little boys into their car seats before I began driving towards the restaurant matters little. Max reminded me, after all, so it's all okay. It could have happened to

138

anyone. It probably does happen to anyone. Besides, I'd only driven about fifty feet, so it was no problem. No problem, all okay, end of story. Everything is better than okay, actually. It's freaking amazing!

Meghan is in an unusually good mood herself, revelling in the fact that she has a PD Day, while Daniel does not. Max and Sam are busy colouring with crayons, while Meg starts to talk to my parents about an upcoming school dance. I look around the pancake house and smile to myself. *This moment feels perfect. It's goddam perfect! All is right in the world.*

"It's not like a dance they'll have in junior high," Meg says. 'It's for families, too, which is kind of lame, but at least they'll have a DJ. Me and Emma are writing a list of songs to request. Cool songs, nothing Justin Bieber or anything…"

I start to clap my hands to the beat of Baby, humming my little heart away.

"Mom!"

"Alicia," my mother says. "Meghan was telling us about her dance."

I giggle, but force myself to sit on my hands. "Sorry! It's just that whenever someone mentions Justin Bieber, I think of his songs. They're so catchy, don't you think?"

"No, I don't," my mother says.

I giggle again. "Oops! Just me!"

Meghan gives me what seems like an embarrassed look, then resumes talking. "So the dance is for all the grades, but because we're the oldest this year, it's kind of *our* dance. Lots of parents bring food, so there's stuff like chips and pop and brownies…"

"Did Meghan tell you how I made green bread for St. Patrick's Day?" I say.

Sam looks up from his colouring. "It was gween. I didn't wike it."

"Mom!" Meg says. "I was talking!"

"Oops! So sorry!"

"Alicia," my father intones. "Why are you clapping your hands together again?"

I look down at my hands, which are indeed clapping. This is worse than smelling my fingers! I forcibly hold them together in my lap. "Sorry, sorry! I'm just a bit hyper, I guess."

Meghan mutters. "More like just a bit embarrassing."

"Meghan, don't be rude to your mother!" my mom says.

"But she is! Always dancing around the house, doing weird accents in front of my friends!"

I look around the table. "That was an *Irish* accent," I explain. "For St. Patrick's Day!"

"And what about the dinosaur costume?" Meghan asks. "Was that for St. Patrick's Day, too?"

"A dinosaur costume?" My mother sounds puzzled. *Who doesn't love the dinosaurs, those poor, doomed creatures of yore?*

"I wore it because it's green." I pause. "I thought it would be funny!"

"You wore Max's costume in front of my friend to be funny? Thanks a lot!"

This time Max looks up from his colouring. "My costume? Where's my costume?"

I pat him on the shoulder. "It's okay, Maxie. Mommy just borrowed your costume before. Just the hood part. I put it back. It's all okay."

"No!" Max shrieks, beginning to throw his crayons. One hits a diner at a nearby table. "My costume! Not yours! Mine!"

My mother pulls Max onto her lap and he leans against her, petting her hair.

"He gets loud when he's upset," I say.

"Alicia," my father says, "he's not the only one who's being loud today."

I can feel myself blush. I look down at my damn hands and notice I'm clapping again. I push my chair back and stand. "Meg, you keep telling Papa and Yaya your story. I'm going to the washroom."

I rush to the Women's Room and stare at myself in the mirror. I turn on a tap and splash cold water on my face. *What the hell is happening to me?*

******

It's D Day, to be hereby forever known in my family as shit-or-get-off-the-pot day. I'm rushing about the house, afraid of being late for a pre-kindergarten meeting with Max's future principal. It seems like I'm always rushing lately, always having that het-up feeling of running late. I've noticed that I'm a bit more agitated lately, a bit less "fun", but it's all still good, everything's still okay. I've never missed an OT session for Max, and I'm never late picking him up from preschool. I always, always, *always* get him to his appointments on time, so I'm a stellar mom in that way. But yet I feel so damn rushed.

I run out of the house, checking my watch as I go. I unlock my car and quickly start the ignition. The school is a five-minute drive away and I have two minutes to get there. *Shit.* I put the car in reverse and begin to move backwards. Suddenly I hit my forehead with my hand, remembering a forgotten task.

"Dammit! Girl Guides!"

I jump out of the car door and run up the front steps of my house, the car still moving backwards. I rush up to the door and begin banging on it.

"Meghan! Meghan! Don't forget to call your Girl Guide leader to tell her you're not coming today! She'll be worried!"

My daughter opens the front door and begins to scream hysterically, pointing at the road. "The car, Mommy! The car, the car! It's moving!"

I turn to look at where she's pointing and then I see it. The minivan, my minivan, is indeed heading backwards down the street, making a bee-line towards a parked car mere metres away. I remain motionless for a moment, before jumping down the steps. My husband appears from nowhere and is at my side.

"Oh my god!" he shouts. "What did you do?"

I don't answer, but instead pull open the front door. I try to force the car to stop with my body, before I realize that the ignition is still on. I jump into the car and turn it off, just before it backs into the other vehicle. I stay seated in the minivan for a few moments, stunned.

"Are you all right?" Joel asks, his voice loud. "What happened?"

I slowly get out of the car and reach for my husband. He holds me and I let myself fall against him, a puddle of confusion.

"I don't know," I whisper. "I got out of a moving car and I didn't even notice. I don't fucking know."

******

Joel and I sit side by side on the sofa, with Dr. Kelly across from us. Joel sits with his back straight and his arms crossed. I keep jiggling my leg and occasionally reach out to touch Joel's arm.

Dr. Kelly clears his throat. "Well, it's clear to me from everything you've told me that you're experiencing a hypomanic episode."

I snort. "HA!"

"A hypo what?" asks Joel.

The psychiatrist turns to speak directly to my husband. *I am the patient here. I no longer count*. "A hypomanic episode. From what your wife told me before, she likely also experienced one as a teenager, when she ran away to Niagara Falls."

Joel looks at me. "Didn't you tell me that you were depressed back then? That you kept cutting yourself and stuff? I don't remember anything about hypomania."

Dr. Kelly shuffles through his notes. "Alicia, didn't you tell me that you mainly brought summer dresses when you ran away and that you told your mother that you planned to wear them while walking by the Falls, writing poetry? This despite the fact that it was February?"

I grin, then jiggle my leg some more. "I know, ridiculous, huh?"

"No, not ridiculous," the psychiatrist says. "But quite likely hypomanic, which of course is an aspect of Bipolar Disorder."

Joel suddenly leans forward, as if shot out of a cannon. "Whoa, now wait a minute here! I don't mean to be disrespectful, but first we were talking depression, now we're talking hypomanic, and we're also taking Bipolar? Even if she did have that episode as a teenager, how could Alicia be Bipolar if she hasn't had anything like this happen between seventeen and forty?"

Dr. Kelly holds up his hand for a moment. "I understand that as a husband this is a lot to take in. but Alicia is clearly hypomanic or 'high' right now. Look at how agitated she is."

Both men turn to look at me. My leg is now doing its own version of the St. Vitus' Dance. I suddenly notice that I've been slapping my hands together without even noticing. *Interesting*. I stop moving my hands and sit on them, but allow my leg to continue its jig. Maybe it'll remind Dr. Kelly of his homeland.

"You only need one episode of hypomania or mania to get a diagnosis of Bipolar Disorder. Only one. And from what you have told me, Alicia, it is highly likely that you had an episode as a young person as well. My guess is that in the years since, you experienced ups and downs in your mood but have been able to manage them, because you have decent coping skills and because they haven't been too extreme. Am I correct?"

I nod. I reach out to touch Joel's face, but he jerks away. "Can you believe how good-looking my husband is?" I blurt out. "I mean, not to embarrass anyone in the room here, but he is one good-looking man!"

"Alicia!" Joel hisses.

"Sex drive increased?" Dr. Kelly asks.

"How did you know?" I say, startled. *Am I that easy to read? Or maybe it's more that I'm just easy! HA!*

"A common symptom of hypomania," Dr. Kelly informs us. "Difficult at times for the partner to cope with, especially when it's uncharacteristic of their spouse. Still, be assured that it's very common." He clears his throat. "For someone who has an underlying vulnerability to Bipolar Disorder, a high dose of an SSRI may actually help to trigger a hypomanic episode. The fact that Alicia became hypomanic while on Cipralex further proves the diagnosis."

I glance at my husband. You wouldn't be able to loosen the grip his hands have on each arm with a crowbar. "So if she hadn't had the medication she wouldn't have become Bipolar? Is that what you're saying?"

"No, no." The psychiatrist shakes his head. "She has likely been Bipolar on some level for years. It would have been triggered eventually."

Joel looks at me and gives *the* sigh. He slowly uncrosses his arms and does something that surprises me. He takes my hand and holds it between his own. His skin feels warm and I like it.

"You *are* a sexy man, hubby, hub-hub-hub of mine," I purr.

Joel again ignores my flattering overtures. *Is he perhaps forgetting that I'm an entire decade younger than him and that he is thus a damn lucky man?* When he next speaks, his voice is quiet. "Now that I think about it, there was an episode last year at the newspaper awards banquet."

Dr. Kelly raises his eyebrows. "Oh?"

"I'd been nominated for an award. The ceremony was a pretty big deal for me. Alicia had a few glasses of wine and then insisted on dancing the night away on the dance floor. Danced like a crazy woman —the only one out there."

I pull my hand away. "A crazy woman? They had a dance floor and a DJ for a reason, you know!"

Joel's voice gets louder again. "It's just that no one else was dancing, sweetie. And you were going at it like a teenager. It was kind of embarrassing."

I look at Joel, then the psychiatrist, then back to my husband once more. "You were dancing, too!"

"That's because you forced me too. You wouldn't let go of me until I joined you." Joel edges away from me ever-so-slightly on the sofa. "So looking back that could have been some sort of hypomanic state. I mean, it's not like she had that much wine." He pauses and gives his best stare towards the psychiatrist. "So what comes next?"

"What comes next is that we try and get your wife on the proper medication. We'll begin by lowering the antidepressant dose immediately." Dr. Kelly looks towards me. "I'd also like you to begin taking a mood stabilizer. We don't want to have to hospitalize you, do we?"

"Hospital! No way!" I start to giggle like an insane person, both legs dancing now.

"Alicia…" says my husband.

"No! This is surreal! Can you imagine me, in a psych ward? I mean, I'm managing things at home, aren't I? I've been taking Max to his OT every week and I've been practising all the deep pressure stuff to calm him down and I've made a pretty amazing visual schedule for him, too! I even practice all of ABA stuff with him! Could I do all of that if I were Bipolar?"

Both men are silent.

Suddenly a thought enters my head and I feel compelled to share my wisdom. "Isn't that a weird name to call a therapy? ABA? Why don't they just call it MNO or XYZ instead? Who picked it anyway, the writers for Sesame Street? HA!" I start to laugh and find that I can't stop. Joel begins to rub my back. He sighs, but this time it's a caring sigh, mixed with some fear. Joel looks at Dr. Kelly and nods. The psychiatrist takes out his prescription pad and then hands the paper to me. *And next up to bat, folks, is Lithium.*

******

I'm driving down Highway Seven as I do every other weekend, taking Daniel to visit his father. Thanks to Lithium, I'm now able to remember the speed limit and to follow it like a good citizen. I take in a few deep breaths to prepare myself for the conversation I'm about to give. I feel incredibly nervous, more nervous than the time I had to explain to him at age four why penises are great, wonderful parts of your body but that anything you do with it on your own has to remain *private* (I may be mistaken, but I believe that discussion might have been our last mother-son chat).

I take one final deep breath, then begin. "So, there was something I kind of wanted to talk to you about today," I say.

Daniel sighs. "I said I was sorry for handing in that paper late! I just thought it was due in another week!"

"No, not that. Nothing about you, actually. I wanted to talk to

144

you about me. About how I've been doing."

Daniel becomes deeply interested in the pastoral scene that flies by our window.

I take another deep breath. "So, as I'm sure you've noticed, I've been a bit hyper lately."

"By hyper do you mean crazy?"

"No, I don't mean crazy, but fine, sure. I've been a bit crazy lately. The dancing around, the listening to music really loud, the talking sometimes in French..."

"Yeah, that's really messed up."

"And the scary thing that happened with the car," I add.

Daniel turns to look at me. "How could you not realize that the car was still moving? Even a monkey would notice that a car is moving!"

"Dan, can you just let me finish here please?"

Dan looks away again. "Yeah, sorry."

"Anyway, to backtrack a bit, after Max was diagnosed with Autism, I became depressed. Depressed in the way that means someone needs to take medicine to feel better."

"Because of Max?"

I shake my head. "No, not because of Max. It was the situation itself that was so stressful. And that combined with the fact that I have an underlying vulnerability towards depression..."

"A what?"

"Mood problems run in my family a bit, which means that if I'm under enough stress I'm more likely to get depressed than the next person. Joel, for example, didn't get depressed throughout all of this."

"Does that mean I'm more likely to get depressed, too?"

I nod. "I guess it kind of does. You'll need to take care of yourself and..."

My son interrupts. "Crap! So I've got Autism and depression in my blood! Nice family!"

"Every family has something. And Autism isn't something that you're going to get. You're either born with it or you're not."

"Well, that's something, I guess."

I continue driving for a few minutes, the silence between us a heavy thing that tastes sour when you breathe it in. "Anyway, they needed to give me medicine to make my mood improve. Antidepressants. The only problem is that the medicine improved my mood too much."

"That stuff will mess with you. Weren't you taught to 'just say no'?"

"*Daniel*! Will you just listen?"

"Okay, sorry. Are we almost at Dad's yet?"

"Soon." I pause. "Anyway, the reason that the medicine made my mood too high is because I must be vulnerable to something called Bipolar Disorder."

Daniel turns his head abruptly to face me, a look of shock and maybe disgust on his face. "You're Bipolar? Like Bi-Winning? Like Charlie Sheen? So you *are* seriously crazy now?"

"No! I'm not crazy now! And no one even knows if Charlie Sheen has Bipolar Disorder..."

"Well, he's high on something and it sure ain't life!"

I reach the outskirts of the city. *Only a few more minutes to go.* "I was actually what's called hypomanic, not manic, which means that I have something called Bipolar II Disorder, which is a milder form. Like Catherine Zeta Jones." The image of the actress jumps into my mind and I instantly feel better. *I'm like a movie star.*

Daniel blinks. "Who?"

"Or Demi Lovato."

"That chick Meghan likes?"

I nod.

"Didn't she, like, cut herself or something messed up like that?"

"I think she might have, but I don't do that, so don't worry."

"Well, now I will."

I turn onto my ex-husband's street. "No, you really don't have to worry! I was just trying to explain what's been going on, to make things make sense. I'm now on another medication to help stabilize my mood. Something called Lithium. So far it's working really well."

"Lithium! Omigod! I've heard of that! That's for crazy people!"

"It's also for people like me." I pull up against the curb and park. "We're here. Do you have any questions for me before you go see your dad?"

Daniel shakes his head, then speaks in his best big-brother voice. "Just don't tell Meghan what you told me, okay? She's still a kid. She won't be able to handle this stuff."

Daniel opens his door and climbs out, taking his knapsack with him.

"I'll have to think about that," I say. "Bye, Danny!"

"Later."

Daniel closes the door and lopes up to his dad's house. I watch him go, suddenly aware that I called him by a nickname I stopped using when he was ten.

Section Seven Hope

CHAPTER 23

Over the course of the last few days, my hybrid family has celebrated not one but two major holidays. On Friday Joel and I packed up the four kids and took them off to Toronto, where we took part in a seder that my mother-in-law hosted in her seemingly effortless way (I say seemingly, because, despite being a "shiksa", I have come to learn that there's an extreme amount of prep work involved when it comes to Passover). Around the long table sat three of her sons, including their spouses, children, and in my own husband's case, stepchildren. In front of each of us was a Haggadah, the Jewish text which tells the story of Jews' liberation from slavery in Egypt, all those many years ago. Hours before the multi-course dinner was served, each person around the table took turns reading from the book, and numerous rituals took place (e.g., the washing of hands at certain times, the dipping of egg in salt water, etc.). As an outsider, a seder is a beautiful, somewhat mysterious tradition, and I look forward to it every year.

But what about to an almost-four-year-old, who just so happens to have Autism, and thus finds large gatherings, lengthy periods of sitting, and delayed eating to be overwhelming, to say the least? All the way to Toronto, I worried. While I knew that my other three would be well-behaved (and I included in this crew Sammy, who can remain seated for an entire day if food is involved), I had doubts about Max. Were we expecting too much from him, to bring him to this family event? Would he have a meltdown even before the meal was served? How would we cope? How would *I* cope? While the Lithium was keeping my mood in check, my anxiety was going off the charts. I popped one anti-anxiety pill, then two, unable to handle the anxiety without some reinforcements.

It turns out that I shouldn't have worried, for you see, my little boy had taught himself the time-honoured skill of retreat, then return, a skill that as a psychologist I have previously taught numerous clients struggling with anxiety. Feeling too overwhelmed/over-stimulated by a situation? Then retreat to a quieter, safer place, calm down, and when you feel ready, return.

Throughout the lovely but lengthy seder, Maxie did just that. Here he is sitting next to his cousins. There he goes again, running off to a quieter room. Here he is once more, not at the table, but rolling on a sofa, humming to himself, watching us from the periphery. And there he goes once more, off to a quieter space. To my endless gratitude, my relatives all acted as if such behaviour was of course entirely normal, and carried on with the beautiful ceremony. No one demanded that Max stay seated, like all the other children were doing. No one expected Max to be anyone other than he was, a sweet, highly curious, but easily overwhelmed little boy who had decided to experience the ancient holiday in his own, Max-like way.

Retreat, then return.

Then yesterday came, the day that began with the excitement of Easter baskets and candy, as well as the promise of an afternoon egg hunt. Once again, the four kids were packed up and off we went, this time to my parents' house in Waterloo for an elegant Easter lunch. The dining room table was covered with linen, beautiful dishes were used, and a candle glowed brightly. While the number of people at the lunch wasn't unwieldy, the guest list did include several near-strangers for Max.

Again, I worried. Again, I popped an anti-anxiety pill. How would my little boy react? Would he begin screaming when asked to sit for such an elegant meal? And how would the guests (lovely people, but still individuals who don't know Maxie the way that we do) react? Once again, while Sammy sat through the entire meal, shovelling in forkfuls of new foods (beet salad, devilled eggs, lemon mousse, bring it on!), Max spent much of the meal playing by himself in the adjacent sun room, occasionally returning to peek into the dining room to see what was what, and then retreating once more. As had been the case at the seder, the Easter guests took such behaviour as normal, happily enjoying the good food and conversation, and not minding the little boy whom now you saw, now you didn't.

Retreat, then return.

Thanks to my little boy, my two spring holidays were wonderful, anxiety and mood problems be damned. And thanks to my little boy, I was reminded of a time-honoured skill that I had almost forgotten. Retreat, then return. A good lesson for us all, I think.

* * * * * *

Max begins his integrated social skills group next week and I can't wait. Ever since hearing about this community-based program, we've been waiting for it to be Max's turn. Having just come off a successful round of group-based ABA treatment, our little boy is more than ready for the next step. Called "Stay and Play", the integrated social skills group is for high-functioning preschoolers with developmental needs, with each child in the group expected to bring a parent, a childcare teacher (if they have one), and most importantly, a normally developing ("neurotypical") peer.

Did you read that last part? Each child is expected to bring along a friend, a little boy or girl who will be involved in modelling appropriate social behaviour. And that for us, is where the whole trouble begins. For you see, at almost four, Maxwell doesn't *have* a friend.

When I look back to being almost four, my memories are imbued with kids. Neighbourhood kids, kids of my parents' friends, kids at church, kids at nursery school. While my parents were a constant, safe presence, they were a solid backdrop for my world of play, rather than being on centre stage. There were my best friends on the street, like Linnie and Sofia, Lucie, and John. There was my God-sister, Rachel. I lived in a world populated with little people who often ran out to play each afternoon and didn't come back until their parents called them in for supper (*Anyone out there remember the 70s? A damn good decade to be a kid*).

While I realize that logistically Maxie's world is different, the same fact keeps coming back to haunt me: Maxwell doesn't have a friend. While it's true that there are no small children directly across from or beside us, there is a little girl his age at the end of the block and there is a little boy one street over. Are they his friends? No. And while it's true that he doesn't have the benefit of attending a church parish or synagogue on a regular basis to form friendships there, he does attend preschool three days a week. Does he have friends, true friends? No.

For Maxie, his friends are found within our family—Mommy and Daddy and his siblings, not to mention his loving extended relatives. Most of the time this seems enough, especially with an adoring little brother following his every move. But then came the request from the integrated social skills group, with us incapable of finding anyone (*anyone!*) who would be willing to have their child attend this all-important program with our son. After we failed miserably in our search to find a friend to go with Max, the head of the program finally found someone for us. A pale victory, at best.

And that leads us to today. It's almost suppertime and Max is in the kitchen with me, making supper. Rather than ask to stir, he just sits there, quiet and unmoving. I ask him what's wrong, but my questions lead nowhere fast.

Eventually, he comes out with it. "I asked the boys to play and they told me to go away." As Max says this, he turns to look at the wall, far away from my eyes.

At this moment, I'm glad he isn't looking at my gaze, because my eyes have become shocked with tears. Max actually asked children to *play* (a hard-earned skill from ABA), and the little shitheads said *no*?

"What did you do next, Max?" I ask, hoping that he had perhaps decided to ask other children to play instead.

He puts his chin on his chest, not answering.

"What did you do next, Maxie?" I ask again.

"Get sad," he whispers, before leaving the table.

And that's when it hits me again. Maxie doesn't have a friend.

So while I'm thrilled that good interpersonal abilities may result from Max's time at the integrated social skills group, my biggest hope is that he'll come away from it with even one blossoming friendship as well, because I can tell already that the world of family just isn't quite big enough for this particular boy anymore.

******

Max's integrated social skills group is run out of a hospital whose patients are primarily there for the long haul. On our first day of the program, I hold Max's hand tightly as we walk through the main doors, feeling oddly disoriented. The hospital lobby is bright and pleasant, seeming to have the same decorator as the River Glen Centre. Other than the fact that there is artwork associated with the hospital's Roman Catholic lineage, it's like I'm back in the same place, and I can't help but feel that Gail's face could pop up at any moment. As we walk through the lobby, I notice a few older people sitting on sofas, with others in wheelchairs. Each person is elderly, several look frail, and many are all alone. *This is so depressing.* I squeeze my son's fingers, not certain how he will react to this scene. As we reach the elevators, however, Max begins to hop up and down, doing his happy dance.

"Are you excited about going to meet the other kids?" I ask.

Max ignores my question, but keeps on hopping.

"Maxie, sweetie. Is everything okay?"

"I like this place! I really like it!" Hop. Hop. "When we were walking over here I saw so many people and so many people smiled at me! They all smiled because I made them so happy! I did it! It was me!"

"You sure did, sweetie," I say, feeling a twinge of shame that it's so easy for me to see situations from the glass half-empty perspective.

We enter the elevator and go down a floor, Max pressing a few extra buttons before we exit. We walk down a hallway until we see a sign for Stay and Play. As we approach the doorway, Max begins to cling to me, hiding his face against my waist.

"It's okay, Maxie," I whisper to the top of his head. "You're going to love this place, just like you loved Playtime Pals. I promise!"

After being warmly greeted by the two therapists who run the program (Nancy, an OT, and Greta, a Speech-Language Pathologist), we're pointed in the direction of a table that's in the middle of the room.

"If you go over there, you can get a name-tag," Nancy says, leading us to the table.

Max stumbles by my side, his eyes squeezed shut, and one hand firmly pushed against an ear.

"Maxie, open your eyes or you'll hurt yourself!" I say. I turn to look at the OT. "He doesn't usually do this!"

Nancy waves away my concerns. "This is a huge room. It's bright, it's colourful, and it's new. Sounds echo off the walls, and with at least twelve kids, not to mention all of the adults here, there's a lot of sound. I'd probably want to keep out the noise and colours, too!"

Soon we reach the table, which is surrounded by little children, their parents, and a few preschool teachers who've agreed to come observe the program. I quickly spot Cheryl, a teacher from Max's daycare, and one of his favourite people on the planet.

"Cheryl's here," I whisper.

Despite himself, Maxwell opens one eye, then another. He takes a few steps over to Cheryl, his left hand still held over one ear.

"Hi Max," she says cheerfully. "I wrote your name on a name-tag. Do you want to colour it with a marker?"

Maxwell nods, then lets go of his ear and makes the final few steps closer to his teacher. I take a deep breath in, then out. I can already tell that this is the place where we need to be.

******

Once the children have all arrived and name-tags are firmly affixed to chests, everyone sits down in a circle and waits for Greta and Nancy to begin. I quickly learn that each session will have a fun theme for the children, with a specific targeted goal to be taught to kids and parents alike. The sessions will be highly structured, with a visual schedule used throughout to let the children know what comes next. Even more importantly, each child is given their own visual schedule with Velcro on it, so that they can pull off a picture each time they finish a task, and put it on a "Done" pile. Once circle-time is over, I watch as Max gleefully pulls off that picture, clearly enjoying the sensation and sound of the Velcro ripping, not to mention being able to show himself that an activity is done.

After being informed about the basic goals of the program (transitioning, communication, self-regulation, imitation, listening and responding, sharing, etc.), the parents are asked to follow Greta out of the room and to their own intervention space. After many reluctant goodbyes, we leave our children and walk in single file towards the elevators. Once in, we stand in silence, all watching the floor numbers and waiting for the ding. *We could use communication as a basic goal, ourselves.* With Greta as our leader, we quietly herd ourselves into a conference room, and take seats (note: during the next five weeks, each of us will choose the same seat every time, a routine set in stone after just one day; it seems that our apples may not fall that far from their parental trees).

After we've settled down in our chairs, Greta begins our first parent education session, and for the next few hours the room is filled mainly with the sounds of the Speech-Language Pathologist speaking about issues related to self-regulation, listening, and responding, our pens scratching on paper, as well as the voices of the few mothers brave enough to ask an occasional question. A garrulous group we are not.

By the second parent session, however, this all changes, with Nancy or Greta (they take turns) lucky if they're able to get in a ten minute education blurb before we moms begin our coffee klatch. While we all appreciate the information the therapists provide us, our mutual intense desire to connect with other parents who *get it* sidelines most of the group's formal teaching component. In sharp contrast to my former workplace self (*I won't let you get close! I won't let you know me!*), I find myself so eager to share myself with these fellow moms that my words almost stumble over each other in their need to get out of my mouth and be heard. If anything, I have to hold myself back from talking too much and not letting the shyer, quieter moms, like Annie or Megan, also get a chance to share. *Did this happen to you, too? Does your child do this as well? How do you deal with it? How do you actually...cope?*

In response to our increasingly loud, raucous group, both Greta and Nancy sit back and let us connect, quietly giving us handouts to read on our own, and trusting us to be grownup enough to ask questions as needed. By allowing our ragtag group of often isolated, often lonely mothers to share the stories with each other that we've been holding on so tightly to for so long, to actually grant us a few (child free!) hours to connect with the people we clearly needed to connect with, these two therapists show themselves to be the true professionals that they are.

Greta and Nancy's ability to pick up on what is most needed is not just restricted to the Stay and Play mothers, but to their offspring as well. During one of the parent education sessions, I happen to mention in passing that while Maxwell seems to love his time in the intervention program, he has indicated to Joel and I that the room Stay and Play is held in can be "too loud".

When I drop him off the next week, Nancy gestures over to me. "I'd like to show you and Max something," she says.

Max grabs my hand and together we follow the OT over to the other side of the room. We walk towards what looks like a long table covered with a blanket that reaches to the floor.

"Oh," I say. "Nice."

Nancy smiles at me, my obliviousness clearly obvious. "Bend down," she says.

I get down to Max's level and wait as Nancy lifts up one side of the blanket. In front of us is a make-shift cave, complete with welcoming pillows and a few stuffed animals. I can feel Max begin to vibrate beside me.

"Do you see this, Max?" Nancy asks. "This is a quiet spot, just for you. Your Mommy told us that sometimes it gets too noisy for you here. Is that true?"

"Yes," Max whispers.

"It can be very noisy in here sometimes," Nancy agrees. "If it gets too noisy for you, tell me or Greta, and then you can come into your quiet spot. Does that sound good?"

In response, Max climbs into the cave.

"Maxie," I say. "I don't think she meant right now…"

Nancy gently waves me away and then pokes her head in herself. "Do you like it, Max?"

Max nods, his face one giant smile. He picks up a stuffed animal and rubs it against his face.

"Do you think you'll want to come in here when it gets too loud?" Nancy asks.

"Oh, yes," Max says.

I watch my son, looking so dignified in his own quiet spot, a place made just for him. I then glance at Nancy and feel my eyes fill with tears. How is it possible that it took so little to make my child so happy? I get the urge to curl up next to Max myself, to stay here forever.

******

Unfortunately, I can't stay there forever. The six weeks of Stay and Play fly by and all too soon, it's over. Unlike ABA, which was helpful in a didactic way and taught me several valuable techniques, this program has become my own personal haven. During the short time that I've come here, I've learned to trust these other women, therapists and mothers included. I'm not ready for it to all end. I'm not ready!

During the final parent education session, we casually talk about having possible play-dates between our children, as if this was a run-of-the-mill idea (ho-hum!), rather than one that would be like a gift rimmed in gold for our quirky, socially awkward children. *A play-date! For Maxwell!* Jennifer, the alpha mom of the group, suggests that we all exchange email addresses or even create a group on Facebook. Quickly, we all agree. I look around the table at these women, each one with a story so different than mine, and yet each one so similar. Just the way I've always assumed that sisters would be.

CHAPTER 24

World War Three has erupted in the tween world for the fourth time in as many weeks. After leaving cheerfully with her BFF for a trip to the local department store, Meghan comes storming back into the house alone, slamming the front door behind her. She pushes past me without taking off her boots first, wet footprints marking her path.

"Where's Emma?" I ask, trying to follow her to the mud room, but slowed down by thirty-five pounds of boy wrapped around my legs. "What's happened?"

"Emma's a jerk is what's happened!" Meghan barks. "I never want to see her again!"

"But you guys left an hour ago so happy," I say. "You said you were going to go look at clothes and maybe buy a bag of chips to share. I don't get it."

"I can't talk right now," my daughter hisses. "She'll be here any second!"

And sure enough, the front door opens once more and the enemy in question steps tentatively across my threshold.

"Hi, Emma," I say.

"I *knew* you'd pick her side!" Meghan shouts, running into the washroom (with her boots still on, I might add), and slamming the door.

I turn to look at Emma (not an easy feat, given that Max is still clinging to my leg and Sam has toddled over to grab at my shirt) and raise my eyebrows. "What's going on, kiddo?" I ask.

"We got into another fight," she says, shrugging. She takes off her boots and places them on the mat, then unzips her jacket and hangs it up in the proper spot. I look at her face more carefully and notice that she's been crying. This is so *not* okay.

"Meghan!" I call out. "Come in the den this instant!"

"No!"

"Get your butt in this room *right* now!" I shout.

Max lets go of my leg immediately and covers his ears with his hands. "Library voices! Library voices!"

"Sorry, Maxie," I say. I bend down and hand him his favourite toy car. "Why don't you and Lightning McQueen go to the quiet spot for a little while so Mommy can talk to the girls?"

"Is Meghan being naughty?" he asks, a smile breaking out on his face. For some reason, Max seem to experience unparalleled glee at the thought of his siblings getting into trouble.

"No, Max, she's not being naughty," I say.

Max's smile turns to a deep frown and tears fill his eyes. "She's being naughty!" he shouts. I notice his hands start to shake and decide that one instance of giving into him is excusable, if it's for the greater good.

"Actually, now that I think about it, you might be right," I say. "Meghan *has* been a little bit naughty."

"Yeah! Naughty!" Max shouts and goes running into the other room with his car. "Naughty! Naughty! Meghan is naughty!"

"I am not!" comes a muffled yell from the washroom.

I pull Sam off my shirt and pick him up, then march both of us over to the bathroom where I open the door. "Right now means *right now*!" I say to my pouting daughter.

Meghan grudgingly follows me to the den. I point to the sofa, where Emma is already dutifully sitting, hands in her lap.

"I'm not sitting next to *her*!" Meghan says.

"*Meghan!*" I raise my voice once more. She sighs and ever-so-slowly perches her behind on the arm of the sofa. "Good," I say, putting Sam down on the floor. "Now girls, I want you to tell me one at a time what is going on here."

"Emma said she had a dollar to give me but then when we got to the store she wanted two dollars from me instead and when I said no she started to cry like a baby and..."

I hold up my hand. "I don't mean what just happened today, but what is happening in general in this friendship. I don't get it." I look the two twelve-year-olds full in the face. "One day you're best friends and the next day you hate each other. It seems like every week there's at least one huge fight. So much drama! What's up?"

Silence from the sofa.

"Look, Meghan, I know how much Emma means to you. I know it, okay?"

"Why are you picking on me?" she asks, crossing her arms. "I knew you'd do this! It's so unfair!"

"I'm not picking on you," I say. "I'm fully aware that there are always two people in a friendship and that both of you have a role in this. It's just you're my daughter, not Emma."

"I consider *you* to be my second mother," Emma says sweetly, looking at me with wide eyes.

I turn to smile at her in gratitude, but then quickly recognize that manipulation may be in play as a distraction technique and put my focus back on the topic at hand.

"Guys?"

"Oh my god! You're being a therapist again!" Meghan rolls her eyes.

"I'm not being a therapist, I'm being a concerned mother who doesn't want to see this friendship ruined. Now what is going on?"

"Well, I *might* get kind of jealous when Meghan says she's also best friends with Sarah," Emma admits. "It hurts my feelings."

I look from one face to the other. "You know, I have three best friends and they are all really important to me."

"It's true, she does," Meghan says. "One she's been friends with since she was our age."

"And it's also true that how I feel about one best friend doesn't affect my friendship with another. As long as I make time for all of them and they make time for me, it's okay."

"Really?" Emma asks. Again, the wide, unblinking eyes.

"Really," I nod. "The important thing is to try and talk to each other about things that are bugging you without being mean or hurtful about it. And also to try and talk about what you actually like about each other."

"We could do that," Meghan nods. "As long as Emma wants too."

"I do!"

"Okay," my daughter says. She then looks at me. "So, are we done?"

"We're done."

I watch as the two girls go rushing off to the downstairs playroom, giggling once more. I pick up Sam who has been chewing on toy food and head to the quiet spot, where my third child is hum-singing "naughty Meghan, naughty Meghan" to himself in a soft, contented voice. And as I stand here watching him, a warm feeling spreads throughout me. My daughter was right, I was acting as a therapist, and what's more, I can tell that despite continuing to work at stabilizing my own mood, I've still got my basic therapist superpowers. *I've still got it.* However, I also know, more firmly than ever, that I still don't want to use that ability anywhere but here, at home.

I'm driving with my two oldest kids back down Highway Seven, this time headed to the River Glen Centre. Daniel is beside me and Meghan is ensconced in the back. I glance towards my son, who has been ever-so-polite and tiptoe-y around me since our little talk (*how I yearn for some surliness, just a little backtalk or sarcasm!*), and see that with his earphones jammed in and a video game between his fingers he is doing everything in his power to avoid any more of our fireside chats.

I clear my throat. "So, do you guys have any questions before we get there?"

Meghan mutters something from the back.

"What did you say? I couldn't hear you?"

Meghan talks loudly. "Just that this is stupid. Why do we have to see a therapist just because you're crazy?"

"First of all, I'm not crazy! Second of all, Joel and I thought it was important for you guys to have a chance to meet Gail and to ask any questions you might have about what's been going on with me or Max."

"I don't have any questions. Why would I have any questions? *God*!"

"Fine," I say. "You can just enjoy the time off from school then."

Meg lowers her voice, this time muttering again. "That's great, except for the minor fact that I'm missing a major test today and I'll probably get a zero on it. Except for that!"

I begin my deep breathing once more and remain silent until we reach the driveway to the retirement complex. I park the car, then attempt my chirpiest voice. "We're here!"

Meghan begins to unbuckle herself from the backseat, while Dan remains seated, fixated on his video game. I poke him in the side and he turns to me, startled.

"I said we're here."

Still playing his video game, my son manages to get himself out of the minivan in one fluid motion. Soon we are in the main hallway of the River Glen Centre, Meghan walking as slowly as humanly possible behind me. We pass the Great Hall and the Muskoka Lounge, before heading towards the ever-cheerful Carousel Lounge and the reception desk.

From behind me I hear a shriek. "Omigod! Is that a toy horse?" My daughter rushes towards the carousel horse and reaches out to touch its plaster mane.

"Don't touch it!" I hiss. "See the sign!"

Meghan pulls her hand back, then begins to walk around the lounge, making herself quite at home. "Gonna explore a bit," she says.

I glance at my watch. "Don't go too far. We're just visitors here, remember."

I sit down in a nearby chair, while Daniel remains standing, his thumbs permanently glued to the tiny screen he's holding.

"I hope Joel gets here soon, before Gail comes," I say to the air. "I really want him here."

"He'll come," Daniel says, using his big-brother voice on me. "Why do you always worry so much? Is that part of your Bipolar thing, too?"

I open my mouth to answer, but don't bother, my son's attention clearly recaptured by his game.

Meghan comes back from exploring and sits down in the chair next to me. "I wonder if we're allowed to sit here?" she asks. "I mean, there's a sign that says don't touch the horses, and there's a sign that says don't touch that toy train, so maybe there's a sign somewhere that says don't sit in these chairs!" Her voice sounds higher and higher, until it reaches a Minnie Mouse squeak.

"Meg, honey, it's fine. Calm down."

"I am calm! What are you talking about?" She whips her head from side to side, as if looking for the Gestapo. "I'm going to go ask that secretary woman over there if we can sit here!"

"Meghan," I whisper-speak. "Please mellow out a bit. We're here as guests, okay? I don't want anyone getting too loud or being a nuisance."

"Exactly!" she answers, of course getting louder. "That's why I'm gonna find out about these chairs! Be right back!" Meghan jumps up and skips over to the receptionist's desk.

"I *told* you she's too young for all this," the big-brother voice next to me mutters.

Suddenly Gail is in front of me, her hand extended. I quickly stand up.

"Alicia, how wonderful to see you! It's been a few months since we last met."

"Yes. You were really, ah, helpful during the fall and winter."

Gail smiles, a genuine smile. "Good to hear."

We then both turn to look at my son, who continues playing his damn game. *Manners, my boy, manners!*

I speak loudly. "This is my son, Daniel." I pause. "And Daniel, this is Gail, my therapist."

"Very nice to meet you, Daniel."

Dan thankfully looks up, his face reddening. "Hi. Um, thanks."

"Joel should be here any second," I say. "And Meghan is just over there…"

I point to the receptionist's desk, but my daughter is gone. *Where the hell could she be?* I glance towards the carousel horses, just to make sure she hasn't decided to do a pirouette off one of its backs. When I turn back again, I see her walking towards us, Joel in tow.

"Look who I saw coming from the parking lot!" my daughter shouts. "And he was almost late, too!"

"Good to see you, Joel," Gail says. She then looks directly at my daughter. "And you must be Meghan."

Meghan lifts up a hand and waves. "Nice to meet you." WASPy greetings over, she then

faces me. "Mom! You were right! We are allowed to sit on those chairs. That secretary woman said that we could sit on them any time we want too!"

"Why don't you all follow me to my office?" says Gail, beginning to walk away as she speaks. "I tried to get a larger room for us today, but unfortunately they were all taken. We'll have to make do with my own little space."

"I'm sure it's fine," Joel says.

Gail leads my motley crew down the hall and then around a corner. She unlocks the door to her office, a room I have never paid much attention to before. Now I notice that besides her desk chair that swivels (an important detail to remember, gentle reader), there are only two other chairs. I quickly do a headcount of our group. Five people, three chairs. *One of these things is not like the other…*

"Oh," I say.

"I do apologize," says Gail. "But I'm sure that we can somehow make it work! Perhaps if I perch on my desk here, and then…"

Meghan grabs the swivel chair and starts to spin it around. I glance at Joel, who gestures with his chin, spouse-speak that I'm free to take a chair. Gratefully I sit down. Daniel and Joel remain standing.

"Um, what should I do?" Daniel asks.

Joel looks at his stepson. "You go ahead, Dan. I can sit on the floor."

"Are you sure?" Gail asks. "There still room on the desk, if you want to lean on the other side."

"The floor is fine."

Daniel sits down next to me and slumps in the chair. Meg continues to turn back and forth in her chair, likely thrilled that if she can't be on a carousel horse, at least she's found some sort of carnival ride. There is a small fan blowing on a side table between me and my son, but otherwise the air circulation seems to be nil. I look at Joel, who's begun to sweat.

Gail smiles at each of my children in turn, before beginning. "So, your mom and Joel asked me to have this meeting today in order to let you guys have the chance to ask any questions you might have about what's been going on in your family, both with your mom and your little brother."

Daniel stares at his lap while Meg begins more twirling. I cross my leg, then switch to the other.

"Maybe I can get started?" my husband asks. "If that's okay with you, Alicia."

I nod. "Yeah, I kind of want you to take the lead on this one."

"Well," says Joel, "as everyone in this room knows, Alicia became quite depressed in the fall, not long after Max was diagnosed with Autism."

I interrupt. *I've never wanted my husband to take the lead on anything before, so why start now?* "It wasn't so much the diagnosis," I say, "but how hard his behaviour was to deal with and how upsetting it was to see him in pain like that."

Joel glances at me, a flash of irritation in his eyes. "Yes, that's what I meant. Anyway, as we all know, your mom became depressed in the fall and found it very hard to cope."

Meghan pipes up, still spinning. "I didn't notice anything!"

"Meghan, is that really true?" Joel asks. "You used to come tell me that you were worried about your mom."

My daughter glares at her stepfather. This was clearly a *secret*, and my husband is even more clearly one big blabbermouth. "Well, so maybe then. But I'm not worried anymore! It's all good now." More twirling.

"Anyway, your mom became depressed and began to meet with Gail here for counselling. She also started a medicine for depression. The thing about that medicine is that it triggered what's called hypomania..." Joel looks at Gail for help.

"For someone who is vulnerable to Bipolar Disorder, the medicine used to help depression can sometimes turn their mood in the complete other direction, so that they become too happy, too excited, too up."

Daniel speaks quietly. "So the drugs *are* the problem."

Gail and I answer at the same time. "No!"

"Daniel," I say, "the antidepressant only did that because I'm someone who is at risk for Bipolar Disorder. Remember what I told you before? I could have become hypomanic for other reasons, too. And now I'm on a drug meant to stabilize my mood."

"Stabilize?" Meg asks.

"Your mom is taking a medicine called Lithium to help make her mood more normal again," says Gail. "It helps to reduce the chance of getting depressed or too up. Your mom will probably need to take the medicine for a very long time, maybe even her whole life."

"But the main thing to remember is that she's *not* crazy, she's still your mom," my loving husband adds. "She might do things more impulsively at times, or become oddly emotional..."

Meghan twirls faster. "Like dress up as a dinosaur and talk with a really bad Irish accent? God, that was embarrassing! Emma thought you were really weird!"

"Mom would have done that even when normal," Daniel says. I smile at him brightly. *Finally! The sarcasm is back!*

"Regardless," Joel says, "the main thing to remember is that your mom is not crazy."

"I think you already said that," I say. "But thanks for clarifying."

"Have you heard of Diabetes?" asks Gail.

Both of my children nod.

"Well, Bipolar Disorder is a medical condition just like that. A diabetic needs to have treatment all of their lives to keep their blood sugars normal. And someone who is Bipolar needs to take special medicine to keep their mood normal." She smiles at them and the image of Gail as a highly successful third grade teacher flashes through my mind (*I mean that in the best possible way, just so you know*).

Daniel shrugs. "Makes sense, I guess."

"See, just like a medical condition." Again from my husband. "Not crazy at all!"

Both Meg and Dan look at Joel.

"Do you have any questions to ask me?" Gail asks.

"I'm fine," says Meg. "I think Mommy's normal right now."

"I'm fine, too," Daniel says.

"And what about Max?" I ask. "Is there anything you want to mention about all you've had to go through with him, or how his behaviour impacts you guys?"

Meg shakes her head.

"Max probably impacts Sam the most," says Dan. "Maybe you should bring him along next time?" *Again with the sardonic wit. Hallelujah!*

"One thing I did want to mention is that because of Alicia's struggles, there have been times where she is way more irritable than normal. Especially when very hypomanic," Joel says.

I turn to stare at my husband. "That bowl of ice cream never even grazed you!" I say. "I aimed it at the wall!"

Joel ignores me. "Whenever Alicia gets that way I just stress to the kids that their mom *isn't* crazy, just experiencing some mood problems, and if she gets upset, to walk away, if needed, or to talk with me."

Gail nods at Joel, my ice cream comment clearly shifting the balance of who has all of their marbles and who may not in the room. "That makes sense, Joel. I think as long as you all remember that communication and respect are two vital things for everyone in a family, with no physical violence of any kind, you'll be doing well."

I can feel my face flush. *It was one time that I totally lost it, just one! I mean, come on, Joel's kvetching about who left out the milk would ruffle the feathers of a saint! And I aimed at the wall, dammit, at the wall!*

"So guys," says Gail, turning back to the kids. "Do you really have no questions?"

Again my children shake their heads.

"Sometimes parents worry about how their children are reacting to things more than the children actually react," says Gail gently. "Why don't we leave it there for now and maybe meet again in a few months, as a group? We can see how things are going then."

"That sounds good," I say.

Meg reluctantly stops her twirling and we all stand up, each shaking hands with Gail in turn, as if in some sort of line at a reception.

As we walk down the hallway, Joel turns to me. "I'm going to head back to work now. See you at home?"

"Okay," I say. "Bye."

Joel walks towards the back exit of the building, while the rest of us head towards the front doors. As we get to the entrance I notice that it's pouring rain outside. Sheets of water are flowing from the sky. Not normal, run-of-the-mill rain, but fake-looking, let's-have-the-stars-make-out-in-white-shirts-standing-outside Movie Rain. I turn to look at my kids. Meghan's face suddenly breaks into a smile.

"Did you notice how many times Joel said that you're crazy? I couldn't believe it!"

Dan starts to grin. "No, he kept saying how she *isn't* crazy. Big difference, there!"

"'Now kids, please remember above all else that your mother is not crazy! I repeat, she is *not* crazy!'" I say, mimicking my husband without any trace of guilt.

We all burst out laughing, and Meghan reaches over to kiss me on the shoulder. Together we watch the Movie Rain, in no rush to be anywhere else but here.

CHAPTER 25

"Mom, wait until you see what I just got!" Meg bursts through the front door and into the den.

"Not so loud." I point a finger towards Max, who's busily working on a forty-piece puzzle. "He's been kind of fragile today."

Meghan shrugs and leans against the arm of the sofa. "So, anyway, Emma and I went to this vintage shop downtown. I think it's called A Cat Meowing, or something crazy like that."

"It's called The Cat's Meow," comes a voice from around the door. Emma.

"Guys, please tone it down a bit, okay? Max has been having a hard time."

At the reminder of his recent "hard time", Max looks up and lets out a growl. "Too loud!"

Meg rolls her eyes. "Do you want to see what I got or not?"

"You actually bought something? Without asking me first? I thought you were only going out to get ice cream."

"It was money from Grandma. She said I could spend it on whatever I want."

"But why didn't you wait to go shopping with me, when I was free?"

My daughter stares at me. "When are you ever free to shop, Mom, at least without Humpty and Dumpty with us?"

"I just bought you those new jeans and the sweater you wanted, or have you forgotten?"

"That was for my birthday, like three months ago, and it was on-line. On-line doesn't count!"

I'm about to remind Meghan that when it comes to my Visa bill, on-line does indeed count, when the look on her face stops me. It's an *I'm excited and feeling grown up so please don't ruin this moment for me* look. I remember that look well, as it used to sit on my face when I was twelve-years-old, too.

I take a deep breath. "So, big spender, what did you get?"

Meg grins and shakes her bag. "I got my dress for graduation next week! It's perfect! Wait 'til you see it!"

"But what about that dress from last fall? The one we both really liked?"

"I've matured a lot since then. See?" Meghan stands up tall and sticks out her chest.

"She's definitely grown a lot," Emma says solemnly. "I'd say she's at least two inches taller, and she's starting to grow in the, ah, chest area, too." She gestures with her hands. "Maybe were just too busy to notice?"

I take in another deep breath and force a smile. "No, I noticed."

Meg opens the bag and pulls out a strapless pink concoction, covered in what looks like black lace. The dress reminds me of something Molly Ringwald might have stitched together from a bag of cast-off nighties in a John Hughes movie, rather than acceptable formal attire for a girl in the sixth grade.

Meghan holds it up against herself, her face one huge grin. "What do you think?"

"I think it might be a bit too mature."

"It's actually not, Alicia," says Emma. "When it's on Meghan, it actually looks very appropriate, I think." My daughter's biggest defender smiles sweetly at me.

"We'll see," I say. "Maybe if you put a nice white cardigan on top, buttoned up, along with some long socks..."

"Mom! I'm not wearing a sweater like some old lady!"

"Too loud! Too loud!" Max kicks at his puzzle, scattering the pieces, then bursts into tears. I open up my arms and he scurries into them, his hands covering his ears.

"It's going to be an old lady sweater or another dress," I tell Meg, trying to keep my voice calm over the crying. "This is not negotiable."

"You're so unfair!" Meghan shouts, before running up the stairs, Emma in tow.

I close my eyes as I rock Max back to calm, the image of that tarty dress still in my mind. *Not in this lifetime, dear daughter.*

******

A week later, I'm standing at the bottom of the stairway next to my parents and Joel, camera in hand. Meghan is upstairs with her oldest friend, Sarah, a girl who moved to another city over a year ago, but who has made a point of being here today to watch her former classmates graduate and to cheer on my daughter. I'm relieved that it's Sarah who is helping Meg get ready, as she's always been an incredibly grounded child, the very much needed Yin to my daughter's Yang. Having pulled Sarah aside ahead of time to tell her about my concerns in terms of (ahem) wardrobe, I feel confident she'll be able to persuade Meghan that the white cardigan really *is* perfect for the dress, stunning in fact!

"Time to go, girls!" I call up for the third time.

Sarah rushes out of Meghan's room, stopping at the top of the stairs. "Okay! Get ready, folks, because here she comes!"

Joel lets out a long whistle, while my mother and father start to do a drum roll. I get the camera focused on the stairs and wait. Within seconds, the image of my sweater-less daughter fills the lens. *Where the hell is the cardigan?* As I lower the camera and truly take in my ecstatic child as she skips down the stairs, however, something occurs to me: *I was wrong.* For it turns out that when the supposedly tarty dress is clothing the slender, coltish body of a twelve-year-old girl, it doesn't look tarty at all. It turns out that my daughter, her makeup simple and her golden-red hair down her back with a Grecian braid running through it, looks both lovely and age appropriate for a sixth grade graduation.

"What do you think?" she asks, as she rushes over to hug me.

"You look absolutely beautiful." I take one photo, then another, making sure to forever capture this fleeting moment, making sure that this is oh-so-brief period in time does not skip by when I'm *too busy to notice.*

An hour later, I'm sitting between Sarah and Joel in a darkened auditorium, watching my daughter as she walks down the aisle to Fun's *"We Are Young"* with her classmates, her spine straight and her head erect. She looks so unabashedly proud of herself, it makes me want to weep. I reach over and grab Joel's hand. Emma was right. My little girl, my youngest child for over eight years, has grown so much in the last twelve months, and I almost missed it, my focus pulled elsewhere. As I squeeze my husband's fingers I let the tears fall where they may, so damn relieved that at least I didn't miss this.

CHAPTER 26

At first Lithium seems like a wonder drug. Not only does it stop my hypomania in its tracks (hypomania which has, over the course of many weeks rudely switched from glee and boundless energy to mind-blowing irritability/agitation, without bothering to consult me), the side effects I'm experiencing seem relatively manageable. Sure, the constant mild nausea reminds me of a boat trip I took at age eleven with my father across the English Channel, but it's nothing compared to the severe morning sickness I felt in two of my pregnancies. And sure, the biweekly blood tests (gotta check those kidneys to make sure they're still functioning!) are inconvenient, to say the least, but nothing I can't handle. And so okay, I feel as if my body has become the first human salt lick and thoughts of sex or chocolate have been replaced by an all-consuming lust for water (*water, water, everywhere…nor any drop to drink*), but still, if this is the price I have to pay in order to experience true mood stability, then I'll gladly ante up. For a few months I continue to feel this way, stable, content. It's a nice feeling, being content, mild seasickness, bottomless thirst, and all.

Until. Until I start to notice some weird things occurring. Not with my body, per se, but with my mind and my ability to remember and to think. It's like my brain has been captured against its will and is being held prisoner within a fog. Not an unpleasant fog, necessarily, if you're British and like that sort of thing. But I don't. I'm not a fog kind of gal. I prefer my mind to be cloud-free and clear. I'd rather be able to process information, and not only to process it, but to retain it. Yes, I experienced severe concentration problems when I was depressed in the fall and early winter, but this is different. This is about forgetting-to-buckle-up-my-two-boys-in-their-car-seats-four-frigging-times different. This is about telling my husband that Ernest Borgnine had died and then adding that I got to meet him as a child (*an actual movie star!*) at the annual Milwaukee fair, and having my husband then stare at me bug-eyed, because I supposedly had just finished the exact same conversation a mere five minutes before, with *him* telling *me* about Mr. Borgnine's untimely demise. This is about me eagerly waiting to watch the end of a movie with my husband, only to be told that we finished it the night before and moreover, had a heated half-hour conversation about the ending. This is about putting water onto boil and then forgetting to dump the pasta in (*oopsy-doopsy, no dinner again, guys!*). This is about me putting my keys on top of the refrigerator and later trying to find my watch (to no avail), despite it being securely fastened to my wrist. This is about me driving down the most familiar road in the city and having no idea where the hell I am. This is about those occasional memory lapses that most everyone over forty experiences, except having them occur on an hourly basis. This is, in other words, so not cool.

And so I do what seems perfectly rational to me at the time: I decide to stop the Lithium without bothering to consult my psychiatrist first. When I now think of how judgemental I was of any former therapy client if they dared to confide to me that they had stopped their meds without consulting their doctor first, I cringe. Upon hearing that they'd stopped their medication on their own, I immediately affixed a scarlet "D" to their chests and assumed they would be one of my more "Difficult" patients. It didn't matter at the time why they had decided to stop their medication, the fact remained that they had made the decision on their own, without parental (oops, I meant "expert") supervision. To do so was not only dangerous (note: it certainly can be), but also evidence of a desire to get high (for the Bipolar types) or self-sabotage (everyone else).

It was only through making the decision myself *by myself* that I came to realize how wrong I had previously been. My decision to stop taking Lithium was not in the hopes of catching a ride on the hypomanic wave again, or to sabotage my recovery. The reason for stopping was simple—for me, the consequences of the drug were not worth the benefits. I can only speak for myself, but being a thinker is what makes me most me. An introvert since adolescence (except when tipsy), I crave time to escape within my brain and just think. Not worry things over, but *think*. To think deep thoughts, to think stupid thoughts, to think totally ridiculous thoughts. To spit out poetry or stories or far-fetched theories about this or that. To question everything I'm told, roll it over in my mind, and usually come to the same conclusion.   In a less pretentious vein, the not-being-able-to-think thing meant that I was acting like a less than stellar mother to my kids. Yes, having me dress as a dinosaur or attempt a not-half-bad Irish brogue (just end every sentence in question form) was embarrassing for them, but was a better option than having me potentially burn the house down by repeatedly turning on the burners/over/toaster oven all at the same time and then go leave the room to watch reruns of Little House on the Prairie (*gotta love that Dean Butler!*).

My highly introverted thinking-ness is *me*, has always been me, and for fuck's sake, I intend for it always to remain me, until old age or an encroaching brain tumour forces it to no longer be so. In other words, agreeing to take a drug is different than ageing or developing brain cancer. While often an extremely good thing to do, taking a drug is a decision, a personal decision. The very acts of opening the bottle each morning or night, shaking out a pill or two, and downing them with a half-glass of water are purposeful choices, each one a decision in and of itself. Once I realized that these daily choices were robbing me of *me*, I stopped. My guess is that an awareness that one has lost an integral part of themselves while on a drug is why many of my former clients (and many people out there, wherever there might be) also stop. Yes, some people want to feel high again. Yes, some people need to self-sabotage. But for a lot of us, the decision to stop taking a particular medication is about empowerment and a sense of self.

Do I recommend doing it without discussing it with one's health practitioner first? Of course not (for the time being I remain a registered psychologist and in general consider suggesting that someone ever go off their meds on their own as boneheaded as telling them that riding camels will cure all children of Autism). So yes, not consulting Dr. Kelly first was an idiotic, unsafe, highly risky move on my part, with the strong potential of triggering a true manic episode, or worse. I mean, we aren't talking about a yeast infection, here. The bald truth is that many, many people who struggle with Bipolar Disorder also experience psychotic symptoms or suicidal thoughts. Going off my meds without at least speaking with Dr. Kelly about the right way to do it could have led me to the roof of the nearest high building or a bottle of Tylenol. So do I recommend first speaking to one's health practitioner about your decision, but knowing that you are the one *making* the decision? Yes and yes.

So now that I've hammered the point of drug safety (and hopefully prevented myself from potential law suits), let's put that aside to focus on how deciding to go off the Lithium (on my own or not) made me feel after months of delightful chats with Jenny and showing ID at the pharmacy for potentially addictive drugs and having an Independent Medical Evaluation with a kind but distant psychiatrist to prove that I *was* in fact slightly insane. Deciding to go off my medication made me feel like an adult for the first time in too damn long. And that feeling, that grownup feeling was better than any drug I've taken before or since.

CHAPTER 27

It's coming. Can you hear it approaching? Turn off your TV, your stereo, any mobile doohickey, and just listen. There. That. Did you hear it, now? It's the soft, insistent sound of fall approaching. It may seem far off, it may be barely discernible, but the sound is there, and with it comes full-day Junior Kindergarten for Max. I try to calm myself with the reminder that hey! The summer has barely begun! And that hey! There's really no need to waste time thinking silly things like school starting when there's so much family fun stuff to do now, especially since I've kicked that ol' Lithium to the curb!

But it doesn't work. Because the truth is that Maxie (aka Mr. Wide-Eyed Innocent) is about to begin "real" school for the first time, and I won't be there to protect him. At this point I probably sound like any other helicopter parent out there, unable to give that necessary first little push to my baby bird and let him take a try at flying on his own (if by on his own I mean "under the watchful eye of two fully trained teachers"). But it's not that. Not really. You see, I've been through the whole first-day-of-kindergarten thing before. After all, Max is my third kid. With my older two, I felt sentimental, sure, but never panicked, because neither of the older two were autistic. And that makes all the difference in the world.

In a matter of weeks, Max will move away from the relative safety and understanding of his highly supportive daycare to begin kindergarten at a *real* school (Grades JK to Eight) with real "big kids" (including those who can shave, for god's sake!). Even the other children at Max's daycare help to create that sense of safety and support for him, having known my little boy since he was in the Infant room. So Max tends to walk around the periphery of the class during free time rather than actively join in the play? So Max typically won't ask for a turn at an activity or even to have his hands washed when finished at the lunch table? So what? Max is Max and that is fine. More than fine for a lot of the kids, actually, with several of his peers calling out to him when Joel drops him off three days a week. But what about at his new, two-storied school, where the kids in his class will not have known him since he was a fellow baby, drooling and chewing on plastic rings, just like the rest of them? *What the hell will happen then?*

While I know my current anxiety could be waved away with my own diagnosis, I also know that Joel and I have been repeatedly warned by other parents in the know that real school isn't just a bigger version of daycare and that we should not assume that the wonderful resources and interventions our son has had access to in preschool will be as readily available for him in JK. From parents already in the trenches, we've been told to be prepared to *Advocate*, to *Not Take No For An Answer*, and to *Demand Support*. We've been told that we are the voice for our child, who is depending on us to get him the help that he needs. We've been told about IEPs (Individualized Education Plans), about EAs (Educational Assistants), and about not assuming that our son will receive what we've been told by professionals that he ideally needs. Add into the mix that our little boy will have to make what may be for him Herculean adjustments to new teachers, a new principal, new children, and an entirely new daily schedule, and my heart flips over.

Don't get me wrong. We've all come far since Max's initial diagnosis, mainly thanks to professionals who have taught Joel and I how to stop responding to meltdowns/upsetting behaviours in bungling, ineffective ways. Max is a bright, verbal, curious child who actually *seeks out* social activities. But don't let that last characteristic fool you. For while Max may seek out friends, he remains clueless about what to do once he's found his potential playmates. Max does his best, which is both lovely and occasionally heartbreaking to watch. He remembers what he's learned in ABA and his integrated social skills group and will formally stick out his hand to shake, introduce himself, and ask the child what their name is. And, more often than not, the other child will look at him baffled, roll their eyes, or worst of all, just ignore him.

When children do respond, Max will eagerly start to play with them, following their lead. From a distance, this looks like fun, very interactive play. *Maybe the Autism is now cured, like a bad case of strep throat!* When one gets closer to the action, however, one quickly learns that Max finds it difficult to follow even slightly complex play, and will instead follow one "instruction" from his playmate over and over.

I watched this happen just yesterday, when a little girl at the park asked Max to play. He jumped at the chance and followed her initial direction to sit under the slide while she went down it. Things began to fall apart, however, when she suggested that they now switch roles.

"Okay, Max!" the girl chirped. "Now you go down the slide and I'll hide under it!"

Max smiled but remained where he was. "Okay!"

"No! *You* go down the slide and I'll hide under it!"

"Okay!" Max said. He climbed out from under the slide, ran to the ladder, then ran back under the slide, smiling all the while.

The little girl put her hands on her hips. "*No*! You go down the slide! You!"

Max stayed under the slide. "Okay!" he said.

The little girl then turned to me for answers. "Why is he so confused?"

I then jumped in and tried to help Max understand what the girl was asking him to do. Once I led him step-by-step through her game he seemed to *get* it and they played happily once more. As I sat on the park bench, the fact that I had to coach my four-year-old in a game that his little brother would immediately understand made my chest squeeze. For Max, this wasn't so simple. For Max, the quick-changing world of social interactions is confusing at best, bewildering and alienating at worst. Watching Max try to "play" is like watching the Little Engine That Could as it attempts to huff and puff up the hill, always so optimistic, always so eager and wide-eyed, yet always so small.

Yesterday at the park, I was there and it all went well. At preschool, I'm not, and I've been told by the professionals who come visit that he often wanders around the room, lost. In kindergarten, where there will be twice as many kids and a forty-five minute recess involving four kindergarten classes let loose in a fenced-in area, what will happen to my Little Engine then? And so, as I keep listening to the sounds of fall approaching, all I want to do is become that helicopter watching over my sweet son and somehow keep Max safe forever.

CHAPTER 28

It's August. Meghan's father emails me, asking if there is any way I can pick up our daughter at the end of her annual one-week stay at his house, rather than have him drive her back. The request is more than reasonable, given that he and his wife have done the lion's share of driving when it comes to Meg, and also given that it will be their anniversary. Hell, he even throws a hotel stay into his offer, so that Meg and I can have some well-needed girl time, before heading back the next day to our house filled with *boys*. While going to get her will mean that Joel will be left alone for twenty-four hours with our two preschoolers, I know he'll do fine (even if he's not so sure).

My instant response to Mark, however, is no, I can't do it. There are, after all, solid, practical reasons standing in my way. Joel's relatives might be visiting for the weekend. Joel might have to do extra work at the office. There could be a solar eclipse. Clearly, unfortunately, this new plan just isn't meant to be. Another time, perhaps? Until I realize the *truest* reason for not agreeing to do the three hour drive to go get my daughter: last autumn.

In the past, I used to drive Meg to see her dad and step mom a few times a year, with them coming to our city regularly in turn. When it was our time to take Meg to Trenton, either Joel or I (or even better, Joel *and* I) would make a weekend out of it, dropping Meg off on a Friday, staying in a hotel for two nights, and then driving back home on the Sunday. A nice break from the regular routine, with everyone benefiting.

Then came last autumn. Now the very idea of driving my daughter to see her father and staying in a hotel there floods me with anxiety. Images of staying in the same damn Holiday Inn that I did last October with Maxie make my stomach do its best imitation of a pretzel, for it was there, of course, that I realized for the first time that I was seriously losing it. In the months that have followed, I've avoided going to Trenton. Take Meg to visit her dad? How could I, given my mental breakdown? How could I, with horrible winter weather on its way? How could I, with possible flash floods in the spring (I didn't say even remotely likely, given this is Southern Ontario, I said *possible*)? How could I, when Max/Sam/Jessie the cat had the sniffles? It was just too difficult and challenging to even contemplate. No, it could not be done quite yet. Maybe when the boys were a bit older? Maybe once Max had finished his next integrated social skills/ABA/OT program? Maybe once Max/Sam/Jessie the cat were all toilet trained (I have heard of cats using the toilet—once again, it *is* possible)? Yes, maybe then.

Until the email request from Meg's father arrives in my inbox and my hibernating psychologist rears her know-it-all-head, poking at me repeatedly, until I have to listen.

"What do you want?" I finally ask Dr. Alicia. *Why won't she take a hint already and go away?*

Dr. Alicia responds in her typical nasal way. "If a situation triggers intense anxiety, how do you get rid of the anxiety?"

"Um, I forget," I say.

"Do you continue to run from it, or do you take a few deep breaths and get in its face?' asks Dr. Alicia.

"Stop sounding like a smart ass," I say. "It doesn't become you."

"What will it be?" Dr. Alicia sniffs. "Continued retreat, or actual return?"

"Okay, I've got it. Now will you please shut up?"

******

I'm driving away from my house, feeling the anxiety waking up once again. By the time I drive through a traffic-jammed Toronto, the fear is clogging my throat, threatening to take over. I try to channel Dr. Alicia once more, but unfortunately she's left the building. *Typical.* I force myself to take a deep, slow breath. Then another. And another. *This is not last autumn. It is not.*

By the time I reach Trenton I'm feeling a bit more relaxed and am able to focus on how much I've missed my loud, dramatic daughter during her week away. By the time I knock on her father's door, I'm able to feel excited about the fun things I'll get to do with my twelve-year-old girl, things that aren't always possible in a house filled with *boys*.

And for the next twenty or so hours, that's exactly what we do. We swim in the hotel pool, we buy a cheap copy of Twilight from Walmart and watch it on Meg's new laptop, we eat picnic suppers on our beds while making fun of Edward shimmering in the sunlight (*I mean really, shimmering? Who the hell are we kidding here?*). We talk, we laugh, we confide, we have fun. It's just me and my Meg, no anxiety invited. By taking this trip I get to learn new things about my kid, such as that she has entered that oh-so-fleeting stage where a young girl is becoming aware of her loveliness yet is still child enough to make a joke out of it; that she has created a "bucket list" that involves seeing every Meryl Streep movie before the age of twenty (she is a *serious actor*, after all); that she is incredibly pleased with herself for her ability to make waffles on the hotel waffle cooker; and that when she sees the little shampoos and conditioners all hotels provide, she still squeals like a small child, as it means she'll have more for her hoard-like collection. Most importantly, I get to learn that despite this challenging year for our family, my daughter is still a wonderful, amazing young girl who loves the chance to have private, quality time with her mom (*please remind me of this in two years*).

I also get to learn new things about myself. Most importantly, perhaps, I learn that what I've told countless therapy clients in the past is surprisingly not just psychobabble bullshit: That by revisiting a situation that caused you such anxiety or sorrow in the past, you can actually shed that pain once and for all. Psychologists call this extinction. I call this victory.

CHAPTER 29

Before Max's diagnosis, I could have given you reams and reams of information about Autism, being the smart-ass that I considered myself to be. I would have said, for example, that Autism is a pervasive developmental disorder that involves a significant impairment in one's ability to communicate (both verbal and nonverbal) and interact socially, with a restricted range of interests as well as stereotyped behaviour (e.g., hand flapping, rocking) present. Compulsive adherence to specific, often nonsensical routines or rituals is often evident. Problems with direct eye contact, reciprocal social interaction, and imaginative play can often be noted.

I would have explained that it is a condition for which we know no exact cause, although genetics and environmental factors may both play a role in some manner. I would have said that we thankfully no longer blame the condition on "refrigerator mothers" (a lovely theory made by mostly male psychologists in the past). I would have said how it is a condition that overwhelmingly affects boys, but that girls can develop the disorder as well. I would have said that there is a lot we still don't know, but that new research is being conducted all of the time and new advances made. *Blah-dee-fucking-blah.* After throwing all of this information in your face, I would have sat back and smugly rested on my laurels, confident that I had told you all that you needed.

Since Max's diagnosis I know better. I know that Autism is a game changer, an agitator, a troublemaker, a rabble rouser, and a shit disturber. I know that at times it can seem like a torpedo that is aimed directly at your child and your family and that once it hits it will take years to try and reassemble the pieces. I know that Autism can be an entity that is mercurial and thin-skinned, demanding its own way or else there will be hell to pay. I know that occasionally it can be a sweet presence that helps to highlight all that is good in your child's personality, rather than merely a dark shadow that blankets everything. And rarely, oh so rarely, I know that it can even be (dare I say it?) a joy. Most importantly, since Max's diagnosis I have come to realize that all of the didactic, pedantic, ultimately useless information I would have spouted in the past merely provides the outline for what

Autism is. It is up to your child, your unique little boy or girl, to colour the rest in.

******

I'm doing the dishes when a stranger calls. It's a woman, with a breathless voice, seemingly desperate to tell me about some sort of treatment she "knows" will "cure" my autistic child. She explains that she had read a column by my husband just this morning, and considered the situation to be so terribly *urgent* that she immediately looked up our name in the phone book and gave me a call. This woman, albeit well-meaning (let's throw her that bone) is a complete stranger to me and knows nothing about my personal thoughts or views regarding my son. Who I am seems irrelevant to her. All that matters is that she gets her message expressed, and gets it expressed *immediately*!

I listen to this woman, stunned, wondering if I can possibly hang up without somehow putting my husband's job in jeopardy. I know that he gets lots of emails from readers about his columns. This is expected, given that, to a certain extent at least, he invites people into our family with his words. But that is email, written to the address that he provides at the end of each column. Not to mention the fact that each email is sent to him, the writer of the column, and not his wife, who is merely a bystander in all of this. As the woman rambles on, I feel increasingly anxious about even politely interrupting her to explain that I did not write any column and that she thus needs to *shut the hell up*. But if I refuse to listen to this unsolicited advice, will there be a nasty Letter to the Editor splashed in next Monday's paper? As the woman continues in her breathy, urgent way, I become increasingly aware that an invisible line has been crossed. This stranger calling my house, demanding that I listen to her wisdom, assuming that she knows best when it comes to *my* son?

For the rest of the day I feel unsettled and almost dirty, as if in need of a shower. Many times I pace the main floor of my house, trying to collect my loose thoughts into a coherent whole. What is it about this woman that bothers me so, other than the obvious fact that she felt the need to hunt down our home telephone number (a task that was slightly more difficult than it sounds, as we do not live in the same city in which the paper is printed). When I finally figure out what I am feeling, it comes together in one word: *Enough*.

After months of books filled with competing, often contradictory information, numerous treatment interventions, and signing up for endless waiting lists, I'd had my fill of receiving any unsolicited advice from people I don't know (and more importantly, who don't know Max), about how to help my child. This is not to say that the strategies we've learned haven't been helpful in teaching us and our little boy how to manage intense emotions. By and large, the skills we've gleaned in the last year have been wonderful and quite beneficial. I also recognize the need for ongoing skill-learning and intervention-seeking. Max continues to need help to navigate the highly complex social world that exists around him. He just does. I'm not a pie-in-the-sky idiot. I recognize that if it's tough at four, it's going to be that much tougher at fourteen, especially once hormones are involved.

I know that. I get that. But here's the thing. Here's the really big, gigantic, in your face thing: Most of who Max is (and that includes many of his so-called "quirks"), I wouldn't want to change at all. Not one iota. Nada. For example, I find many of his stims endearing, I find his ways of showing affection lovely. I find the way he often looks at life to be uniquely Max. I don't think that there is a wonderful little boy hidden within the Autism. I think that the wonderful little boy and the Autism are one. Max is autistic, just like he's half-Jewish, and has brown hair, and is a spitting image of his Daddy at age four. Autism is part of what makes Max *Max*.

The level of desperation that the woman expressed on the phone doesn't match up with the sweet little boy who just this morning asked me, "And how is your day going so far, Mommy?" It just doesn't. He isn't an emergency that needs to be dealt with STAT. He isn't someone who should be tossed into this experimental intervention or that, just in the hopes that it *may* work. My child is not a guinea pig. He is a delightful autistic little boy, end stop.

When people learn Max is autistic, there's a question I sometimes hear. Not often, but often enough. If you are a parent of an autistic child, maybe you've heard it, too. Maybe you've even asked it of yourself, as I once did, when all alone, late at night.

If you were told that there was a complete cure for Autism, would you give it to your child?

In order to answer that question, I want to talk a bit about Sam. While it seems like Sammy has been in my life forever, it wasn't that long ago when he was a little zygote in my tummy, a very welcomed, but still abstract idea to Joel and me. In those seemingly endless months before I met him, people would ask me what I wanted:

A boy or a girl? While I always gave the safe, politically correct answer ("It doesn't matter, as long as my baby is healthy, blah, blah, blah"), the truth of the matter is that I did know what I wanted: I wanted a girl.

While I *knew* I'd love a boy equally (the two sons I already had were proof of this), a part of me wanted one more daughter. As a female myself, I just *understand* girls better than boys. While I realize that every girl is different, there's a connection that I feel with my lovely, twelve-year-old daughter that is different than what I feel for my equally wonderful boys.

And then came Sam's birth, my only c-section baby. Soon after it was announced that he was definitely a boy, I got to meet him for the first time. And, as my squalling little bundle of eight pounds and twelve ounces latched his then grey eyes onto mine, I knew. Of course I knew. The only child that I could have possibly been happy with was Sammy, my new son. He was exactly what our family needed, a perfect fit.

In the almost three years that have followed, the idea of having had a second daughter instead has faded completely away. Have I ever looked at my youngest child as he jumps on me to wrestle or he cuddles his beloved stuffie in his tender-rough way and whispers in her soiled ear that he loves her best, and longed for him to be a girl? Not once, because if I had this imaginary daughter, I wouldn't have Sam. And if I didn't have Sam, my world would be empty indeed.

Now back to Max. If I'd been asked before he was born if I would prefer to have an autistic child or a "neurotypical" child, the answer would have been simple. I am neurotypical, thus I understand what that's like. On the other hand, I don't know what it's like to have Autism, just like I have no clue what it's like to be a boy and have to lug around all those male parts everywhere I go.

So yes, when Max was an abstract idea and not actually *Max*, the answer would have been simple.

Now that Max is a solid, three-dimensional child who lives and breathes, the answer remains simple.

If there was a guaranteed cure for Autism, I would not give it to my child. If someone came up to me with a miracle pill today, without hesitation I would turn them away and wait for Max to make that choice if he wanted, as an adult. For you see, just as Sam cannot be separated from his maleness, Max cannot be separated from Autism. The child I know and adore is autistic. It may have taken me months to get where I now am, with tidal waves of grief and helplessness to learn how to swim through, but now that the learning has at least started, I can say this definitively: Max's Autism is not an ailment that he needs medicine to recover from. It is not a blanket that is hiding the true child underneath. It is a part of him, interwoven into his unique personality and temperament. If Autism was somewhat removed from Maxwell, what would be left?

Without Autism, would Max have turned to me on a nondescript day filled with errands and have proclaimed, "It's a Mommy-Maxwell day but I call it a Dinner Date. You and Joel go on Dinner Dates. It's a sweet thing!"

Without Autism, would Max (with a cold) have told me in all seriousness that he was a "storm", because he had "thunder" in his throat?

Without Autism, would Max have pointed to our house and told me, "We live in a fancy house. Everywhere, there's fancy to see."

And without Autism, would Max have sadly whispered, "Daddy went to work so my mouth can't smile."

Without Autism, would I have been able to witness a child who, when excited vibrates (from top to toe) with a pure glee that's privilege to witness? And finally, without Autism, would I receive the gentle, repetitive "bonks" that Maxie gives me against my chest when he's feeling particularly affectionate?

It's important to add that the fact I wouldn't take Max's Autism away doesn't mean that I think intervention is unnecessary. As I said, I'm no pie-in-the-sky kind of gal. How could I be? After all, I still have bruises from my child's most recent meltdown. I'm more than aware that for Max, the world is often a highly unpredictable, anxiety-provoking place, and that he needs to continue to be taught the appropriate tools in order to better cope with his intense emotions and his intense desire for control. However, I do not see wanting to help Max learn how to manage his feelings, connect socially with others, or rein in certain behaviours as the same as wanting him to be "neurotypical". I see it more as wanting to teach any of my children how to ride a bike, or use a stove without getting burned, or say please and thank you when wanting a treat, or cope with bullying when they experience it. Keeping that in mind, just like with my other children, when it comes to Maxwell, I want to parent him in the best way I know how, by focusing on his strengths and helping him to learn how to navigate his areas of difficulties.

Please don't take my words to mean that I judge any parent who feels differently than me. I can't know what the experiences of other mothers or fathers are like. I can only speak of my own experiences with my own, often high-functioning child, and for me, Maxwell is Maxwell, a delightful, brown-eyed, curious *autistic* boy. He is who he is, and, just like with his brothers and his sister, it is an honour to know him.

There is something out there called the Neurodiversity Movement, which views Autism as a normal human difference, rather than a disease to be stamped out at all costs. I don't necessarily agree with everything the movement is saying. I have seen my little boy in intense emotional pain and believe that he will need to continue learning how to cope with such feelings for a long time to come. I also believe that he will continue needing to learn and practice basic social skills in order to have the friendships he so desperately seeks (there's been enough rejection and confusion on playgrounds to realize why this is so important). Fine motor and gross motor skills also continue to lag and will need help to develop. Additional integrated social skills groups, ABA, or OT? Bring it on.

So no, I don't necessarily agree with all of the Neurodiversity Movement's views, and as a mom, that's my prerogative. That being said, when breathy strangers call me up to beg me to try this treatment or that "before it's too late", it can make me understand so much better why there's a need for the Neurodiversity Movement, and to be thankful for their existence. And maybe, just maybe, a grown-up Maxwell will someday be thankful for them, too.

CHAPTER 30

"I'd like to stop taking the Lithium," I say. "You know, maybe start gradually and see how it goes?"

Dr. Kelly scribbles something on his notepad and then raises his eyes briefly to mine.

"I can handle the nausea," I say, "but the memory stuff is just too much. It's gotten to the point where I'm having serious memory glitches every day. I've forgotten to buckle Max and Sam into their car seats about four times now. I just think it would be a good decision to stop."

More scribbling, more furtive glances in my direction. I can feel my cheeks start to burn, the flush spreading from forehead to chest, like a wild river that's jumped its banks. *Why the hell isn't he saying anything?*

"Actually, um, I already stopped taking it," I blurt, the truth coming out of me like a belch. I've never been able to lie effectively, despite my many attempts to do so. I consider this pull towards honesty to be one of the more unseemly things about myself, as it stems less from any built-in decency and more from a desire to make my life as easy and seamless as possible, by avoiding conflict at all costs. I'm one of those people who can make friends gasp in horror if I dare to say anything remotely profane: "Did you just say shit instead of shucks, Alicia? Did you actually *swear*?" (Yes, I know. I hate those kind of people, too). I notice my fingers moving towards my nose for a quick sniff and I force them back down. "Actually, the last time I took a pill was last week."

"Oh?" His eyes jump.

My hands reach for each other across my lap, my fingers knotting together to form a protective barricade. "Yes. Um, sorry I didn't say that right away." I pause. "I'm just nervous."

"You're nervous about your decision?"

"No! I'm nervous about telling you about stopping. I know I should have checked with you first. It was an idiotic thing to do."

Again the raised eyes.

"And your reason for not taking the Lithium is that you believe it's been impacting your memory?"

"I don't just believe it, I know it." My voice gets louder and the room smaller. "I'm not *me* without my ability to think. It's what I identify most with about myself."

"You identify with thinking?"

"Yeah," I nod. "I'm not trying to be cocky, but I've always known that I'm bright, ever since I was a kid. I like being able to really process ideas and work through things in my mind. And I know that after ten years of being a psychologist I have a great memory. It kind of goes with the job. I normally have an amazing memory!" Again, my voice gets too loud. *Who am I trying to convince?*

The psychiatrist puts down his pen and stares at me. I blink rapidly.

"I'm not trying to be cocky," I repeat. My finger barricade loosens and my heart starts to bounce, all confidence now gone.

"Alicia." The psychiatrist says my name with such concern that the balance between feeling like a shitty, ungrateful patient and feeling like an independent, self-assured woman who knows-her-own-body-and-can-make-her-own-damn-decisions-about-it shifts completely and I'm covered from head to toe in crap.

"Yes?" I say.

"After all of those years of being a psychologist, do you really think it's a wise idea to suddenly stop taking your prescribed medication when you've been struggling for almost a year with your mood?" Pause. "When you in fact experienced what was a quite significant depressive episode, followed by a prolonged period of hypomania?"

"Um…"

"A prescribed medication, I might add, that was working well at stabilizing you and that seemed to be causing minimal side effects?"

I stare at my lap, I fidget, I start shaking my leg, I smell the fingers on my left hand, I bite my lip, I turn prepubescent. *Fuck. Shit. Hell.* "Well…"

The psychiatrist looks at my again and nods, before scribbling once more.

"I just want to give myself a chance, you know? I just want to see…"

This time he doesn't look up, he just keeps scribbling.

"I can always go back on the Lithium if I need too," I say, back-peddling . "I mean, I still have a full bottle at home!" If my ability to think is number one in terms of how I identify myself as a person, then the need to please others comes a close second. "If Joel or my parents or even the kids tell me that I'm getting too up, I'll take a pill that day, even that minute, I swear!"

"I know you're aware of how long it takes for any mood stabilizer to truly work. That it is weeks, not minutes, before you experience significant benefit of even the best medications."

I nod. "Yeah, I guess that there is that..."

"If I were to prescribe you an alternate mood stabilizer today, not Lithium but something completely unrelated, would you be willing to at least try it?"

"I just want to *see*," I repeat. I can feel my eyes fill. "I mean, I went through over twenty years without any real mood problems. It's not like I've had a lifetime of extreme highs and lows. This whole thing was triggered by not knowing how to cope with Max and *his* diagnosis, with not...I just want to *see*, on my own." Pause. "I've been happy lately. Truly happy!" Fat, sloppy tears roll down my cheeks, each one belying my professed mood stability.

The psychiatrist hands me a box of Kleenex. "Let's meet next week and talk about this more, shall we?"

"I'll be at a cottage with my family next week," I say. "Um, it's our only true vacation all summer and it's three hours away, so..."

"The following week then," he interrupts. "After what you've experienced this year, I truly believe you need to be on a mood stabilizer. If not Lithium, then something else."

I wipe at my face, but the tears won't stop. The psychiatrist stands up and waits for me to follow. I fist my hands at my sides and dig my fingernails into my palms in an attempt to stop the damn crying. *Enough with the tears, already. Enough.*

"Just think about what I said," he tells me, gesturing towards the door.

"I don't want you to think I don't respect you as a professional or appreciate all you've done," I start to blather. *Why did I think I could make medical decisions on my own, after this man has spent months trying to make me whole again? Who do I think I am, anyway?*

The psychiatrist nods once more. His face looks almost sad, as if he's gone through this same worn scenario a few too many times before. "Until our next session, then," he says, his voice kind.

I nod like the fool I now recognize myself to be, and let myself be led out to the waiting room, to the receptionist, to the exit. I glance at the next fool who is sitting docilely in a chair, an out-of-date magazine open in his hands, and then proceed to bolt out of the office.

This so did not go as planned.

＊＊＊＊＊＊

I decide to go for a walk, the summer evening weather at the sweet point of warm but not humid. Joel is home with the kids, I have time to aimlessly wander about. And so I do. At first I head towards the newly built school that will be Meghan's home for seventh grade and Maxie's home for kindergarten, but seeing it triggers anxiety about my little boy, so I quickly walk away. Eventually I find myself nearby the grocery store, one of my favourite places to be. I've always felt that you can divide the entire population of North America by who not only enjoys *but looks forward to* going to get groceries and who finds this chore to be like a weekly visit to Hell. My guess is that most parents of squalling infants or small, sticky children are in the former group, with the caveat that they are of course going to the grocery store *alone*.

I head to the doors, deciding to continue my aimless wandering within the aisles of my favourite store. As I'm about to enter, I notice an older, somewhat dishevelled woman sitting on what seems to be the back of a walker, clearly in some sort of distress. My instincts kick into high gear. I go over to her and ask what's wrong. The woman is semi-coherent, but makes it obvious that can't breathe. From a few yards away, another woman signals to me that she's going into the grocery store to call an ambulance (*not a great day to forget a cell phone*).

While I'm clearly not an MD or a paramedic, it's obvious to me that, regardless of any possible medical problems, the woman in front of me is also having a panic attack. I begin to rub her back and speak gently to her. At first she remains highly upset, yelling at times, but gradually she calms down under my touch and my words, words that I know to give.

The manager of the store comes out and heads over to the woman. "I'll take it from here," he says to me.

"I'm a psychologist," I say.

He immediately nods and moves back as if I've parted the Red Sea. I forgot about this reaction to being a *psychologist*. I forgot. I keep talking gently to the woman, reminding her that the very fact she can talk (and yell) means that she isn't going to die, something she fears. I also promise her that I won't leave her side until the ambulance arrives. She looks at me trustingly. Eventually a fire truck arrives and

188

the fire fighters jump out. I give them room, but immediately tell them that I am a psychologist and intend to stay. While they do not seem as in awe of my profession as the grocery store manager seemed to be, they do nod in recognition and allow me to continue rubbing the woman's back (I will keep calling her "the woman", but please know that I asked her name within ten seconds of being with her). By this point her breathing has slowed and she seems to enjoy the back rub. Finally the ambulance comes. The paramedics seem to know the woman well and also clearly know what to do. I can tell by their interactions with her that they are kind, they are respectful, they are compassionate. The paramedics thank me for my help and I quietly slip away.

It is only then, only when I have continued my aimless wandering, that I break down. For you see, I haven't really considered myself to be a psychologist at that level for almost a year. Yes, on paper I remain a registered psychologist in Ontario, albeit an "Inactive" one on leave. But I'm fully aware that if I were to go back tomorrow to work and combine my not-fully-stabilized (and perhaps never permanently stabilized) mood with the reality of Max's Autism, not to mention up to six distressed clients a day, the result would not be pretty.

And yet my instinct was to immediately use my skills to help the woman and to not leave her side until other help was there. In the future, will I do that as a non-psychologist? I hope so, but I can't really say, for at that moment, I *was* a psychologist. I *am* a psychologist. Except, just as strongly I'm not. Hence, the limbo. And hence, the tears.

CHAPTER 31

It's late summer and we're back in Southampton at the cottage we rent most years. Coming back to this place feels bittersweet. It was here, after all, that the fact all was not well with my little boy truly hit me. It was here that I already knew, without being told, that Autism had made its nest in our family and was going to stay. And it was here that the seeds of my depression were planted and began to take root. Despite this, or maybe because of it, all year I've felt the pull to come back, to watch the roar and the calm that can be Lake Huron.

Once again my father-in-law Al is with us, his caring, go-with-the-flow presence a good balance for Joel's kvetching and my dramatics. If there's one thing that my hubby and I have in common it's our intensity levels and our annoying inability to be easygoing. Type Bs we are not.

My eighty-one-year-old father-in-law happily agrees to sleeping on a blow-up mattress in a corner of the living room ("What could be better?"), while everyone else gets a bedroom, Joel and I sharing what in comparison to Al's corner truly is a master suite.

We are here during the end of the summer, the only week that was available for rent. During the past few months Joel has hemmed and hawed about the wiseness of booking now, given that late summer is notorious for cool days and even cooler nights. It turns out that there was no need for worry, as the week is one of the hottest on record. Did I mention that like most cottages, this one does not have air conditioning? And did I mention that my youngest children have trouble falling asleep at the best of times, let alone when under a blanket of humidity and heat? Well, now you know.

Despite the horrific humidity and despite the lack of sleep due to two unhappy, sweaty little boys, the first day or two go very well. The cottage kitchen is large and roomy for a family of seven, the counters generous and long. Given that I am (by choice) the cook for this vacation, I find the sheer size of the kitchen soothing. Whenever possible, I head in there to make a meal or a snack, just to get out of the fray. My unflappable father-in-law compliments each and every food item I put before him, whether it's a pasta, garlic bread, and salad dinner or a bowlful of Cheetos.

"Alicia," he says," patting his stomach, "you have clearly done it again! Bravo!"

I smile back at my father-in-law, a man I consider my second Dad, to be honest, and stick out my tongue at my oblivious husband.

"What?" asks Joel. "Am I expected to say thanks, too?"

To be fair, throughout the trip Joel does the lions-share of caretaking when it comes to Sam and Max. While the frequency of Max's meltdowns has lessened dramatically, adjusting to a new space and a new routine is still hard for my little boy. Increased bonking, the need for more quiet breaks, and a lot of tight hugs are needed.

During the first day there, I'm not only pleased by how well I'm doing meds-free, I feel cocky about it. After all, I was able to manage packing for a large family, loading up the minivan, driving for three hours, unpacking, soothing an often uncertain Maxie, going off to the grocery store for a week's worth of food, unpacking that load, and then making a delicious supper for my beloved family (in horrific heat and humidity it must be added), all the while maintaining at least a modicum of decorum towards my relatives. *Take that, Dr. Kelly*! It's only the next morning, during our first visit to the beach, that the realization that everything might not be so peachy, after all. Instead of feeling too up or too low, I feel overwhelmed, over-consumed, over-the-top with anxiety.

When we first arrive at the beach, all is right with the world. Max is proudly in his first bathing suit (no more diaper swimmers for him!), and all four children have been successfully slathered from head to toe with sunblock. While there are a lot of people at the beach already, we manage to secure a large space for our blanket, which we anchor with shoes and water bottles. The little boys are ecstatic about the idea of using their new sand toys, and Max is eagerly making plans for what he and Sam can do together. My two eldest kids have raced down to the water and begin to swim with one another, reminding me of our early days here, when they still did everything together.

Yes, all is right with the world until my husband decides to take Maxie and Sam for a ride on a blown-up raft that was lovingly given to them by Al. Despite the fact that the tide is far out and the water is all of six inches deep for many yards, despite the fact that Joel is a former lifeguard not to mention a devoted father who would never do anything to put his small sons in jeopardy, despite all of that, as I watch my two babies sit in what suddenly seems like the most precarious of water vessels, I begin to experience a full-blown panic attack.

"Too far out, Joel! Too far out!" I call.

My husband waves me away.

"No farther, Joel! They could fall out of the boat!" I call louder.

"It's fine," he calls back.

This time, I scream. "JOEL! GET BACK NOW!"

Several fellow beach goers turn in my direction, clearly startled by my shrieking. At this point, I could care less. What the fuck is my husband doing? Does he not realize that they don't know how to swim and are not wearing life jackets? Has he completely lost his mind?

My husband also looks startled, as well as a bit embarrassed. Who is this screaming woman, standing on the edge of Lake Huron? I begin to wade into the cold water, gesturing wildly to Joel once again.

"GET BACK NOW!" I yell.

Joel now looks irritated. "I know what I'm doing," he says. "Please let the boys have some fun."

"JOEL!" I can hardly breathe. Oh my god, my children are going to die. I am going to actually watch them slip under the water and drown before I can ever reach them. Oh my god! I start to cry and cover my face with my hands. "Joel!" I plead through my fingers. "Please! Please! I can't handle this! I can't see this!"

Hearing the change in my tone, Joel begins to pull the little boys back to shore. "Rides over, fellas," he says.

Once he reaches me, he touches my shoulder. "Are you doing okay?"

I shake my head, then nod, wiping my face with my arm. "It was too far," I whisper.

******

As the days pass, the anxiety increases, most of it directed at the safety of Max and Sam. I begin crying at the thought of Max rolling over in his sleep and suffocating Sam, and demand that Joel check on them regularly (whose lame-brained idea was it anyway, to let them sleep in the same bed?). Each beach-visit is a nightmare, with me demanding that we instil the one-on-one rule at all times, whether in the water or building sandcastles. That means two adults to two little boys, no ifs, ands, or buts. The anxiety spreads to Dan and Meghan, too. Despite the fact that they've each had years of swimming lessons under their belts, and despite the fact that the tide remains far out throughout the week, if they look too far away from me when swimming, I start to yell. The fact that they might still be just waist-high in the water matters not. *This is a fucking Great Lake, everyone! A Great Lake!*

Finally, the anxiety spreads to the cottage itself. The cottage is up a few flights of stairs, stairs which little Sammy could *fucking fall down* if someone isn't right behind his little bum to stop him. And look at the balcony, that death trap. Who cares that the bars are close together and all that could fall through are Sam's little chubby legs. Under *no* circumstances is Sammy allowed to be out there without a grownup holding his hand at all times! And what about those hot dogs that my husband barbecued for his excited little boys? If they are not cut into at least a zillion pieces first, not even one bite will pass Max's lips, let alone Sam's. Do you hear me, everyone? Do you hear me?

Mid-week, my parents come to visit. While also affable, loving grandparents, they wisely choose to stay in a bed-and-breakfast across the street, rather than bunker down in the living room's remaining available corners. With my mother and father present, I make a concerted effort not to show so much anxiety, but during each beach visit, the threats of Lake Huron overshadow the concern my parents might feel if I seem a bit "off".

"Too far out! Too far out!" I again shriek at Joel and his father, as they each hold a little boy as they tramp through the water.

"Waves are coming! You could lose your grip! It's time to come out and get ice cream! Right now!" I notice my mother looking at me, but choose to ignore it.

And so it goes, the waves of my anxiety so much more powerful than the little ripples that go back and forth across Lake Huron this week. Along with the anxiety there are crying jags, which include me crumpled in the cottage bathroom once more, six other people taking turns banging on the door because they have to pee already.

By the time the week's over, I've come to two conclusions: 1) I'm still glad that I went off the Lithium; and 2) I'd better get the hell back to see Dr. Kelly as soon as possible to try another medication.

******

I'm back in Dr. Kelly's office, Joel at my side. I've just finished describing our vacation in Southampton, watching the psychiatrist as he occasionally scribbles.

Once I'm done, Dr. Kelly starts to speak, his voice kind. "Do you think you might be ready to try a mood stabilizer now?"

I look at Joel, then back at the psychiatrist. If it's possible, my anxiety level is even higher today and my desire to have the feeling go away is now coupled over worry about any possible horrific side effects of a new medication.

"Um, what mood stabilizer exactly?" I ask.

"Either Epival or Lamotrigine, otherwise known as Lamictal," he says. "Given your history and what you've recently been experiencing, I would prefer to try Lamictal."

I look again at Joel, who shrugs. "I'm out of my depth here," he says.

I close my eyes for a moment and try to access the Psychologist drawer in my brain. *Lamictal. Lamictal.*

"It's an anti-seizure medication that is also used to treat Bipolar Disorder. It's been found to be particularly effective for those prone to depression," Dr. Kelly says. "I believe that the anxiety you just described, along with the crying and how you presented during your last appointment suggest to me that you're beginning to become depressed again."

Lamictal. Lamictal. Lamictal! "That's the drug that can cause you to die from a skin reaction!" I blurt. I turn again to Joel. "You can get this horrific rash, with sores in your throat and your groin and then you die! You die! It's called Steven something. It's fatal!" An anxiety wave starts to crest.

Joel frowns and looks at the psychiatrist. "That doesn't sound too safe," he says. "Maybe we should just wait another week or two and see..."

Dr. Kelly raises his hand. "I've been down this road with both of you before. You over-think my recommendations and then Alicia's mood worsens. I don't want to see that happen again!"

"But the Steven thing!" I say.

"It's called Stevens-Johnson syndrome, and yes, it can be fatal," he says. His voice sounds matter-of-fact, as if he's telling me that my mouth might get too dry and that I'd better carry around a bottle of water. *What the fuck?*

"I've had two severe reactions to medications before," my words spilling out. "Did you know that? I'm a highly allergic person! Penicillin and aspirin! I had hives from head to toe and my lips and hands swelled up!"

Joel nods. "She does react to medication," he says. I can tell from his voice that he's beginning to get worried.

Again the psychiatrist raises his hand. "Before you both start worrying even more, let me emphasize that a serious skin reaction is extremely rare, while the possible benefits of the drug are high."

"But what if I was one of those rare people?"

The psychiatrist sighs. "If you begin to develop a rash, we stop the Lamictal."

"But..."

"Would I even suggest a medication that was likely to harm you?" he asks.

"Um, no..."

Dr. Kelly grabs his prescription pad, scribbles something down, then hands it to me. "Here it is. You start very slowly on this drug. The instructions will be on the bottle."

"But..." I say.

"I really don't think," says Joel.

"Alicia, Joel." We both look up. "You can look up information about the medication if you choose to. You can decide not to even take it if you choose to. But just in case, I want you to have the prescription before our next session. My goal is to help stabilize your mood, Alicia, nothing else."

I take the prescription from him and nod, images of skin falling off my body in layers as my organs fail filling my mind. Joel and I stand up together, as the team we are (*a little fact we both typically forget*).

"I'll see you in two weeks," says Dr. Kelly. "I'm on your side," he adds, before shutting the door behind us.

******

For the rest of the afternoon and again after the children are in bed, I compulsively check internet sites, letting myself be drawn back time after time to horrific photos of the victims of Stevens-Johnson syndrome. *That could be me! Lamictal! Lamictal!* During my more sane moments I also read testimonials from many people who, just like me, have struggled with their mood, and who, unlike me thus far, have taken the plunge and tried the drug. The overwhelming reaction of people (people who do not seem to be paid by any drug company) is that it has helped them, at least somewhat.

I spend most of the night awake, a big ball of sweat and panic. I toss and turn, leading Joel to gently nudge me away from his side of the bed. *Skin falling off! A horrific death! I'd be crazy to try such a risky drug!*

But then, a quieter, so much smaller image enters my mind—the image of my little boy. Max is about to start kindergarten and is vibrating with excitement. While clearly nervous about the change, he is excited, and he is brave. He is, in fact, acting like he did when his father suggested he hop on the raft at Lake Huron, to take a ride. My anxiety at the time wrecked the experience for him, effectively stomping over his attempts at bravery and his eagerness to at least *try* something both scary and fun. If I refuse to take this stupid medication, to at least give it a chance, could my all-consuming anxiety once again stomp on my child's bravery and joy? I let my body still for a moment, and just focus on my child, on Max. He's come so far during the last several months. He still has so far to go. Will I let myself hold him back, or will I choose to somehow walk beside him, no matter how long the path? Most importantly, will I choose the fear of an incredibly rare side effect over helping my little boy? Will I for once let myself be brave, too?

By the morning I've made my decision, a decision that initially shocks both me and my husband: I will take the Lamictal, and if that doesn't work, then fuck it, I'll try whatever's next in Dr. Kelly's arsenal of psychotropic medications.

******

Out of the blue, Jenny from Northern Life Insurance calls me. It's been months since we last spoke, and I had successfully eliminated her existence from my mind. My initial telephone conversation with her almost a year ago was like a mirage for masochists. *La, la, la, Ms. Meanie isn't part of the picture anymore. I hope the door didn't hit her ass on the way out.* Except, of course, that she *is* still in all of this, her voice in my ear proof that she continues to be a living, breathing bane to my existence. Her voice this time is perky, friendly, almost a carbon copy of the voice I used to use with Max when attempting to somehow corral him. Hairs on the back of my neck stand on end (at least, I assume they do—who the hell would be able to empirically *prove* this about themselves?).

But I digress. Here I am in my bedroom, a basket of laundry at my feet, my parents one floor down playing with Sammy, and here is Jenny's sunny voice, chirping into my ear. I prepare myself for battle, I stand on point, my fight-or-flight response kicks into overdrive. What does Northern Life Jenny want this time? Do I again have to argue for my insanity?

Except this time it's different. This time not only do I remain calm throughout the conversation, but Jenny seems warmer, more helpful, more interested. Not fakey-fakey interested, but exhibiting at least a modicum of concern about my well being. Don't be misled here. During the course of the phone call I remain acutely aware of Jenny's allegiances (she does work for the insurance company, after all, a business that does not like to bleed out money to anyone who is not certifiably nuts). It's more that whatever Jenny's role is as we talk, she seems respectful of me, and that makes all the difference in the world.

After I hang up the phone, I check myself for bruises. There are none. Shockingly, despite an awareness that at any moment I could be informed that the university is expecting me back tomorrow, thus forcing me to make a final decision about work, I feel okay, I feel fine. A thought begins to tease with my mind that perhaps, just perhaps, I was a tad too hard on Jenny following our first phone call. Yes, she may have been a bit too aggressive, a bit too impatient with my ramblings, a bit too distant in tone. But is it just possible that my severely depressed mood at the time played a role (even an itsy-bitsy one) in terms of how I perceived the conversation? Is it conceivable that listening to a professional, one-step removed Jenny was too much for me when in such an emotionally fragile place and that I thus viewed anything but buckets of warmth and compassion thrown my way as rejection or cruelty? I roll this idea around in my head for a while, and grudgingly acknowledge that Jenny may not be an incompetent witch, after all. I leave the unfolded laundry and instead head downstairs to be with my parents and my happy little boy, still feeling okay, still feeling fine, and, most shocking of all, still free of fatal rashes. *Damn, this Lamictal is good.*

CHAPTER 32

The first day of kindergarten arrives, and I wake up more thankful than you can ever know that I've got a steady level of Lamictal in my bloodstream, as the mood stabilizer is the only thing that is keeping me from becoming a completely panic-stricken, frothing at the mouth basket-case, when it comes to releasing my autistic child to the potential wolves that roam the playgrounds of elementary schools. While Joel seems confident that we've done all we can do to prepare for this day, for me there can never be enough professional reports sent, emails messaged, meetings with teachers scheduled, or even early visits to the classroom to make me feel ready for what's about to occur. Today marks the first time that Maxwell will go to real school for an entire day, and this inevitable fact scares the hell out of me.

Like most mothers who feel anxious for whatever their child is about to face, I do the only thing that I can do in this situation, which is to pretend that today will *be the best day ever*, perhaps overdoing it in the exuberance department. Lucky for me, the entire family has pumped up Max enough about the joys of big-kid school so that he seems truly excited to start. As Joel grabs the requisite jackets and shoes, Max does a few happy circles around the den, keeping one hand on me as he races around my body, as if I'm his maternal Maypole.

"I'm wearing my new knapsack and it has Elmo on it and I get to bring a snack and a lunch and I get to play on the new playground and I'm a big kid now!" he crows, his circles becoming faster and faster.

Sammy sits on his daddy's lap as his feet are stuffed into shoes, clearly jealous of his big brother. "I wanna go, too," he says.

Max sticks his arms out as he continues to circle, as if preparing for take-off. "You can't go to big-kid school because I'm a big-kid and you're a little kid, so you can't go!" he shouts repeatedly, about to cross the line where excitement becomes over-stimulation.

During his next lap, I reach out and pull Max towards me, giving him a tight squeeze to help him (and me) calm down. "You're going to have a great time," I whisper in his ear. "You're going to make new friends and it's going to be so much fun!"

Within ten minutes, we're out the door, Joel pushing Sam in his stroller, me holding Max's hand as he skips next to me, and Meghan trailing behind, her new seventh grade nonchalance worn like an old jacket.

"Meghan's going to be at the same school as me and the school is a new school and they just built it for Meghan and me, right Meghan?" Max calls out to his big sister.

Meghan walks quicker and reaches out to grab Maxwell's other hand. "That's right, Baby," she says, her big-sister sweetness coming through (it should be noted at this point that Meg is the only person who's permitted to call Maxwell 'Baby'). "Just remember that I'm in the school if you ever need me. Just tell someone and they'll come get me."

"I won't need you, because I have a teacher and then another teacher and even another one and then a principal, too!"

"You're right, Max," I say. "There are two kindergarten teachers in your class, and then that nice woman we met."

"Becky," he says. He keeps skipping beside me, humming as he goes. It's his content hum, as opposed to his anxious hum, and I start to feel soothed by the constant sound.

The walk to the newly built school is over quickly. Once we arrive, Meghan lets go of her brother's hand and rushes off to find her friends. Our remaining group of four heads to the kindergarten playground, which is securely fenced in, an entity onto itself. I stop just outside the gate, my anxiety overtaking me once more, letting other parents and children file through instead.

"Alicia?" Joel asks. "Ready?"

I glance towards my husband, so much weight hidden in that question. No, I am not ready. I'm far from ready. No amount of Lamictal in the world is going to make me feel ready to let go of this vulnerable little boy's hand and just leave him here, without me. To be ready, I need someone to let me stay here for an hour, a morning, even a day. Let me be a shadow in the back of the kindergarten classroom. I won't make a noise, I swear. Just let me be the ears and the eyes that might be needed to make sure that my Maxwell is okay. Just let me stay and I'll be ready for anything, I promise.

I glance away from Joel and squeeze Max's hand tighter. Then I notice that a young woman is striding quickly towards us. It's the aforementioned Becky, an Education Assistant (EA) who's been assigned to Maxwell and to a few other special needs classmates. While I know that Becky is going to be helping three children and therefore will not always by my son's side, I also know that she has been placed in his class to be that extra set of ears and eyes. I watch as Becky reaches out her hand towards Maxwell and he gently takes it. I listen as she welcomes him into her fold and he shyly whispers in return. I then glance back at Joel, my answer now different. Yes, I'm ready. Yes, at least this morning, I can let my little boy go. And that, I would argue, is a start, for everyone.

******

Before kindergarten even began, we were told by both professionals and other ASD parents that communication between staff and parents on a daily basis is essential in terms of our son's learning and were urged to insist on using a communication book in order to make that happen. The communication book we end up using happens to be a lined notebook that's been chopped in half, but no matter. It serves its purpose, which is to send little notes back and forth between home and school. Inevitably, given that Max is Max, the notes sent by Joel and I often detail recent meltdowns and aggressive behaviours ("Maxwell woke up screaming this morning and refused to eat or pee"), whereas the notes sent back home often describe what a sweet, charming little boy our son is ("Max seemed to enjoy going to an assembly today").

Day after day we're told that Max seems to be adjusting well to the new routine, that he seems cheerful and happy, and that there are no behavioural concerns. We read that he is a pleasure to have in the JK/SK classroom, a sunny, agreeable child, not one of the ruffians. A bit shy, perhaps, more content with playing *near* other children rather than actually with them, but still a pleasure. And while Joel and I believe that this more passive version of our firecracker of a son exists, our antennae can't help but be raised, as we know too well that a passive, make-no-waves Maxwell can also mean a highly unassertive Maxwell, a child who, for example, doesn't use the water fountains in the classroom for more than two weeks, because another child supposedly told him that it isn't allowed. Given that Max has Autism, what this also meant for him is that not only did he avoid the water fountains, he also never drank the juice box I faithfully packed in his lunch bag each day. Rather than tell a teacher that he was thirsty or (*screw it!*) sneak a drink anyway, my law-abiding little boy went all day without even a drop of liquid. This pattern would likely have gone on and on, into the late fall and winter, had I not brought a bottle of water for him after school on a particularly hot day.

Seconds after handing him the bottle, I watch in shock as my four-year-old proceeds to guzzle the entire thing down in no time flat.

"Whoa, buddy!" I say, watching him drink. "Slow down!"

Max ignores me and continues to guzzle. Finally done, he hands me back the bottle. "Thank you for the drink," he says sweetly, before letting out a loud belch.

"You're welcome," I say. "But Maxie, why are you so thirsty?"

Max looks to the ground, suddenly interested in a pile of rocks near a tree.

"Maxie?"

Max kneels on the grass, picking up this stone and that. He mutters something into his t-shirt.

"Can you speak louder, sweetie?" I say. "I couldn't hear you!"

"Not allowed," he mutters again.

I lock the brakes on Sammy's stroller and then kneel down next to Max. "Not allowed? What do you mean?"

"Not allowed to drink," he says, still picking up rocks.

"But that's silly!" I say. "Of course you're allowed to drink!" I pause. "Is that why you haven't been having your juice box? Because you think you're not allowed?"

Max nods, a gesture that seems to be meant more for the rocks than for me.

"Maxwell, look at me please," I say.

Max keeps collecting rocks.

"Maxwell, look at me!"

Slowly Max raises his gaze to mine, his eyes wide and brown.

"Please tell Mommy why you thought you weren't allowed to drink at school."

"He said," Max whispers.

"Who said?"

Max takes in a deep breath and then begins. "An SK said that you can't drink from the water fountains in the class because the water fountains in the class are for SKs only, so I can't drink water from the water fountains because I'm a JK!" His speech finished, Max turns towards the stroller and proceeds to plunk handfuls of tiny rocks into the bottom basket.

"I wanna rock, too!" Sammy yelps from his seat.

I grab a stone and hand it to Sam, feeling dazed. No matter how well I know my four-year-old, I still can't fathom how he could force himself to not drink all day, every day. What must it have been like for him on hot afternoons, or after recess, or during lunch? Had it been fortitude, fear, or the sheer inability to express himself that led my child to ignore what is a most basic need?

The next morning I tell the teachers in detail what happened, and their reaction is equally concerned. They reassure me that of course Maxwell is allowed to drink from the fountains during the day. That's what they're there for, after all. They tell me that they will speak to Max individually about what happened, and will also explain to the entire class about the fountains and about letting adults know when they are thirsty. Finally, I'm told that they'll make a point of checking if Max drinks his juice at lunch and will occasionally prompt him to use the fountain after recess or playing in the gym.

All of this is good and highlights how professional and on-the-ball my son's teachers happen to be. But despite this, what I'm left with is a hard pit in my stomach and the knowledge that the water fountain incident is just the first of what will likely be many misunderstandings for Maxwell. This time, a grownup noticed something was a bit off. But what about the next time my child misunderstands something or is too fearful to speak up, remaining sweet-natured but silent? *What about then*? And for a moment, if only for a moment, I wish that the firecracker, overly domineering Maxwell, the one who, when at home, may demand that you play with the red car or risk having it thrown in your direction, would occasionally rear his head at school.

CHAPTER 33

As the weeks go by, and Max's experiences with Playtime Pals and Stay and Play move further and further into the past, Joel and I are left to see which of the skills he learned actually stick and which do not. The good news is that thanks largely to both programs, our son is less "zoned out" in kindergarten than he was in daycare (*stick*), will make eye contact with others in class at least some of the time (*stick*), and will happily, if very quietly, respond when a teacher speaks to him (*stick*).

At home, Max consistently uses a skill practised in the integrated social skills group—how to get another person's attention appropriately. At Stay and Play, Max was taught that he should tap a person on the shoulder, say their name, and then wait until the person turns to look at him before speaking. Time and again, Max performs this skill very well, with the tap often replaced in his Max-like way by cupping a family member's chin tenderly in his hand, before forcibly turning their head towards him. Still, in my mind at least, this is a triple stick!

Unfortunately, at the same time that these skills seem to become lasting, we also notice a huge, frightening step backwards. What we notice, what each member of our little family can't help but notice, is that Max's relationship with his little brother begins to deteriorate with a disturbing alacrity. This change seems to be at least partly rooted in the fact that Sammy is growing into his own independent person. The Sammy of old was an affable, easygoing little brother who was at Max's beck and call ("If you want to be my best buddy, then you have to hold the red train, not the green train!"). In recent months, however, Sammy has slowly changed from being Maxwell's yes-man to a child who will occasionally shake his head in response to his brother's demands, suggesting that perhaps instead of playing with trains for the umpteenth time they might make a craft with Mommy, or squish Play Dough, or even pretend to cook! While Joel and I are pleased that Sam is turning into a little boy who likes to make choices for himself, thank you very much, Maxwell is (ahem) less than thrilled.

When Sam's desire to be allowed to take turns choosing activities with his "best buddy" is combined with said buddy's intense desire to control situations, not to mention mind blindness, the result is not pretty. Unfortunately for their friendship, unfortunately for us all, the oh-so-important lesson of letting others have a turn at play seems to have *not* stuck. Having Sam not do exactly what Max has told him to do is not only unacceptable to my four-year-old, but absolutely unbearable. Thus, like a captain faced with a mutiny, each time that Sam makes an unexpected move, Max reacts in attack mode.

While Max has been aggressive with Sam many times in the past, this is different. Each attack is a no-holds-barred, full-on take down, with Maxwell leaping across the room to try and pulverize his baby brother by any means necessary. Within seconds he could be lying on top of Sam, or have his hands around his little brother's neck, all because my youngest had the audacity to suggest that they play house instead of Thomas and Friends. If my four-year-old cannot reach Sam quickly enough, he will try and destroy whatever is nearest to him, be it a fort made out of pillows or even a tower that Maxwell himself had just finished carefully constructing. And what does Sam do in return? Sam looks bewildered and then bursts into tears, as no matter how quickly Joel or I reach him to end the attack, it's never quite quick enough.

What I find hardest to wrap my mind around is the fact that Max still hasn't accepted (or at the very least, become inured to) the idea that his brother may not always do what he had expected him to do. As a result, each time Sam makes a suggestion, it's as if Max has been betrayed for the very first time. Each "no" is an insurrection, like an arrow to the heart. No lesson is learned from past experiences, nothing sticks. Despite hearing Sam say no the week, day, or even hour before, Max will react with the same shrieking, the same outrage, the same intense, raw aggression.

That's not to say that someone else isn't learning a lesson. Within weeks of this new dynamic, Joel and I start to notice that Sammy's newly found confidence as a separate social being has already started to ebb. Slowly, but surely, Sam begins to back down in the face of Max's fury, quickly agreeing to whatever it is that his brother demands. *Watch the same Bubble Guppies episode for the third time? Sure! Keep putting stickers on paper in a very specific way? You gotcha!* No matter how quickly we admonish Max when he attacks, no matter how firmly we explain to them both that *of course* Sammy gets to choose games, too (*Remember turn-taking at Stay and Play, Maxie? Remember that?*), our baby starts to lose bits of himself under the steady gaze of his dictator. And that, folks, cannot happen. Not on my watch.

And so, when we are contacted by the local agency about the possibility of having ABA intervention take place in our home, with the focus being primarily upon Max's interactions with his little brother, we jump at the chance.

******

Rescue comes in the form of a lovely woman named Karen. A highly trained therapist with years of ASD experience under her belt, Karen brings an instant air of professionalism and calm into our home at a time when it's needed most. Officially called a "Functional Behavioural Assessment Interview", our initial session involves Joel and I repeatedly interrupting Karen and each other, desperate to let this expert know just how dire the situation has become between our two little boys. Following the interview, an action plan is developed. It's explained to us that during future sessions one "target behaviour" will be our focus, with the hope that any gains made will then generalize to other situations over time.

It's agreed that the behaviour in question will be Max's "tantrums" when playing with Sam. Together we define tantrums as Maxwell screaming, with "dropping to the ground, hitting self and/or others, and throwing items" also included into the mix. We're told that a tantrum will be considered to have begun when our child has been screaming for at least ten seconds and it will be considered over if he stops screaming for at least thirty seconds (in other words, longer than it takes to draw in another deep breath). We're also told what does *not* constitute a tantrum, a list which includes shouting, growling, angrily performing the activity, or general, little boy rudeness. It's explained that anytime Max actually uses his words to tell us how he feels, we're to reinforce it, even if telling us his feelings involves saying he "hates" us and wants us to "go run away now". Goals such as learning how to accept "no", social skills training, and flexibility training are also to be addressed, with adult prompting and guidance ideally faded over time. In other words, we're told to roll up our sleeves already and actually get to work!

During each session that follows, Karen sets up a simple play situation for Max and Sam to take part in, with very specific rules to follow. Before the activity even begins, we review our expectations

205

with the children (*"Today we are going to build a tower together. Max will get a turn picking a block and putting it on the tower, and then Sam will get a turn picking a block and putting it on the tower. After Sam's turn it will be Max's turn again. Then after Max's turn, it will be Sam's turn again. You will each get six turns and then we will be done."*). During the first play session, things go well, with both Maxwell and Sam seeming to bask in all of the attention and praise heaped onto them by three fawning adults. No significant target behaviour is noted, and Joel and I are proud parents indeed.

During our next sessions, however, the tide begins to turn. At the beginning of Play Session Two, Karen suggests we choose an activity that Max clearly prefers, to see if he will remain calm when one of his favourite toys is the focus of the sharing and turn-taking. We all tromp upstairs to the boys' room, and decide that the activity for the day will be putting trains on a simple railroad track, using Max's train set. As before, the expectations are once again laid out and the play begins. Within about two minutes, however, the train literally and figuratively goes off the rails, and all hell breaks loose. This starts as all such things start, with Sam doing something *wrong*.

It's Sam's third turn, and as he places a train a bit too close to one that Max had just put on the track, the latter train falls over.

"NO!" Maxwell shouts, leaping up and over the train track. "Your Henry made Thomas fall! Your Henry made Thomas fall!"

"I put him back now, Max-well," Sammy says, carefully placing the fallen Thomas back on the tracks with his chubby fingers. "See?"

"NO! Put him back on the ground! Put him back on the ground! Put him back on the ground!"

Sam looks at his brother, then towards the adults in the room. It's clear that he has no idea what the hell he should do next. Seeing him so confused makes my stomach tighten.

"Sam had his turn, now you can have your turn," Karen says, ignoring Max's continued shouting. *A shout is not a scream. A shout is not a scream.*

Max rushes over to me and pulls me into a bear hug, completely ignoring Karen. "Mommy! I don't *want* to play with Sam! He's *not* my best buddy anymore! I'm all done!"

"Thank you for telling us your feelings, Max," Karen says. She pauses.

"Yes!" I say. "Good job saying how you feel!"

"Yeah, good job," Joel echos. He raises up his hand. "High-five!"

I look at my husband and vigorously shake my head. *Has he even been paying attention?*

In response to our praise, Max gets angrier. "I don't like this game!" he shouts. "I'm done!" He squeezes me tighter and rubs his cheek roughly against mine.

"You have three more turns, and then you can be done," Karen says firmly. "Sam just had his turn, so now it's your turn!"

In response, Max lets go of me and starts to run out of the room. As he passes Karen, she reaches out and gently grabs him, preventing him from leaving. Max pulls away from her, but she firmly places him onto her lap. "It's your turn now," she repeats, sweetly but firmly.

"NO!" Max shouts, thrashing in her arms. "I don't *like* this anymore! This is *boring*!"

"Good job with the feelings, there, buddy," Joel calls out. "Fist bump!"

Max glares at him and lets out a growl.

"Your turn," Karen reminds him, acting like anything else that's occurring is just white noise. "Sammy had his turn. Now it's your turn."

"*No*! This is boring! *BORING*!" I can hear the panic begin in my child's voice. Karen's hold around Max tightens. I look towards Sammy, who has suddenly burst into tears. Joel reaches towards his littlest son and gives him a hug.

"We need to finish putting the trains on the track," Karen says. "I will help you have your turn."

Max begins to try and head-butt the therapist, but she turns her face away.

"No, Maxwell!" I shout, horrified. While I've seen Max strike out against his family members many times, he's never been violent with anyone outside of his pack.

Karen looks at me. "It's okay," she whispers. "It's fine."

In response, Max's head successfully makes contact with the front of Karen's face.

"NO!" I scream at him. *My very own target behaviour.*

"Alicia," Karen says. "Please trust me that this is fine. I've seen much, much worse."

"But he's not allowed to hurt anyone!"

"Of course not, but right now the priority is having him learn that he's not the one in charge. Bruises go with the job." She looks directly at me. "Do you want to keep going?"

I dig my fingernails into my palms, but nod. If this doesn't work, then what will?

Karen nods, then turns her focus back to my son. "It's your turn, Maxwell," she says. "You can put Thomas on the track or you can put Gordon on the track."

"No!" Maxwell screams. "Mommy! I want Mommy! MOMMY!" He thrashes against the therapist once more.

I lock my arms around my chest to prevent myself from jumping in. Seeing my son become aggressive against an adult other than me or his father is one of the worst experiences I've witnessed. It's like watching the wounded horse with Robert Redford in The Horse Whisperer, except that the wild animal in question happens to be my little son. My throat goes tight, then tighter still, my sorrow stuck there like wet sand I can't seem to swallow.

In response to the thrashing, Karen takes Max's hand and firmly moves it towards a train. With her hand covering his, she forces them to together pick up a Thomas train and place it on the track. As soon as the train is in its spot, she lets go of him.

"Good job, Max!" Joel calls out, giving him a thumbs-up.

Max puts his knees up to his face and starts to sob.

"It's Sam's turn now," Karen says brightly.

Sam smiles, then moves towards the trains to select a new one. I watch for a moment more, then jump up and race to the bathroom, keeping my tears at bay until I'm safely locked in the bathroom. *I cannot do this. I'm sorry, but I cannot.*

******

It turns out that the hard work is yet to come. We're told that between sessions we're to schedule one-hour structured activities ourselves, to set up expectations and guide play, then to document what takes place. Not only that, we're to record any other situation in which the targeted behaviour occurs. At this point, Max's outbursts and meltdowns have become like the sound of the ocean to Vancouverites, something Joel and I are aware of, but common-place, familiar. Just like any experience that happens day after day, I've become used to occasional hits and growls, heat-butts and shrieks. After all, it's not as if that's my only experience of my child. Maxwell spends much more time being a happy, delightful little boy, a sweet presence in my life. Max's episodes of upset flow into his periods of joy, curiosity, and charm, then back again. Sometimes the waves are gentle, sometimes they are strong, but always, they are there.

Through the task of data collection, however, I'm required to pay more attention to each and every time a strong wave strikes land. And to not only pay attention, but to actually document what occurs, why, and for how long. In other words, I'm required to bear witness. The data sheets themselves are familiar to me, similar to the pages I used to give out willy-nilly to former clients of mine who were struggling with binge-eating, phobias, or obsessive thoughts.

"Here you go," I'd say, passing out pieces of blank paper to be filled. "Whenever you binge/become anxious speaking/worry about having not turned off the oven, just write it down for me, 'kay?"

Easy-peasy. Except, it turns out that it's not. Each time I document an instance of Max's "target behaviour", I feel as if my face is being forced into a puddle of my own incompetence. Titled "Antecedent, Behaviour, Consequence Data Sheet", each page is simple enough to figure out. First, record the context of what is happening (*"Meghan makes a 'fun' drink for her brothers. They seem excited."*). Next, record the antecedent event (*"Sam finishes his drink, so he gets more. Max immediately wants more, too, despite having a full glass. Meghan says she will give him more once he drinks his glass."*). Third, record the target behaviour (*"Max roars in Meghan's face, hits her, and tries to throw his glass at her."*). Finally, record the consequence (*"Max is given no more to drink. He is told to say sorry. He growls 'sorry', and I praise him."*).

Or another: Context (*"Max and Sam begin to play with toys in the quiet spot together"*); Antecedent Event (*"Max wants to play with the car garage. Sam tries to play with it, too, taking turns."*); Target Behaviour (*"Max screams, grabs Sam by the neck, and head-butts him."*); Consequence (*"I tell Max that either they both play with the garage or else only Sam will play."*).

Or still another: Context (*"A TV show just ended and it is time to eat breakfast. I turn off the TV, like always"*); Antecedent Event (*"Max is excited to eat, until he sees that a new show is about to start"*); Target Behaviour (*"Max screams at me. When Meghan walks into the room, he attacks her—hitting her with his fists"*); Consequence (*"I ignore Max's screaming. I have Meghan get down face to face with Max and tell him that attacking her is upsetting."*).

All too soon, I have page after page listing instances of target behaviour. Page after page documenting just how much further we have to go until Joel and I have truly made a difference in how our child copes. The growing pile of pages feels like a hill that may be insurmountable, no matter how much hope or energy we muster up to climb it. I begin to wonder if Joel, Karen, and I are nothing more than a bunch of silly Sisyphuses, and if, through our earnest badgering, we're forcing our small child to learn how to roll a heavy boulder up a mountain, only to watch it fall back down again.

And yet, during our second last session, a tipping point is reached. The structured activity for the day has just been finished successfully (Max and Sam making a block tower together), and Joel and I are using the remaining time to debrief a bit with Karen. I'm eager to share with her that I've actually noticed true improvement between the boys when they play together. While Max still dislikes Sam making his own choices, he has begun to actually tolerate it. Perhaps even more importantly, there have been a few times in which Max has actually asked Sam what he wanted to play. Hearing my little boy say this to his even littler brother has been like music to my ears.

As we adults continue talking, Sam happily plays on the floor with some toy food. Within minutes, Max walks over to me and pulls on my shirt.

"Maxie," I say. "The grownups need to talk a bit more. Why don't you go use your new markers and draw in your colouring book?"

Max shakes his head. He pulls up the back of my shirt and then sticks his head underneath it.

"Maxwell!" I say. I somehow dislodge him from me, then attempt to keep talking to Karen about how well he has been behaving.

In response, Max starts to bang his chest against my legs. "Go downstairs with me!" he shouts. "NOW!"

"He's trying to force your attention," Karen says. "You've already told him that you're talking with us. Don't engage."

I nod, trying to pull myself back into the conversation. Max lets go of me and heads over to his bed. Silently, but full of purpose, he begins picking up his stuffed animals, and throwing them to the floor.

"Don't engage," Karen reminds me.

I nod, but watch as Max throws off his pillows, then somehow pulls off his blanket, before tackling his sheets. *A new skill mastered. High-five!*

"Maxwell!" I say, not able to stop myself. "You're making a mess! Put everything back on your bed!"

In response, Max starts to laugh. He then grabs a stuffie from the floor and throws it at me.

"Max!" Joel says loudly. "Stop that right now!"

Karen motions for us to come closer. "He's just trying to do something more attention-grabbing and stop you from having this conversation with us, Alicia. Do not engage."

"Well, what should we do?" I ask. "You're about to leave and…"

"Never mind that," she says softly. "What were your plans for once I was gone?"

"To let the boys watch Diego," I say.

"Do you want Max to watch Diego right now?"

"Of course not!"

"What does he need to do before he gets to watch Diego?" Karen looks at me, then at Joel. My husband shrugs in my direction. It's my call.

"Um, he has to put everything back on his bed."

"He'll never do that, sweetie," Joel says.

"Okay, then, he has to put at least one thing back on his bed. One pillow, or one stuffie. One something!" In the background, I can hear Maxwell growling.

Karen claps her hands together. "Maxwell," she says. "Your mom and Sammy are going downstairs now. Sam is going to watch Diego on TV. If you want to watch Diego on TV, you need to put at least one thing back on your bed."

"NO!" Maxwell shrieks. He runs over to me and grabs at my shirt again. "Mommy!"

Karen bends down until she's at my son's level. "You need to put one thing back on your bed if you want to watch Diego. If you don't put one thing on your bed, then you need to stay upstairs."

"NO!" Maxwell screams. He begins to hit at me, but Karen pulls me away.

"He wants you here," she whispers. "You are what is called his 'tangible'. If you think you can stay downstairs and not come back up again, then you and Sam need to go."

I nod and take Sammy by the hand. "Want to go watch Diego with Mommy?" I ask.

I quickly walk down the hall with Sammy and Karen shuts the baby gate behind us. Maxwell runs at the gate, his fury reaching an all-time high. I can feel tears building behind my eyes, but turn my focus onto Sam and make my way down the stairs. In my wake are Max's screams.

After I've plunked Sam down on the sofa and turned on his favourite show, I stand in the doorway, just out of Max's sight line. I can hear him shaking the baby gate and screaming for me. The hardest he shakes, the more I tremble. I can feel my resolve start to crumble. Just as I'm about to head back upstairs, Karen comes down.

"Joel is up there with him," she reminds me. "He's going to be just outside the bedroom, but will go see Max every few minutes and ask him to put something back on the bed." She pauses. "Maxwell is safe up there, he's in no danger. He's just mad."

Suddenly I hear a loud thump on the stairs, followed by another. I stick my head around the door and watch as my son starts to throw his toys off the banister. Karen pulls me back.

"Mommy! I hurt! I hurt! MOMMY!"

"Joel's up there," she reminds me. "He will not get hurt with his father there."

I nod, then move back into the den. I shut the door, to better muffle Max's screams for me.

"How are you doing?" Karen asks.

In response, I cover my face with my hands.

"Ignoring your child when he's calling out to you is the hardest thing," she says.

I suddenly think back to my friend's long-forgotten question on the phone and I nod to myself. *Yes, this is the hardest thing.*

Karen reaches out to touch my arm. "Listen," she says softly. "Don't worry about what I've told you. Don't worry about what 'should' be done. Whatever you feel as a mom trumps everything else."

I lift my face up from my hands to look at her. "But the ABA..."

Karen looks directly back at me. "If you need to go up there as a mom, then you need to go."

I open the door a crack and listen to the screaming and gate-shaking a bit more. Then I shake my head, and go sit down next to Sam. "No," I say. "I need to see this through. I'm staying right here."

The screaming for Mommy continues for over an hour, with an exhausted Joel repeatedly used as Max's personal punching bag. But then slowly but surely, Maxwell's outrage slowly winds down and he quietly walks back into his room, picks up a pillow, and places it carefully on his bed, before politely asking his father if he can please go downstairs to watch TV now, too.

That night, as I go over and over what had happened, I wonder how I managed to stop myself from going upstairs, from responding to my baby when he cried out so desperately for me. Did my psychology training help? No. Did understanding that what we were doing was fundamentally important for Maxwell help? No. What helped, what stopped me from rushing up the stairs (two at a time) and breaking down that damn baby gate myself was the deeply caring, compassionate look that Karen had given me. Even if I didn't trust myself in that moment, I trusted her. And it was that, and nothing else, which kept me rooted to my seat.

Section Eight Acceptance
CHAPTER 34

When I look back on being a little kid, one of my favourite things to do was to have a belly laugh. Not just a mere chuckle, giggle, or even a good guffaw, but a down-on-the-floor, rolling on your back, perhaps even peeing your pants belly laugh. You know the kind I mean; the ones that led you to have an ache in your tummy and a relaxed feeling that lasted for hours afterwards. The kind of laughing that felt best when shared with your best friends, brothers, or sisters, and was typically triggered by something supremely silly. That kind of belly laugh.

Now, as a parent, I've gotten to experience those belly laughs of childhood vicariously, through the laughter of my children. While Daniel has passed the age of laughing with such abandon (at least in front of his mother), Meghan still possesses this lovely ability, with little Sammy quickly catching up.

Of my four children, however, it is Maxwell who has the best belly laugh of the bunch, his laughter often associated with such pure joy you can't help but laugh yourself. Despite the stereotypes about ASD (and there are too many to list here), my son *can* see humour in many situations, particularly when it's writ large. Like many four-year-olds, if Max finds something silly, he will often burst out with unbridled laughter and glee.

But here's the thing.

When it comes to Maxwell, those wonderful, early childhood, rolling on the floor belly laughs can quickly escalate to over-stimulation, which in turn can lead to total emotional dysregulation, involving drooling and shrieking. This can change like quicksilver to Max being completely terrified, screaming, head-butting, and even bolting, an experience well-documented in the final report from his integrated social skills group (note: "[Max] seemed to get 'carried away' with laughing and was unable to return to a calm state"; "during this task, he became quite dysregulated, laughing hysterically…"). I'm sure that no one needs me to tell them that such episodes are neither joyful nor fun for anyone involved.

Here's the other thing.

While Joel and I are able to tell the difference between Max being a "silly" four-year-old and him having "the sillies" (our son's name for what occurs), most others cannot. When in a public situation, Max being over-stimulated, anxious, or scared in this way just looks like a child who's being overly active and perhaps a bit naughty, rather than one who feels completely out of control and needs help to calm down.

Perhaps the most extreme example of Max having *the sillies* occurred this summer, while visiting a drop-in preschool centre with his little brother. Maxie seemed to enjoy himself at the centre for almost an hour, busying himself with different activities. Yes, there were more children there that day and thus more noise, but Max seemed to truly be having fun, so we stayed. Towards the end of our visit, the staff announced that they would be doing a circle before closing for the morning. Sammy was excited to join the circle and when I asked Max, he indicated he'd like to try the circle, too, so against my better judgement, we stayed. Yes, he seemed a bit silly at the time, but he didn't seem to be at risk of having *the sillies* (spoiler alert: it turns out that the line between these two experiences is fine indeed).

The circle started well, with Sammy sitting next to me and Max in my lap. And then, it happened. During a song about trains, Max leaped out of my lap, laughing hysterically, and began running around the room, grabbing at toys that had just been put away. I jumped up after him, leaving Sammy alone in the circle. Max raced faster around the room, now drooling and screaming even more hysterically. Finally I was able to grab him, at which point he screamed louder, still laughing, and began to butt me with his head. While he kicked at me, I held on tight, and led him back to the circle, making a split second decision to try and calm him at the centre rather than in the middle of a mall.

At this point I was aware of many parental eyes looking my way, as well as a few people shaking their heads (heads that should have known better, dammit) and openly whispering to their neighbours. While no one said anything directly to me, it was clear that at least some parents viewed Max as a "bratty" kid, a little boy who needed to learn about what was appropriate behaviour and what was not. I also sensed that some parents might have been wondering why I was holding my child so tightly, refusing to let him go while he thrashed about.

As Max continued to butt at me, I started to rock him,

determined to stay strong. The staff member who was leading the circle noticed the rocking. She nodded gently at me, and then announced loudly that we would now all sing "Row, row, row your boat", actions included. This was quickly followed by "Row, row, row your bus", and then "Row, row, row your car". Finally, it was "Row, row, row your horse". Soon it was not just me and Maxie rocking, but an entire circle of children and parents who were doing the back-and-forth motion. And, as Maxwell saw that everyone else was rocking too, he slowly, oh so slowly, began to come back down again, his body relaxing into my own.

So yes, in terms of *the sillies*, that episode was the worst. Thankfully, Max's family, his OT, his kindergarten teachers, and his EA are all aware of the difference between my son being "silly" like any other small child, and having *the sillies,* and thus desperately needing some help (please and thank you), in order to feel grounded and in control of his body once again. During OT sessions, Joel and I learn different hands-on techniques to help our little boy when he needs it the most. At school, there's a hub room to go for physical calming, there is a weighted stuffed animal to put on your lap to soothe you, there are earphones filled with classical music to bring you down. There is help, when help is needed, and for me as a parent, that is an unbelievably wonderful thing.

Here's the final thing.

After episodes like the one at the drop-in preschool centre, I've thought about what it would be like if Joel and I could somehow bubble-wrap our son's experiences, to ensure that Maxie's level of stimulation always remains at an even keel, like an oven set permanently at 350. Would our little boy's angry meltdowns or episodes of *the sillies* magically disappear if calm was somehow always maintained?

But then I think back to my own early childhood and those wonderful belly laughs. Forcing Max to somehow always stay calm would mean that he'd miss so many opportunities of joy, of laughter, and yes, of true silliness. And that, gentle reader, would not be worth it. No, it would not. So I'll take *the sillies*, however difficult they are for everyone, as long as Max is also allowed to enjoy the sheer bliss of just being silly, belly aches and all.

******

When I go to pick up Maxwell, his EA tells him to go play, then walks up to me. Instantly, my maternal antennae start vibrating.

"Did something happen?" I ask. I search Becky's face. The fact that she's smiling isn't necessarily a good thing. It could be a professional smile, meant to put me at ease before the axe falls.

"Has Max told you about his new friends?" she asks me. Her smile grows.

"Friends?" I say. "Max has friends?"

Becky nods. "There are two little girls in senior kindergarten who have taken quite a liking to your son," she says. "He used to play by himself at recess, but now whenever they see him they run up and hug him."

I swivel my head in Max's direction, watching him try to balance on a wooden alligator. "Does he...like them hugging him?"

Becky shrugs. "I'm not sure if he likes it or not, but he certainly seems to like the attention!" She smiles again. "He's become real buddies with one of the girls in particular. Emily. This morning I saw them playing tag. Max was having a great time!"

"Really?" I say. "He really was playing?"

Becky nods, then quickly touches my arm with a mitted hand. "Anyway, I just wanted to let you know."

She moves to another parent, seemingly unaware that she's just spoken the very words I never expected to hear, at least not without years and years of more intervention. Somehow, with no help from me or his father, our quirky, intense little boy has found a friend. *A friend.* I watch Max try to balance for a few more seconds, before walking over to join him. *This is what people mean when they say their heart is full. This.*

CHAPTER 35

This evening will mark the third night of Hanukkah and I for one am excited. The candles, the songs, the latkes...I love it all. Having been raised in an Anglican home, however, and having only celebrated this holiday with my husband for five years, the "festival of lights" remains a magical, but somewhat foreign tradition to me. While I *enjoy* celebrating Hanukkah with my new found family, I remain a bit on the sidelines, more of a befuddled observer than a full participant.

When it comes to the customs and traditions of Christmas, the same can be said of my Jewish husband. While Joel seems to like the joy and excitement that the holiday can bring, he remains perplexed by the often odd rituals associated with it. Why do we leave out not only milk and cookies for Santa, but carrots for the flying reindeer as well? Why do we pull Christmas "crackers" around my parents' linen-covered table and then don colourful paper crowns, all the while dressed in our best attire? And what exactly is the meaning and symbolism behind the miniature nativity scene at my parents' house?

Keeping in mind our mutual confusion over one another's most sacred traditions, it's no wonder that Joel and I occasionally have trouble answering the questions of the four children in our house.

"Why is the shamash so special, Mommy?" Meghan asked me a few years ago. "And what is it, anyway?"

"Um," I answered, using the tried and true clearing-one's-throat technique to buy myself time. "Why don't you go ask your step dad?"

"Who were the Maccabees exactly?" asked my eldest during our first Hanukkah celebration. "And how many of them were there?"

In response, I smiled brightly at Daniel, then looked desperately towards the stairs, and yelled for Joel.

In my defence, I should point out that my husband is not much better when it comes to the Yuletide knowledge department.

"Why does Santa come down a chimney, Daddy?" Sam asked this year, his forehead furrowed with concern. "And how do reindeer fly?"

Joel responded with a slow throat-clearing, followed by a quick yelp for his non-Jewish wife.

And so it goes. While as a family we may observe both Hanukkah and Christmas, as interfaith parents we continue to bumble through each other's holiday, with Joel pretending to be fine with having his sons eat chocolate each morning from something called an "Advent calendar", and me pretending to understand the Hebrew words he says while lighting the Hanukkah candles.

Enter Maxwell, stage left.

As a fervent devotee of all things ritualistic, and possessed with a razor-sharp memory, Max kindly gives a helping hand to his often clueless parents.

"The shamash is the candle that is used to light all the other ones," Max informs me as I pull out our Hanukkah and Christmas books. "You put it in the middle spot of the menorah."

Later, as I search the basement for a box marked "Hanukkah", Max follows me downstairs. "Don't forget to use the menorah you got Daddy," he says sternly. "We have to use that menorah because it's important to our family."

"Santa is like magic for Christmas," Max later tells his little brother. "We will leave him two cookies that we made and also a carrot for Rudolph and also a piece of cheese for Santa Mouse" (*yes, Santa Mouse, just trust me on this*).

"Is Hanukkah magic?" asks Sam.

"Er," I answer. I look towards Maxwell for help. "Well..."

Max seems to think deeply before replying. "The magic part is how the oil burned for eight nights and there was only enough for one. That's the magic."

"Oh," Sam says solemnly, the awe he holds for his big brother suddenly tripled.

"Mommy and us use the Advent calendar to count down the days until Christmas," Max explains to his hapless father one morning, as he opens up the first window and pops a tiny chocolate into his mouth. "And the baby in this book here is baby Jesus. He had to sleep in hay."

"Read this book to Sammy," Max later demands, handing me a family favourite called *My Two Holidays: A Hanukkah and Christmas Story*. "It's important."

And so, I do.

How a child who is only four-and-a-half even remembers the existence of his Daddy's pewter menorah or the use of an Advent calendar is irrelevant. What is important is that, thanks to Maxwell, our family becomes less at risk of muddling through the holidays with each passing year. Thanks to Max, the traditions and rituals that are so near and dear to me and my husband will eventually become familiar to and understood to us all. *So happy holidays, Maxwell. We are indeed lucky to have you in our fold.*

CHAPTER 36

I sit here on my den sofa (propped up by many pillows), feeling more than a little bit sorry for myself. Not only did I succumb to the nasty virus that hit my family with a vengeance in mid-December, this current bug has recently blossomed into pneumonia. It isn't so much the being sick that leads me to such self-pity (although it certainly helps), but rather the knowledge that I'm missing out on so many of the traditions and rituals of this season that I've grown to count on and love.

The first person in our house to become extremely sick was Max, whose virus made itself known late into the night on the sixth evening of Hanukkah, only to quickly develop into pneumonia (thankfully for him, it was caught at its very early stages). Max's illness happened to coincide with my mother-in-law's annual Hanukkah party, an event our entire family looks forward to. While sad to be missing it, however, I didn't feel "sorry" for myself at the time, as all that mattered was Maxwell's health, and his level of sickness frightened me.

Once Max was out of the woods and I became ill with the bug, however, how I felt about missing out on holiday events began to change, as my worsening health coincided with my birthday. At this point I should probably mention that my excitement about turning forty-two was no less over-the-top than how I felt about turning eight. Despite the fact that my birthday isn't until December nineteenth, I begin to get excited about its imminent arrival the day after Halloween. *It's going to be my birthday! My birthday and not yours!* I'll say, badgering my older children whenever possible. *We're going to celebrate my birthday in five weeks, days, hours!*

Every year in the past, my birthday "script" has gone as follows: My parents come over in the late afternoon, laden with gifts and birthday greetings. Soon after, we order takeout from my favourite restaurant and we all sit down to eat in the dining room (note: my family only eats in the dining room for birthdays—please do not question this, as it's an unspoken yet sacred rule of the Hendley/Rubinoff household). The delicious dinner is then followed by someone turning down the lights, Meghan carefully coming in carrying a plate filled with bakery cupcakes (*thank you, Cake Box*), and my family singing Happy Birthday to me, while I blow out the candles. Finally, this is followed by us all tramping into the den, where I sit on the sofa like a queen-for-the-day and am given various gifts and sundries.

Except this year was different.

This year there was no visit from my parents, who were fully occupied with taking care of Max so that both he and I could recuperate. This year there was no takeout from my favourite restaurant (who has an appetite when hacking up a lung?). And this year, there was definitely no gift-giving (I refused any offers, as it was essential for me to have my little gift-unwrapper by my side when the ritual happened).

So how did I feel on my forty-second birthday, besides sick? I felt frustrated, I felt sad, I felt sorry for myself, and yes, even a little bit anxious. All was not right with the world. After all, my birthday has a script to follow and that script was not followed. *This is not acceptable!* But then things took a turn for the worse, and my nasty virus morphed into a much more nasty pneumonia. As a result, my extremely supportive parents offered to not only keep Max for several more days, but to also take care of little Sammy, both to lighten our load and to hopefully soothe Max's intense anxiety at all the huge, unexpected changes which were occurring by having his "best buddy" at his side. A few days later, Daniel and Meghan joined the group over at Papa and Yaya's house, as my husband succumbed to the viral monster.

Right now, as I type this in my freakishly child-free home and wait impatiently for my antibiotics to kick in, how do I feel? Other than incredibly grateful to my parents for all that they are doing, as well as to my husband, who is attempting to catch up on all the sleep he missed, I feel anxious, upset, and frustrated. It is one thing to not have my birthday go as planned, but what about Christmas, the holiday I look forward to all year? Last year, it was all a blur of forced cheer and overwhelming greyness, as I remained stuck in the fog that is depression, but this year, it was supposed to be different. What about spending an entire day baking and decorating cookies with my children, putting these treats on holiday plates, and then delivering them (children in tow) to each of our neighbours' doorsteps? *What about that?!?* This tradition is as important to me as any other and has always taken place several days before Christmas, with me using both the recipe and the special cookie cutters that my aunt from

Connecticut gave me so many years ago. Right now instead of the sweet scents of butter, sugar, and vanilla, all I inhale is Vicks VapoRub, and that makes me angry, sad, and a little anxious, too. *I mean, what the hell?*

Finally, as the days tick away and I remain quite sick, it is more than possible that the most essential part of Christmas may not even happen this year—spending most of the day (and all of the subsequent night) at my parents' home, where the script for what should happen has been set for years.

All of these traditions I love. All of these "scripts" I count on. *How dare they not happen!*

And then, this morning, in the midst of my private pity party, it hit me: How is my strict adherence to these holiday scripts, not to mention the feelings I'm having when they don't get followed, any different than what happens to Max when things don't go the way he planned? Yes, Max's reactions to changes in expected routines may be more extreme than mine (e.g., I fully expect him to head-butt, hit himself, and shriek when he returns from his prolonged, highly unexpected stay at my parents' home, whereas all I'm doing in response to my unexpected changes is to wallow in self-pity). Yes, the scripts I want to follow are based on traditions that have been set for years, whereas many of Max's scripts often seem nonsensical and can develop after just one occurrence (e.g., when Max used a striped straw once to drink his glass of milk, he thereafter demanded that he *always* drink milk with a striped straw and would become hysterical if it was not offered forthwith).

However, given that Max has Autism and I do not, and given that Max is only four-and-a-half, whereas I'm a newly minted forty-two, our intense dislike of having what we expected to have happen not happen (*goddammit!*) isn't so different, after all.

And, while this new awareness of yet another way in which my child and I are similar may not change my disappointment about the holidays, it does help, and more than just a little. After all, anything that leads me to better understand the thoughts and feelings of my beloved little boy has value, value that I would argue is worth even more than bakery cupcakes, birthday gifts, and homemade cookies, combined.

******

As sit in this quiet house, I think over the last several months. Filled as the fall has been with Max's transition to junior kindergarten,

Joel and my intense preparation for his IPRC (Identification, Placement, and Review Committee) meeting (*Advocate! Advocate! Advocate!*), our weekly sessions with Karen in home-based ABA, and my adjustment to occasional tweaking of my Lamictal dosage (pharmacology, it seems, is as much an art as a science), I'm more than ready for a new season to begin.

That's not to say that this fall was in any way comparable to its predecessor. While stressful, this year's autumn and early winter lacks the overwhelming heaviness of the one just past. Instead of flailing in grief, it seems that I've begun to dog-paddle in hope. Given that approximately a year has passed since Max's diagnosis, I decide that the time is again ripe to make a list of all of the things I've learned since being told that my son has Autism. Once again I turn on my computer, create a new word file, and begin to type.

MAX DIAGNOSED WITH Autism MEANS THAT:

1)   Max is still the same little boy he was as before the diagnosis.

2)   The meaning of Max being the same little boy as before his diagnosis is similar to the fact that I am the same woman as before mine.

3)   During this past year I've explored some of the darkest caves imaginable, often going in blind.

4)   During this past year I've managed to come out of these caves, not so lost, after all.

5)   I've found guidance and support in both expected (e.g., professionals) and unexpected (e.g., other ASD moms) places.

6)   I'll never be able to thank all of the women who patiently taught me the tools needed to connect with my son and help both he and I cope.

7)   Daniel, Meghan, and Sammy each possess an inner strength that I didn't think possible in such young people.

8)   Maxwell does, too.

9)   This is still just the beginning and that there are many miles to go before I sleep.

EPILOGUE

This morning was terrible for Max and me. Mini-meltdown was followed by mini-meltdown, which in turn was followed by an episode of intense silliness, my three-year-old son at one point so out of his head with wild glee that he was drooling on himself. But that was then. Now we are lying on our backs in the early autumn grass, staring up at the blue sky. There are hazy, thin clouds that seem to be slowly floating by, but otherwise the sky is clear, flawless. It was Max's idea that we do this, lie side by side and just look up. Sammy thinks we're nuts and occasionally toddles over from where he's playing with trucks and cars to ask what we're doing.

"Mama? Are you sleeping, Mama? Are you and Maxie sleeping?"

"No, Sammy," I say. "We're relaxing."

"We're relaxing," Max repeats.

And for the next ten minutes that's exactly what we do—relax. We occasionally comment to each other about the clouds we see, but otherwise just focus on looking up contently, our breathing slow. It seems that Max has learned a new way to calm down all by himself and has been kind enough to teach his overwrought mother the much needed skill of self-regulation.

In an hour or two, there could be another meltdown, another silly episode. Hell, something highly upsetting could happen in the next ten minutes. Right now, however, none of that matters, it's just white noise. All that matters is the beautiful sky and the beautiful boy who is lying next to me. All that matters is right now and all that I have, here, in this backyard.

Biography

Alicia Hendley is the mother of four children, including a son with Autism. She has a Ph.D. in clinical psychology and worked for a number of years as a psychologist.

She is the author of two novels (*A SUBTLE THING*, *TYPE*), with poetry and nonfiction pieces published in *Room* magazine and *Hippocampus Magazine*. Dr. Hendley was long-listed for the Vanderbilt-Exile Short Fiction Award in 2010 and 2011, and was short-listed for the 2014 CBC Canada Writes Stories of Belonging competition.

Dr. Hendley is an advocate within the Autism community. She blogs regularly for an Ontario Autism website, with a particular post ("Mommy, do I have Autism?") published in the winter 2014 issue of *Autism Matters* magazine. Dr. Hendley is asked to speak regularly about her experiences regarding Autism and parenting.

CPSIA information can be obtained
at www.ICGtesting.com
Printed in the USA
FFOW02n0053060416
23002FF